365 Activities for Fitness, Food, and Fun for the Whole Family

Super Sports, Great Games,
Exciting Experiments, and
Nutrition Nuggets

JULIA E. SWEET

Foreword by Michael Jacobson, Ph.D.
Center for Science in the Public Interest

**Mc
Graw
Hill**

New York Chicago San Francisco Lisbon London Madrid Mexico City
Milan New Delhi San Juan Seoul Singapore Sydney Toronto

Library of Congress Cataloging-in-Publication Data

Sweet, Julia E.
 365 activities for fitness, food, and fun for the whole family : super sports, great
games, exciting experiments, and nutrition nuggets / Julia E. Sweet ; foreword by
Michael Jacobson.
  p. cm.
 ISBN 0-8092-9767-1
 1. Physical fitness for children. 2. Family recreation. 3. Games. I. Title:
Three hundred sixty-five activities for fitness, food, and fun for the whole family.
 II. Title.
 GV443.S95   2001
 613.7—dc21   00-59012

6 7 8 9 10 11 12 13 14 15 16 17 18 19 20 21 22   MAL/MAL   0 9 8 7

ISBN-13: 978-0-8092-9767-2
ISBN-10:   0-8092-9767-1

Cover design by Jennifer Locke
Cover and interior illustrations by Andy Anderson

McGraw-Hill books are available at special quantity discounts to use as premiums and
sales promotions, or for use in corporate training programs. For more information, please
write to the Director of Special Sales, Professional Publishing, McGraw-Hill, Two Penn
Plaza, New York, NY 10121-2298. Or contact your local bookstore.

This book is printed on acid-free paper.

Dedicated with much love and thanks to my husband, Jon; my children, Marja and Noah; my parents, Stan and Hanni Myers; and to the memories of my grandfather, Dr. Otto Ehrentheil, and my coach, George Jessup, and my friends Nancy Bell and Karen O'Neil.

Contents

Foreword

Face it. America—and our lives—are dominated by automobiles, television, fast foods, and shopping centers. Kids today, living in the richest nation in history, are accustomed to endless gifts and constant snacking on junk food. Many preschoolers have television sets in their bedrooms. Parties are often commercial commodities celebrated at McDonald's or Chuck E. Cheese.

We sometimes forget that 50 or 100 years ago people (us?!) managed to have perfectly happy childhoods without all kinds of electronic gizmos, from Walkman to the Internet, without spring vacation trips to Europe or Disney World. Life seemed—indeed was—slower and less pressured.

This book is an invitation to recall and treat your children to simple pleasures. Julia Sweet has collected and created hundreds of activities that every parent can do with his or her children. The equipment, be it paper bags or stalks of celery, is inexpensive and readily available. Her instructions are crystal clear. And the results are quite predictable: your children will have a blast—and not even recognize that they are ingesting healthy foods or getting rid of pent-up energy.

The main agenda of this book is *fun*. But, between the lines, the message is health (not a surprise from an aerobics champion). Considering that rates of obesity in American children (not to mention adults) are soaring, it's vitally important that parents make ever-greater efforts to find the healthful foods that their kids love. I hope this book will inspire parents to turn off the TV set (with its junk-food commercials) and get rid of unhealthy foods from the cupboards and refrigerator.

Unlike many children's cookbooks, the snack ideas here are healthy, with minimal fat and maximal nutrients and fiber. The hope is that preparing and eating these foods will remind kids that healthful food is not necessarily yucky. The book offers numerous alternatives to going out to the nearest fast-food outlet or reaching into the freezer for chicken nuggets. The activities will help neutralize the junk-food marketers' relentless efforts to addict children to sugary soft drinks, fatty burgers, and salty fries.

Exercise is the essential companion to good nutrition. Most of today's kids are couch potatoes, spending hours a day in front of the boob tube. Many schools are even getting rid of PE classes, many suburban neighborhoods don't have sidewalks, and many parents chauffeur their kids around rather than allowing them to bike or walk to a friend's house. This book has dozens of wonderful ideas for encouraging activity.

As important as physical health is mental health. These activities encourage cooperation, sociability, sensitivity to the environment, relaxation, and all kinds of other "centering" qualities that are lost in the hurly-burly world of soccer games, music lessons, and homework. They get kids and parents working together to build playthings—and friendships.

Not everyone can have Julia Sweet for a mom. But this inspiring book will help you emulate her by creating a healthy environment for your family. Have fun!

Michael F. Jacobson, Ph.D.
Center for Science in the Public Interest
Coauthor, *What Are We Feeding Our Kids?*

Introduction

Fitness has always been a part of my life. As a very young child I remember spreading a towel on the living room floor and doing the Royal Canadian Airforce exercises with my mother. We did them religiously. I remember nightly neighborhood kickball games, masterminded by my parents. And I remember hauling the family up to New Hampshire to hike the White Mountains and camp out. I don't remember ever seeing soda, snack cakes, or fried chips in our home. There wasn't a big fitness or health movement back then, so I am grateful that my parents went with their instincts. And they continue to set great examples: my mother bicycles to work and takes flamenco dancing, my father lifts weights and does laps around their kitchen. I kid you not! Kudos and thanks to both of them!

As a family with four children, a lot of our entertainment was "homemade." We didn't own a television until I was six years old, and there wasn't much in the way of children's programming anyway. I recall shooting hoops, making a high jump and dried leaf pit, hurdling over backyard benches, and practicing gymnastics dismounts on a pull-up bar in my bedroom. When I met my friend Margie Magraw, my athletic prospects seemed to pick-up—she was a gymnast, and darn good too! I hope her parents have forgiven us for dragging the living room couch cushions outside for a tumbling mat. Margie and I trained with Olympic coach Dr. Joseph Massimo for several years as part of "Doc's flock." Margie and I competed together in high school and in college at the University of Massachusetts at Amherst. Margie was always much better than I, and she remains a rock-solid friend. We get a thrill out of seeing our children play together.

After college, I returned to Boston and worked as an exercise physiologist in a corporate fitness center next to Fanueil Hall Marketplace. My responsibility was the cardiovascular program (treadmills, stationary bicycles, rowers). There was a rather handsome guy, Jon Sweet, who would run outside (instead of using the treadmill) and then lift weights at the facility. I actually learned how to teach Nautilus so I could "help" him. I can't say I helped anyone else with the same care! The results were good; four years later we were married. We've been enjoying sharing our love for fitness ever since.

Soon after our daughter, Marja, was born, we started bringing her to the gym with us. She adored watching the aerobics classes. When she was three I began to teach aerobics. Marja always wanted to climb onto the aerobic step with me as I was "practice teaching"—so I relented and made her my first student. She turned out to be a little more coordinated than some of my subsequent students. We made up a little routine and started to compete and perform together as a mother/daughter team. (Later, our business manager, Ian Barrett, a Formula One racing fan, named us "Team Sweet.") We performed on the regional level and then at the AAU Nationals in Washington, D.C. I guess we must have been somewhat amusing because we were invited to be part of the AAU U.S. Team to Pretoria, South Africa. We were lucky enough to have sponsors (including South African Airways) and great friends (the Mokabas) who made this trip possible.

We knew this trip would be lots of fun, but we didn't expect all the media interest. Life wasn't quite the same after that. Marja and I have enjoyed some awesome experiences together, traveled quite a bit, and met terrific people along the way. Our goal has always been to inspire other parents and kids to exercise together.

Hats off to Marja! Marja worked hard, and as a result she really changed my life. I am forever indebted to her for that. This book is a direct result of her being my teammate and workout partner! Many of the activities in this book came from experiences we had and the projects that we did together as a family. At age three, Marja was the youngest aerobics competitor in the world and as a result received a citation from the governor, appeared in the press quite a bit, and performed at various fundraisers and fitness events. At age seven she won the AAU Junior Olympics (competing in the nine to eleven category).

Often I have been asked, "How did you train Marja?" Training a toddler required a mixture of creativity, participation, enthusiasm, and praise. We practiced her aerobics routine just prior to performances (so she wouldn't be bored with it). But we "trained" *each day* using everyday items we had around the house: trash baskets, balloons, broom handles, hand towels, empty water jugs. The outdoors was a big gym to us—walls to walk, cracks in the sidewalk to jump over, trees to climb on. If we were traveling, we found ways to exercise wherever we were. We did knee lifts in our airplane seats, tried chair push-ups in the hotel room, and raced down convention center corridors. The key was we did it together. It was easy, convenient, inexpensive entertainment, and it was one of the ways we played together. This book contains many of the things we did together. My hope is that you, the reader, will adapt each idea according to what you have to work with and, more importantly, what you enjoy. Make these activities your own creation. Have a ball! Become a child once again!

Several weeks after I found out I was pregnant with my second child, I received a contract to write this book for NTC/Contemporary. I was thrilled to have the opportunity to help make more families aware of the importance of a healthy lifestyle and to do it in a fun way! True to the expression, "when it rains, it pours," several more projects fell into my (disappearing) lap. I did a prenatal fitness video and a few television segments, and continued working on children's nutrition legislation (H.B. 1350). At five weeks old, my son, Noah, was part of "Team Sweet" and joined Marja, my mother, and myself for his first fitness event in Boston. I thank Noah for giving me the opportunity to study prenatal and postpartum exercise, and I am now totally fascinated with child development. He is a great addition to our "team."

I've included food information and activities in this book because eating well goes hand in hand with fitness. In my mind, in order to be truly fit and healthy, you must fuel your body with the best nutrients you can, factoring in your budget, time, and tastes. It's not only what you *don't* eat that matters (replacing high-fat foods with low-fat ones), but perhaps more important, what you *do* eat. I prefer foods that are not overly processed, that have labels with ingredients that I can pronounce, and that don't have an unusually long shelf life! I certainly don't mean to imply that our household is perfect. We've had struggles along the way and continuously work toward eating well while living in the "real" world. I empathize with the trials and tribulations of other parents because I know, firsthand, how difficult it is to nourish your child.

I remember once being stupefied by seeing the lunch (home-packed) of a child my daughter sat next to at an elementary school cafeteria. This child's "square meal" consisted of corn chips, potato chips, and cookies, and he washed it all down with soda. Conversely, I was positively impressed by the healthful school lunches I saw in other countries that Marja and I visited: vegetable and pasta soups, stews, and grain dishes. Suffice it to say, they were quite different from those in the United States. With a continuous supply of fat, salt, and sugar in our diets, no wonder so many of our children become unhealthy adults. The question is why such an extreme difference in preference? This whole new area of children's nutrition captured my curiosity. Off to the bookstore I went. My horizons were broadened when I read Dr. Michael Jacobson's book, *What Are We Feeding Our Kids?* I shared the book with a neighbor whose kids ate lollipops for breakfast. Soon she was singing the gospel as well, and her kids came off the bus to be greeted by steamed broccoli. In the book were suggestions of what people could do to effect change. One was to initiate legislation. I called Dr. Jacobson at the Center for Science in the Public Interest and spoke at length with his staff members, Athan Manual and Geoffrey Barron. With the help of their tremendous knowledge and insight, Marja and I submitted a bill on school lunch nutritional disclosure through our state representative. It seemed silly that we could get a nutritional analysis of a candy bar but not the breakdown in our children's school lunches. We feel very grateful for the help we received from State Representative Phillip Travis and his top-notch assistant, Wendy DeClercq. I am also extremely appreciative to Dr. Jacobson for reviewing this book and writing the foreword and to his outstanding staff for all their assistance.

I owe thank-yous to all who have encouraged and supported our mission: "Team Sweet" business managers and agents, past and present—Kristin Kuliga, Esq.; Ian Barrett; Kevin Weaver; Thomas Noel, Esq.; Elaine Rogers, Esq. Thanks for all your expert guidance. Shelley Roth, my literary agent—you are diligent, hardworking, and just plain smart. You could not have found me a better editor to work with. Thank you Judith McCarthy, my editor at NTC/Contemporary. I relied on and fully trusted your expertise, and you exceeded my expectations and made this work easy. Great thanks to project editor Susan Moore-Kruse, editorial assistant Michelle Pezutti, publicist Brigid Brown, designers Monica Baziuk and Amy Yu Ng, and the entire stellar staff at NTC/Contemporary who worked on this book.

My family would like to extend our gratitude to our sponsors who have supported us with kind words, products, and funding. Thank you to our friends at Reebok, PowerBar, Shaklee, Converse/Everlast for Women, the Baby Jogger, L.L. Bean, and the Step Company.

To Jim Karpeichik at Ocean State Video, your work is always first-class. Thank you for caring as much about my projects as I do. You deserve all the success and awards you receive!

To outstanding producer Mary Maguire and top-notch photographer Jim O'Halloran, at Public Eye Media Productions, Inc., thank you for all your help and wisdom.

To Ian Shiff, producer, WJAR NBCIO in Providence, Rhode Island, thank you for airing the original "Fitness Mom" segments. You inspired me to go forward.

To supermom and news anchor Patrice Wood, thank you for all your kind words, support, direction, and enthusiasm—you are a great example to all of us and a dear friend. To my wonderful neighbor and friend Sue Jacobs, bless you for all that you have done! To special folks Donna and Jim Poole, Steve and Jan McPartland, Tony and Liz Pivirotto, Tom and Martina Hightower, Ed and Liz O'Brien, Sue MacDonald, Judy Applebaum, Randy Rockney and Wes and Anne Peterson, Carol MacLagan, Bill and Cheryl Simmons, Hoon and Cheung Kwak, and Mike and Karen Salois—you are all shining examples of outstanding parents who put family first. To Roberta Shafer, our office manager extraordinaire—what would we ever do without you? You amaze us every day.

Many people have shared their advice, wisdom, and ideas with me. Thank you to Dr. Joseph Massimo, Dr. Wayne Westcott, Dr. Avery Faigenbaum, Jeff Chao, Bill Letizia, Mary Ellen Fowler, Andrea Reynolds, Dr. Laurie Grauel, Dr. Gary Wharton, Janice Godfrey, Sherri Higgenbotham, Heather Kahn, Rhonda Mann, Kristine Thurston, Donna Colby, Barbara Morse, Conrad Ostrowski, Dr. Lyle Micheli, Dr. Gina Oliva, Brian Fitzgerald, and the Massachusetts Governors Committee on Physical Fitness and Sports, the National Youth Sports Safety Foundation, and the entire AAU Aerobics Committee. Special thanks to our teachers, trainers, coaches, and choreographers: Tracie Finan, Marianne Renner, Rauly Duenas, Shari Druckman, "Miss Lisa,"

Rena Rinker, Erin Kupcha, Peter Whitehead, and "Coach Grandpa." To Al St. John and the staff at Palmer River School, Joanne Hoffman and Paul Lindenmaier and the staff at Moses Brown School, our heartfelt appreciation for touching our children's lives and sharing your special gifts. To my sister, Kathie; brothers Michael and Kim; their spouses and kids; and to Susi, Jack, Dot, Priscilla, and my cousins—you have all contributed in your own way to this project. A special "hello" to Brittany from Marja and to our foster friend, Son Thanh Ngo. To Marja's wonderful friend Kaia, you are an ace athlete, student, and friend. Thank you to all my spunky students at the Rehoboth Fitness Club and the youthful seniors at Care New England Wellness Center. To the kids who allowed us to use their likeness in the book: Sarah McPartland; Tim and Amanda Dixon; James Poole; Lucas Myers; Mattie Solomon; Katrina and Jessica Karpeichik; Jonathan and Stephanie Pabis; Hillary and Emily Wood; Chantelle, Miya, and Zurich Jacobs; Marja and Noah Sweet—you make great cartoon characters as well as awesome kids!

Andy Anderson worked long and hard on providing the entertaining cartoon illustrations. Thank you so much for your time, effort, and talent!

Thank you to all the parents who recognize that "fitness is a parental responsibility" and lead their children every day by the example they live. To children everywhere, every single effort you make is helping you become stronger, healthier, and more resilient for your life ahead. This is the one piece of advice I hope you'll remember from this book. I wish you all the best and hope you have a great time becoming fit and healthy!

I

Whoop It Up!

Getting your family into the lifetime fitness habit begins with fun and games that you do together starting in early childhood.

1 ✷ Create an Obstacle Course

Materials
Be imaginative and use whatever safe materials are available around the home to create your own obstacle course!
- 2 or 3 hula hoops or inflatable swimming tubes
- 10 to 12 feet of rope
- 2 or more pieces of corrugated cardboard (3′ × 2′) (you can cut up a cardboard box)
- 6 to 8 old washcloths or dish towels
- 2 empty 1-gallon plastic milk or water jugs
- 1 broom
- 1 tennis or other small ball

The only obstacles to becoming fit are the fun ones you use here! Before starting this activity, make sure all furniture is moved out of the way and do the obstacle course on a soft surface (grass or carpet). Put hula hoops or swimming tubes into staggered rows on the ground so you can run through them (putting one foot in each hole). Add a rope outstretched on the ground to hop over in a zigzag fashion. Take the cardboard and fold each piece in half for low hurdles. Place the washcloths on the ground in a hopscotch pattern to jump on. The last station is a goalie shot. Set up the two milk containers as goalposts (two feet apart) and place the broom and ball 10 feet away. Now you are ready to go through the course! The participants can rearrange the pattern each time to make the course more interesting and challenging. This course trains speed and agility.

2 ✷ Mighty Marsupials

Materials
- 6 to 8 feet of large bubble wrap
- clothespins (1 for each child)
- measuring tape
- marker

Fun Fact: Kangaroos can jump as far as 40 feet.

Ask your kids how far they can jump. Lay out a long strip of bubble wrap. (The large bubble kind works best.) Have the children stand at the end with both feet together. Tell them to swing their arms back and then jump forward as far as possible. The bubbles will pop upon landing. (Great sound effects!) Attach a clothespin with each child's name to the side of the bubble wrap where his heels have landed. Children can play this by themselves and try to outdistance their last jump, or they can compete against each other. Ask them what they can do to improve their jump. For example: swing arms back farther, bend the knees more, push harder off the toes. Measure the distance with a measuring tape. Parent or child can write the distance down. Encourage them to practice each day to become stronger. Practice, practice, practice!

3 ✳ No More TV Couch Potatoes

Materials

- none

Here is a way to get your family moving at every commercial. Instead of heading for the kitchen—why not exercise at each commercial? Try this contest over a period of time to create a good habit. At every commercial break get the group doing push-ups, sit-ups, jumping jacks, hops, or whatever gets their hearts beating faster. Try dancing to the commercial's jingle! Usually you will have two to three minutes to do this. A leader can be chosen for each "set" or you can have a contest to see who remembers to start first as soon as the commercials begin. This may help keep junk-food consumption down and also be an introduction to fun group exercise.

4 ✻ "Attention Moms and Dads—It's Playground Time"

Materials
- sneakers
- comfortable clothes

That's right! When you pick up your child from school, wear your sneakers and comfortable clothes. Before you get into the car, go to the playground and spend time on the equipment with your child. When was the last time you went down the slide, climbed through a tube, or went across the monkey bars? All you need is 10 to 15 minutes. You'll get a good workout and your child will be thrilled with your attention and interest. Don't you miss being a kid?

5 ✳ "My Very Own" Workout Music Tapes

Materials

- cassette tape player
- blank cassette tape
- watch with second hand or metronome
- upbeat recorded songs

Do your kids like to dance and move to music? Make a tape of their favorite tunes. Start by listening to all the music that really makes you want to get up and boogie. Then eliminate any song whose beat is too slow or too fast. A professional aerobics tape is 125 to 132 beats per minute. Play each song and count how many beats you hear in the first minute using a watch with a second hand or a metronome. Record one song after another. You should make a tape that is approximately 20 to 30 minutes long. A real aerobics tape will start and end with a slower song. This is for the "warm-up" and "cool-down" segments. Then, play the tape and move with your kids. Older kids will surely give you a thumbs-up or thumbs-down on your musical taste!

6 ✻ Write to the President's Council on Physical Fitness and Sports

Materials
- paper, envelope, and stamp
- notebook
- pencil or pen

Did you know that the entire family can earn a badge and certificate for regularly participating in sports and exercise? Participants must be at least six years old. The President's Council was started in 1972 to encourage Americans to become more physically fit. Write to the President's Council to receive an application and the guidelines. You can help the kids keep a fitness log of their workouts (this aids consistency and motivation). You will need to return the completed form and send $8.00 per participant to the Amateur Athletic Union (AAU). Send your request to:

Presidential Sports Award/AAU
c/o Walt Disney World Resort
P.O. Box 10,000
Lake Buena Vista, FL 32830-1000
(407) 934-7200

7 ✻ Flashlight Limbo

Materials
- flashlight
- limbo music (cassette tape or CD)
- cassette or CD player

This game can be played at nighttime but should not be played in the total dark for safety's sake. (Keep a light on in the corner.) Here is a way to do the limbo without needing two people to hold the rope or stick—find just one to hold the flashlight! Line up the kids, start the music, and have each one take a turn going under the "Limbo Light Ray." The goal is to not have the light touch you. If it does, you are out . . . but at least it doesn't hurt a bit! After everyone has gone under the "Limbo Light Ray" once, lower the flashlight a few inches and try again. Here is a pointer to share with the gang—lead with the chest, arch backward, hop with the knees apart, and make sure the head goes under the light ray last. This is an easy, last-minute game that can channel a little of that extra "before bedtime" energy.

8 ⁕ Athletes' Autograph Book

Materials
- pen or pencil
- autograph book or scrapbook
- camera and film (optional)

Start an autograph/advice collection of athletes you and the kids meet. Take this book to all sports events attended. Instruct your kids to politely ask the athletes, coaches, and trainers for their autographs and sports tips. They can even ask them to pose for photos if they seem friendly. Collect and jot down their training ideas, special health regimens or diets, stories of how they began their careers, and so on. Put their photos or winning statistics in the book. Your kids' friends and classmates will enjoy seeing the end result. Include all levels of athlete from high-school record setter to professional athlete. All of these participants work hard and will have something interesting to share. Remember today's local athlete may be tomorrow's record-setting Olympian. What a great positive example!

9 ✻ Parking Lot Pump

Materials
• none

Even some of the little things that we do in the course of our daily activity can improve our fitness levels. Experts tell us there is a definite benefit to exercising several times a day in small amounts. This is helpful for people who have a very busy schedule and can't get to a gym or health club. Next time you take your children shopping or running errands, park the car at the far end of the parking lot or several blocks from your destination. Instead of walking to the first stop, try playing follow-the-leader. Keep your eyes open for traffic as you hop, skip, leap over puddles, walk on curbs, and jump over cracks. You will all get a miniworkout and have a fun time!

10 ✴ Meet a Mentor

Materials

- none

Everyone needs a hero to look up to! Contact your local high school or college and ask the coach of your child's favorite sport if she can watch or participate in a practice. This is a great way for her to learn drills and technique. It will also help her appreciate how skillful, talented, and hardworking the athletes are. She may also be able to hook up with a mentor who can share inspiration and advice. Now that's a role model!

11 ✳ Water Bottle Bowling

Materials
- 6 one-quart plastic water bottles
  (these should be filled partway) with covers
- 1 tennis or small soft ball
- removable tape or chalk

Quick and easy—this is a fun, last-minute activity at a party or with any gathering of friends. Check and make sure the covers of the water bottles are on very tight so there will be no spills. Place the bottles in the following pattern: one at the front, two staggered behind the first bottle, and then three staggered behind the second row. From the top you will see a triangle. Make a line with "easy to remove" tape or use chalk or a stick when outside. There should be 10 to 15 feet between the line and the bottles. Use a tennis or other soft ball as the "bowling ball." Try to strike down all the pins by rolling the ball along the ground. Each player takes three turns. The name of the game is to knock all the pins down (not destroy the furniture) in as few tries as possible. This game can be played inside or out.

12 ✳ Take Special Notes

Materials
- pencil and paper (optional)

Need some time together with your child? Watch professional sports or major championships on TV or in person with your child. Watch the techniques carefully and compare the results of what different athletes do. Do some athletes get better results? Suggest that your child write down what he observes. Sometimes an athlete is an "innovator." (Dick Fosbury created the backward-flopping high jump and became very successful with this new skill. David Berkoff did the backstroke swimming underwater using both legs together—like a dolphin's tail.) The goal is to have the budding athlete experiment with different ways of working arms and moving legs to become more successful in his attempts. This requires inward focus and "tuning in" to how his body works.

13 ✳ Stomp Dance

Materials
- metal trash cans
- metal trash-can lids
- push brooms, mops, broom handles

"Stomp" is an expressive and loud dance style that originated in Africa. Performing it is a good way to burn off some extra energy. Due to its disruptive noise, though, it may not be suitable for your neighborhood, so use your judgment. Based on a Broadway production, "stomping" uses simple objects to create rhythms and patterns. Have the kids create expressive sounds and movements from banging trash-can lids together, pounding on upside-down metal trash cans, or thumping broomstick ends onto the ground. They can add leaping, hopping, and spinning moves. There is no right or wrong way to do this form of freestyle "dancing."

14 ✷ Stadium Stampede

Materials
• sneakers

Take the children to your local high-school or college stadium. Ride your bicycles if it's close enough. Have the group run up one section of stadium stairs and then down the next. See how far around the stadium everyone can get. "Wind sprints" can be done in a fun way by having two people face back-to-back on the running track. Each runs in the opposite direction as fast as possible. See who can get to the halfway point first. If the runners are in really good shape, see who can get to the beginning point first. (This would be a full lap instead of a half. No cutting across the field!)

15 ✻ "Body by Jake, Emily, James, Brittany . . ."

Materials

- mat
- ruler
- pencil and paper
- clipboard (optional)

Let your child be *your* personal trainer. Your "in-house" personal trainer will tell you which exercises to do. Encourage her to share the exercises that she does in her gym class. Push-ups, sit-ups, arm circles, and windmills may be some of the standard exercises. Let your child tell you how many of each exercise *you* should do and how many *she* should do. She counts for you, and you count for her. Use a ruler and a pencil to make a chart listing the different exercises. You may want to clip it to a clipboard for easy carrying. Try to improve the count over time.

16 ✻ Lost Sneaker Race

Materials

- sneakers

Everyone takes off his or her sneakers (including the moms and dads) and places them in a big pile at the far end of a long room or yard. The gang lines up (shoeless) at the other end, runs to the pile of shoes, digs for their own pair, puts them on, fastens laces (for safety), and runs back to the start. Let the little ones wear velcro shoes or easy slip-ons . . . or how about giving them a head start? All ages can participate in this race.

17 ✶ Ice Bowling

Materials
- candlepin bowling ball (a small bowling ball that fits in your palm)
- 6 to 10 bowling pins
- shovel

Your gang can play on the ice without lacing up skates—no frozen fingers! Ask a bowling alley if they have an old candlepin bowling ball and a few pins that they are willing to part with. Next you need to find a frozen lake. First, make sure the authorities in your town have inspected and OK'd the ice. Shovel off a straight runway 15 to 20 feet long. Take the pins and stand them up three to four inches apart at the far end of the runway. You can put them in a straight line, a V-shape, or a half-circle. Stand at the other end and roll the ball down the runway to knock down the pins. Separate the pins or move them farther away down the runway for a greater challenge. This is one way to wake up sleeping fish!

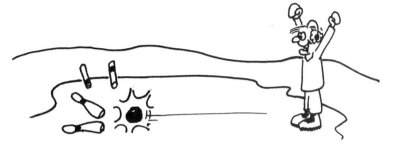

18 ✴ Super Action Socks

Materials
- cotton socks
- cardboard
- pair of scissors
- pencil
- puffy fabric paint in a squeeze bottle
- newspaper to protect the work area

Do your kids want to gain a little more traction indoors from their socks without having to wear sneakers? Pick out some cotton socks and collect a piece of cardboard, scissors, pencil, and puffy fabric paint in a squeeze bottle (choose dazzling colors!). Spread newspaper to protect work area. Start by tracing both feet on the cardboard. Cut the foot shapes out and insert each "cardboard foot" into a sock. You should have two stiff-looking socks. This will give the artist a better working surface, and the paint won't go through both layers of sock either. Have the kids squeeze the puffy fabric paint on the *bottom* (only!) of the socks in a repetitive design. Some designs will provide better traction than others. What can your youngsters think of? Stars, circles, squiggles, or zigzags are some examples. Before the socks are worn, be sure the paint is completely dry . . . especially if you cherish your floors!

19 ✻ Smile, Camera, Action

Materials
- sheet for backdrop
- video camera
- tripod or table
- cassette tape player
- homemade aerobics tape
- exercising mats, sample carpet squares, or small rugs
- clock or watch to time warm-up, aerobic, and cool-down segments

Every celebrity seems to make an exercise video sooner or later—why not your kids? Keep exercise mats or rugs off to the side for "conditioning" exercises on the floor. Hang a sheet up for a backdrop. Set up your tape player with a homemade aerobics music tape (see Activity 5). Next place your video camera on a tripod or a steady table. Look into the lens and make sure you can see the entire set. Recruit talented (or at least willing) family and friends and have the children lead them in continuous "aerobic" movements (e.g., do jumping jacks, kicks, knee lifts, and march or run in place). The fledgling instructors can make up the movements as they go, or each one can take turns being the leader. Always begin with a warm-up of gentle exercises to gradually increase the heart rate and ready the muscles. Stretching exercises should be done after the warm-up but before the aerobic workout. Everyone in the class should be able to carry on a conversation while exercising aerobically or you are working too intensely—slow down the pace! Keep the steady pace going for 15 to 20 minutes and then gradually slow down the routine for 5 to 8 minutes. Add in some conditioning exercises on the mats such as push-ups and sit-ups. End with more stretches. Show the children how to hold each stretching position for 30 to 45 seconds to really feel the benefit. (Look at Chapter 13 for ideas on stretching.)

20 ✶ Climb a Skyscraper

Materials
- journal
- pen or pencil
- box for collecting memorabilia
- sneakers
- water bottle

When traveling to a new city (or even in your own area) find the tallest skyscraper and see if you are allowed to walk up the stairs. Take a family "hike" up the skyscraper— how many flights are there? How many steps? How long did it take? Next time you go to a different city, do the same.

Keep track and make a collection of photos, statistics, and memorabilia of your skyscraper excursion (a button, statue, bumper sticker). This is a great way to get some exercise on a rainy day! (Hint: Dress in layers since you may work up a sweat.) Wear sneakers. Drink water frequently.

21 ⋆ Paper Stepping-Stones

Materials
- 10 to 12 large brown grocery bags
- 12-inch stack of newspapers or magazines
- stapler
- marker

Dig into the recycling bin for this project. Add some creativity and the kids will enjoy moving from one "stone" to the next—contorting, leaping, and squirming along the pathway. You can create stepping-stones out of large brown paper bags filled with small (one-inch) stacks of newspaper or magazines. Staple the bags closed. On the flat side of each bag, draw either two feet, one foot, two hands, one hand, or all four (hands and feet). Next lay out the bags in random order—two to three feet apart. Each person tries to go from one bag to the other, placing only the illustrated "body part" on the bag (i.e., you cannot put both feet on a bag that shows two hands!). Sometimes this is very tricky. If you get stuck or lose your balance, you're out, and the next person in line takes his turn. Rearrange the bags as often as you like. Remember you might have to stretch or jump to reach the next bag!

22 ✳ Adopt-a-Space

Materials
- gloves
- barbecue tongs or scoop and dustpan
- paper bags
- cardboard box (for glass and metal objects)

Need a good excuse for a walk? Take a hike to a park or along a safe road and collect trash. Invite the children's friends—the more the merrier! Hold a contest to see who can gather the most refuse. Be safety conscious—don't stand near a busy road, and don't let the kids gather the trash with their hands. Use tongs or a scoop and dustpan. One child can hold the bag open as the other child puts the trash in it. Only adults should handle glass or sharp objects—place these dangerous items in a sturdy box for disposal. Keep this activity energetic to get the most out of it! Work hard and quickly—you'll feel rewarded in body and spirit!

23 ✳ Paper Plate Frisbee (Plisbee!)

Materials
- paper or plastic plate (1 per child)
- bowl (4 to 5 inches in diameter)
- pencil
- pair of scissors
- crayons or markers for decorating

This is a simple activity even the youngest child can do—with some help. This can easily be done by placing a bowl facedown in the center of a large paper or plastic plate. Make sure the bowl is centered. Trace the edge of the bowl. Cut the circle out of the paper plate. Decorate the edges with markers or crayons. (Crayons won't work on a plastic plate.) Now go outside and play "plisbee." Try to toss to each other, hit an object, have it land in a trash bin or hang on a tree limb. That's a fitness challenge!

24 ✳ Create-a-Sport

Materials "basic list"
- scarf
- tennis ball
- plastic bag
- string
- newspaper

- paper streamer
- empty cereal box
- rag
- piece of aluminum foil
- paper cup
- empty can
- rope
- paper bag to put "basic" items in

Materials for dial
- 2 paper plates
- pair of scissors
- pencil
- markers
- 1 brass fastener

This is a project the kids can do from start to finish (almost completely) by themselves! Collect all the items in the "basic list" before beginning this project. Place the objects in a paper bag. If you can't find all the objects, substitute other items. The next step is to make the dial. Take a paper plate and poke a small hole in the center—big enough for the brass fastener to go through. (An adult should poke the hole using the scissors.) With your markers divide the plate into twelve equal "pieces of pie." On each piece, use a marker to either write the name or draw a picture of one of the "basic" items on the materials list. Take another paper plate and draw an arrow half the width of the paper plate. Cut the arrow out and attach it to the first paper plate with the brass fastener. It should rotate around freely, if it doesn't, make the hole a little bigger. Now you are ready to play! Spin the dial. (If you have four or more players, each person should spin just once; if you have less than four players, each person should spin twice.) Pick out the correct items from the bag and create a new sport or game using just the items you have chosen. This will bring out the creative genius in each child!

25 ✳ Canned Fun

Materials

- 12-ounce frozen fruit juice can
  (made out of cardboard)
- pitcher
- water (according to directions on the can)
- can opener

Kids can practice football goal kicks all afternoon without worrying about having someone hold the ball for the kicker—often the most injury-prone job! Open the top end of the frozen juice can by either using the pull-off tab or a can opener. Remove the contents and make the juice according to the directions. Store in a pitcher in the refrigerator for a post-practice refreshment! Carefully open the bottom end with a can opener. (Adults should supervise or do this for younger children.) Go into a field or yard where digging is allowed and bury the can upright, three-quarters of the way into the ground. Twisting the can into loose soil works best. Try to choose an area without a lot of rocks, tightly packed dirt, or sand. Place the football on top of the opening and practice being a superstar kicker! A coach or gym teacher can help show children proper and safe kicking form.

26 ✴ Slipper Kick

Materials
- pair of soft slippers
- trash bin or basket

Your kids probably do this when you're not looking. Surprise them and try it too! Find a pair of soft slippers—they don't have to be an exact fit—and place them on the bed. Set up an empty trash bin or basket several feet away from the bed. Remove from harm's way any valuable or special items in the "line of fire." Sit on the edge of the bed with your feet dangling down. Put both slippers on partway so they hang off your toes. Cock one leg back by bending at the knee and kick forward so the slipper flies off your foot—and hopefully into the trash bin. Now kick off the other slipper. Let each player try. Did anyone land a slipper in the basket? Who was the closest—adult or child? Probably whoever has logged the most practice time!

27 ✴ Solo Soccer

Materials
- 2″ × 4″ × 8′ wooden post
- electric drill
- ¼-inch eyebolt
- 3-inch hook fastener
- 2 or 3 inner tubes
- pair of scissors
- old pair of pantyhose
- soccer or rubber ball
- fence post digger—borrow a friend's or rent from equipment rental store
- 5-gallon bucket
- quick-dry cement—it usually comes in 40-pound bags but you will not need the whole bag
- 1 quart water

Your child can enjoy endless hours practicing soccer kicks. Lay a wooden post on its side and drill a starting hole into the top end. Twist in the eyebolt. Attach the hook fastener to the eyebolt. Cut the valves off the inner tubes and knot the tubes together. Thread one end of the inner tubes through the hook fastener and knot securely. Place the ball in the pantyhose's torso area. Knot the pantyhose closed at the waist and then tie the legs together. The ball should be firmly in place in the pantyhose. Knot the legs and inner tubes together. With a fence post digger dig a hole wide and deep enough to hold the five-gallon bucket. Place the bucket in the hole and the post in the bucket. Have a helper hold the post upright as you fill the bucket with the cement. Pour in the water and let it harden. (You do not need to mix the cement.) Make sure the post is not tilting! Once completely hardened you can cover the cement with dirt, pack it down, and play a lively game of solo soccer!

28 ✦ Sledding Madness

Materials

- carpet remnants or squares
- carpet cutter—very sharp—
  for adults only to touch!

Going downhill is so much fun, but pulling the heavy sled back up isn't at all! Here is a solution that will make it easier for your kids to enjoy this winter sport. Go to either a carpet or a warehouse liquidator store and purchase carpet remnants or ask for free sample squares. Cut remnants with the carpet cutter to make a one-foot-wide footpath or place carpet squares up the snow-covered hill. Your kids will be happy to pull or carry their own sleds up the hill because the carpet will keep them from sinking into the snow, their feet stay warmer and drier, and their legs get less tired. They will be exercising for longer. Make sure you have some mugs of low-fat hot chocolate ready when they're done!

29 ∗ Slip-Sliding Away

Materials
- sturdy child-sized chair
- ice skates

Standing up is one of the hardest tasks for a brand-new skater! Give your little one a chair to hold on to and push, and it will be like having training wheels—the four extra legs provide support and confidence. Have your child begin by pushing the chair and walking, go to marching in place, marching forward, and then shuffling. Shuffling is a marching step with the feet left on the ice. Let the shuffle steps get longer and longer until they turn into glides and off your skater goes!

30 ∗ Help Out

Materials
- sneakers

Volunteer to take a seeing-impaired person for a walk or jog. Contact a local school or organization for the visually handicapped and offer to be a workout partner. An additional helper will be needed to guide your new partner safely along a pathway or running track. A helper stands on each side. Make sure the trail can accommodate the three-person span. Let your partner hold on to your bent elbows as you lead the way and watch out for road hazards. Announce any upcoming changes well in advance—turf or directional changes, debris and potholes to be avoided. Start off by walking. As your pace, rhythm, and sense of trust develop you can increase the speed and duration of the training sessions. Older children will enjoy this sense of responsibility and community service—and they may make a new friend in the process!

31 ✳ Where There's a Will, There's a Way

Materials

- none

Your family can be able-bodied buddies at a Challenger division baseball game! In 1989, Little League Baseball started a special division for children with physical and mental handicaps. These kids play on the same fields with the same equipment and uniforms but with some modifications in the rules. Help out by pushing a wheelchair around the bases, cheering as loud as you can, or being a coach. See how you can help by writing or calling:

Director of the Challenger Division
Little League Baseball Headquarters
P.O. Box 3485
Williamsport, PA 17701
(717) 326-1921

32 ✦ TV-Free Week

Materials

- 4 bases—cones, old 1-inch-thick chair cushions, or landmarks (trees, telephone poles, and so on)
- plastic, rubber, or soccer ball

Fun Fact: The average two- to five-year-old watches 28 hours of television a week. (*Prevention* magazine, Nov. '91)

National TV-Turnoff Week is the third week in April. Instead of watching TV try playing a game of kickball after the dinner dishes are done. Begin by setting up two teams. You don't need an even number of players because one person can go twice—so invite friends and neighbors. Set up four bases in the shape of a diamond: home, first, second, and third base. The bases should be about 25 feet apart. You will need a pitcher, a home-base catcher, and assorted other catchers spread out in the field—depending on how many players you have. To play the game the pitcher rolls the ball on the ground to the first kicker (from the other team). She kicks the ball with all her might and runs to first base. The catchers all scramble and try to get the ball. If the ball is caught in midair the runner is out. If the ball touches the ground and is stopped and thrown to the base before the runner gets there, she can be tagged out. (This applies to all bases she might run to.) If she is safe she stays on first base, and the next player takes her turn kicking the ball. The first runner gets to run to second base during this time. Sometimes a runner will have time to run to more than one base if the other team is fumbling around for the ball. Maybe the runner can even get to home base. Try to get as many players as possible home before your team accumulates three outs. When three outs are reached, the teams switch places. This game will be so much fun your family will want to be TV-free forever—which is the goal of National TV-Turnoff Week!

For more information on National TV-Turnoff Week call (800) 939-6737 or look up their website: www.tvfa.org.

II

Fun Facts and
Food Folly

There is a lot more to nutrition than just the
food pyramid. Enjoy these interesting food facts
and dig into the unusual recipes and projects to
leave a big impression on your kids!

Note about the nutritional analysis The recipes may call for
a choice of possible ingredients, in those cases the author ran-
domly selected from the list and based the analysis on those items.
Your actual nutritional breakdown may differ from the one
included after the recipe.

33 ✳ Extra Good for You Applesauce

World's Best Applesauce Recipe

Materials
- apple corer and peeler
  (unless you have a
  fruit mill)
- knife
- iron pot
- fruit mill, food processor/blender,
  or metal sieve and wooden spoon

Ingredients
- 10 to 15 apples
- water—enough to cover
  apples
  in pot by 1 or 2 inches
- sugar, honey, maple
  syrup—use any
  combination or amount of
  these sweeteners to taste
  (start with a small amount
  such as ½ cup)
- 1 to 3 teaspoons (to taste)
  cinnamon
- ½ to 1 teaspoon (to taste)
  nutmeg
- ½ to 1 teaspoon (to taste) ground cloves
- 1 to 2 teaspoons vanilla extract (optional)

Fun Fact: According to a recent article in *American Fitness* magazine, applesauce cooked in an iron pot has 22 mg of iron per half-cup serving; applesauce cooked in a glass pot only has 0.2 mg per half-cup serving. Iron is essential for growing a strong body because it helps your blood carry oxygen throughout your body.

Wash apples (even slightly bruised ones) and then cut them into quarters. If you have a fruit mill you don't need to remove the skin, core, and seeds. However, if you don't have one, remove the core and seeds first. Leaving some of the skin on adds a nice pink color to your applesauce. Place apples in an iron pot and cover them with 1 to 2 inches of water. Simmer until soft. This will take 10 to 15 minutes. If you like a firmer texture, cook for less time. You can either grind mixture through a fruit mill, press it through a metal sieve with a wooden spoon, or puree it in a food processor or blender. Add a little sugar, honey, and/or maple syrup and a bit of cinnamon. I like to add a small amount of nutmeg, ground cloves, and a teaspoon of vanilla, too. Serve warm!

Serves 8

Nutrition per serving: 180 calories; 0 g fat; 48 g carbohydrate; 8 g fiber; 2% calcium; 4% iron; 15% vitamin C

34 ✷ Dinosaur Trees

Materials
- fork and knife
- saucepan and steamer
- hot mitts
- serving dish

Ingredients
- 4 baking potatoes, washed and patted dry; leave the skin on (it contains five times the amount of iron as the rest of the potato!)
- 1 large stalk broccoli (preferably organic)
- ½ cup grated low-fat cheddar cheese
- 4 tablespoons real bacon bits (lower fat variety)

Preheat oven to 350°F. Take each baking potato and pierce it

Fun Facts: What would you rather eat: 204 apples or one-third of a stalk of broccoli? A small amount of broccoli has more vitamin C than all those apples! The florets of the broccoli stalk have eight times more beta-carotene than the stem.

✷ CAUTION ✷ Your children can help you do the assembly steps after the broccoli and potatoes have been cooked. Be careful, baked potatoes are very hot, and the steam from the broccoli can cause a burn. Use hot mitts!

with a fork in four places. Place potatoes in the oven and bake for approximately 1 hour at the preheated setting. Test a potato to make sure it is done to your liking. This can be done by cutting it in half lengthwise. During the last 15 minutes of baking the potatoes you can start the recipe for broccoli. Place a saucepan with an  inch or so of water on the stove. Set a vegetable steamer in it and place the broccoli in the steamer. Cover the pan and turn the heat to high. Steam for 5 to 8 minutes until broccoli is tender and still a beautiful, rich green color. There should be a little crunch in the stalks; you don't want floppy, pale broccoli—this would mean you have cooked out many of the vital nutrients. (This is important information that you should tell your children.) After both the potatoes and the broccoli are cooked, remove the potatoes from the oven with hot mitts, cut them in half lengthwise, and place them on a serving dish cut-side down. One potato makes two servings. Cut several small Xs into each potato. They should be big enough to plant the "trunk" of the broccoli. Drain the broccoli and place it upright in the potato halves. Let the children sprinkle the cheese (snow) and bacon bits (leaves) over the "dinosaur forest" scene! Serve warm! **Serves 8**

Nutrition per serving: 170 calories; 3.5 g fat; 27 g carbohydrate; 3 g fiber; 8 g protein; 15% calcium; 10% iron, 50% vitamin C

35 ✶ Flamingo Frappe

Here is a great frappe filled with beta-carotene.

Materials
- blender
- drinking glasses

Ingredients

- ½ to 1 cup pineapple or orange juice
- 1 cup vanilla or any fruit-flavored no-fat or low-fat frozen yogurt
- 1 to 2 cups fresh or frozen papaya, mangos, cantaloupe, oranges, or strawberries—fruit needs to be cut up into chunks with all the seeds and skin removed before it is placed in the freezer
- ½ cup ice cubes or crushed ice
- fresh fruit garnish

Fun Fact: What makes pink flamingos pink? Carotenoids do! They are in the flamingo's diet and give these beautiful birds their color. If they don't eat enough of this important nutrient, they become white! Humans need beta-carotene, a form of carotenoid. Some of the best sources of beta-carotene are papaya, mangos, carrots, sweet potatoes, and red peppers.

Place all the above ingredients in a blender starting with the fruit juice on the bottom. Whip together in a blender beginning with the lowest setting and continuing until smooth. Pour into a tall glass and add a straw and fresh fruit garnish (cherry, watermelon, orange slice, or strawberry). This is a power-packed drink loaded with calcium and vitamins!

Serves 4

Nutrition per serving: 130 calories;
0 g fat; 29 g carbohydrate;
2 g fiber; 3 g protein;
10% calcium; 8% iron;
35% vitamin A; 100% vitamin C

36 ✳ This Meal Is "for the Birds"

Here is a tastier choice than worms for people; try whole wheat or spinach spaghetti. Spinach spaghetti doesn't taste much like spinach, but it is a more nutritious alternative than regular pasta. Whole wheat spaghetti is even more nutritious. You can buy these delicious products at a natural food store or in the health-food section of some supermarkets.

Fun Fact: Our friends at the National Audubon Society tell us that robins eat 14 feet of worms a day!

Materials
- spinach or whole wheat spaghetti, cooked
- plastic tablecloth
- plastic bib, smock, or old shirt
- bowls for spaghetti

To eat like a bird, prepare nutritious spaghetti according to the instructions on the package. Place a plastic tablecloth on the floor or the grass outside. Each of your "robins" needs to wear a plastic bib, smock, or old shirt for this messy dining experience. Have the children kneel down in front of their bowl of pasta and without using their "wings" (hands) eat the spaghetti like a robin. Slurping up the noodles is allowed today!

37 * Great Pizza Creations

Can you discover an unusual and delicious topping combination to place on top of your pizza?

Snowflake Pizza—No Two Are Alike!

Materials
- pair of scissors
- metal baking pan
- aluminum foil
- hot mitts

Ingredients
- 1 package of flour tortillas
- 1 small can pizza sauce or tomato paste
- 1 cup crumbled low-fat mozzarella, muenster, provolone, goat, or feta cheese
- assorted toppings—sliced or chopped, raw or cooked vegetables; low-fat meats; fresh or dried herbs

Fun Fact: Did you know that the favorite pizza topping in the United States is pepperoni (high in fat!)? In Japan it is eel and squid; Russians savor red herring; in Australia they prefer shrimp and pineapple; and in Costa Rica coconut is numero uno according to *Kid City* magazine!

Fold a flour tortilla in half and then in half once again. Cut out geometric shapes in the tortilla with clean scissors. Unfold it and lay it flat on a metal baking sheet covered with aluminum foil. Next spread pizza sauce or tomato paste on top. Sprinkle cheese on it. Apply the sauce and toppings carefully so that they don't end up on the aluminum foil. Try different varieties of cheese (such as goat cheese or low-fat mozzarella) to make your child's "snowflake" truly unique. Let them choose unusual, "kid-friendly" toppings—mandarin oranges, red peppers, portabella

mushroom slices, ham, and pineapple are some suggestions. Finish by sprinkling a dash of herbs on the top. Place it under the oven broiler until the cheese melts. Be sure to watch it carefully so it doesn't burn. Remove with hot mitts and then let it cool down before you serve. Snowflake pizzas are a "hot" item any time of year! **Serves 4**

Nutrition per serving: 360 calories; 10 g fat; 50 g carbohydrate; 4 g fiber; 17 g protein; 30% calcium; 20% iron; 15% vitamin A; 40% vitamin C

38 ✱ Strawberry Shortcakes— a Native American Invention

Here is a quick and nutritious recipe that no parent can object to! Your family will get calcium from the frozen yogurt and vitamin C from the strawberries. Angel food cake is fat free.

All-American Strawberry Shortcake

Materials
- knife
- saucepan
- large spoon

Fun Fact: Yes, strawberry shortcake was invented by Native Americans hundreds of years ago.

Ingredients
- 1 quart fresh strawberries—keep aside 8 whole ones and slice the others for the sauce
- ½ cup water
- ½ to ¾ cup sugar
- angel food cake
- low-fat strawberry or vanilla frozen yogurt

Slice fresh strawberries into a small saucepan, add ½ cup of water and ½ or more of the sugar (depending on whether you prefer a sweeter or a more tart taste). Cook at a medium heat until the strawberries soften. Stir often so they don't stick and burn; add more water if needed. To present your dessert take a slice of angel food cake, add a scoop of low-fat frozen yogurt, and top it off with your delicious, homemade strawberry sauce. Decorate with fresh strawberries. Simply strawberrilicious! **Serves 10**

Nutrition per serving: 330 calories; 1.5 g fat;
71 g carbohydrate; 1 g fiber; 9 g protein; 25% calcium; 2% iron;
2% vitamin A; 50% vitamin C

39 ✹ Sprout Pet

Materials
- 2 damp cotton balls
- small plastic jar (such as a clear prescription bottle)
- 2 dried beans or seeds (e.g., mung beans, soy beans, lima beans, chick peas, alfalfa seeds)

Here is something to "twist and sprout" about! Place one or two damp cotton balls in a small plastic, nonbreakable container. Next select one or two beans of different varieties to make this project more interesting and educational. Place beans in the container with the damp cotton balls. Tighten the cap. Your child can nurture his bean pet along by caring for it—keeping it warm—being careful not to place it directly in the sun or near a heat source such as the stove or radiator. Have the "owner" check and periodically dampen the cotton ball so that it doesn't dry out—it needs to be moist. If the bean is well taken care of, a sprout will develop in five to six days. Sprouts are good in salads and sandwiches and are also low in calories and fat. This project is a quick, easy, and an inexpensive introduction to responsibility. If successful you can go on to something more challenging like goldfish!

40 ✷ Seaweed Pudding

Have you had your *Chondrus crispus* today? Your kids will get a kick out of making this delicious pudding from Irish Moss seaweed (also known as *Chondrus crispus*). It can be purchased at a specialty or health food store. Irish Moss can be found on many food labels as *carrageenan*—a thickening ingredient in pudding and ice cream. This is based on Rose Treat's recipe in *The Seaweed Book*.

Materials
- double boiler
- strainer
- medium bowl
- mold or small bowl
- knife

Ingredients
- ½ cup Irish Moss
- 1 quart low-fat or skim milk
- 1 teaspoon vanilla extract
- pinch of ground nutmeg
- 1 tablespoon (more or less) sugar
- fresh fruit

Wash the seaweed thoroughly—there could be sand or the remains of little guests in the seaweed! Put the milk and the seaweed in the top part of a double boiler. Fill the bottom pan with water. Cook for 30 minutes at a medium heat. (Make sure the water doesn't evaporate in the bottom pan, refilling as needed.)

Strain the mixture into a bowl—keep the milk but throw out the seaweed. Add the vanilla, nutmeg, and sugar to the bowl. You may want to add a little more sugar to taste. Pour the mixture into a mold or into a small bowl. (I love fish molds for this!) Chill the pudding in the refrigerator until it is firm. Cut pieces of fresh fruit and place on the mold to make eyes, scales, and fins. (Try thinly sliced banana for scales, blueberries or raspberries for eyes, and strawberry wedges for fins.) Serve and enjoy! **Serves 8**

Nutrition per serving: 70 calories; 0 g fat; 12 g carbohydrate; 2 g fiber; 5 g protein; 15% calcium; 4% iron; 6% vitamin A; 15% vitamin C

41 ✳ Egg-Cellent Protein

Egg whites contain the highest quality protein available. That is why some bodybuilders drink raw egg-white shakes. But make sure your family never eats raw eggs. They have been known to cause illness.

Egg White "Sleeping Bag" Omelet

This is a good way to get extra protein without the additional cholesterol of the egg yolks.

Materials
- frying pan with cover
- 2 small bowls
- fork and spatula

Ingredients
- 1 cup diced vegetables, any assortment of mushrooms, peas, green or red peppers, zucchini, carrots, onions, tomatoes

Fun Fact: The American Egg Board says that 59 percent of children would like eggs to be blue.

- ½ cup water
- vegetable oil spray (cooking spray)
- 4 egg whites
- ¼ cup fresh or dried herbs
- ¼ cup low-fat shredded American, mozzarella, or cheddar cheese

Place vegetables and water in a frying pan. Cover the pan and simmer for 5 minutes on medium heat. Overcooked vegetables lose much of their nutrients so cook only until tender. Stir with fork as needed. Drain the liquid from the vegetables and set them aside in a small bowl. Next spray the bottom of the same frying pan with cooking oil spray. Spread out the veggies in the bottom of the frying pan. Scramble the egg whites in the other small bowl and pour them over the veggies in the frying pan. Sprinkle herbs on top. Cook mixture halfway then turn the omelet over with a spatula. Add cheese on the second side and then fold omelet over so the cheese looks like it is snoozing in a sleeping bag. When the cheese melts, wake up the omelet by rolling it onto your plate and enjoy! **Serves 2**

Nutrition per serving: 180 calories; 7 g fat; 17 g carbohydrate; 7 g fiber; 15 g protein; 35% calcium; 35% iron; 120% vitamin A; 30% vitamin C

42 ✶ Yummy Log Cabin

This is a fun project that is low in sugar and high in protein.

Materials
- 1 or more empty and clean 8-ounce milk carton(s)
- masking tape, plastic knife, and paper plate

Ingredients
- small jar of smooth peanut butter
- thin pretzel sticks and pretzel nuggets
- ½ cup raisins for decorating
- ½ cup assorted nuts for decorating

Seal milk carton shut with masking tape. Spread peanut butter thickly on all sides, including the "roof." Press the thin pretzel sticks into the peanut butter so they look like logs. Make sure you include doors and windows (break the thin pretzels into smaller pieces for this). Use the chunky pretzel nuggets for the roof shingles. Add raisins and nuts for fancy adornments. The edible ingredients make this a nutritious snack, which is also great fun to demolish and eat heartily with your fingers!

43 ✶ Gummy Jewels

Make these gummy 100 percent fruit juice gems and then string them on a necklace or bracelet.

Materials
- saucepan
- wooden spoon and metal spoon
- cookie sheet

- waxed paper
- needle and thread

Ingredients

- ¼ cup grape, cranberry, or apple juice (100 percent juice)
- 1 envelope unflavored gelatin
- 1 tablespoon sugar
- 1 or 2 drops of liquid flavoring (banana, orange, or lemon)
- Cheerios, popcorn, dried cranberries, or raisins (optional)

Place the juice in a saucepan and heat it to a boil. Set it aside and sprinkle the gelatin and the sugar on the top of the juice and then stir it in well with the additional flavoring. A wooden spoon works best. Remember to use caution—this mixture is very hot. Cover a cookie sheet with waxed paper. Dribble the mixture onto the waxed paper with a metal spoon to make your gems. Allow the precious gems to cool for 10 to 15 minutes. Then peel them off the waxed paper and string them onto a thread with a needle. You can also string Cheerios, popcorn, dried cranberries, or raisins. Wear the necklace until all your gems are eaten off! **Serves 2**

Nutrition per serving: 200 calories; 0 g fat; 49 g carbohydrate; 0 g fiber; 3 g protein; 0% calcium; 0% iron

44 ✱ Make Your Own Pretzels

This is a fun hands-on activity for children of all ages. Be sure to have the kids to go to the washroom and scrub up before starting.

Materials

- cookie sheet
- large mixing bowl
- large spoon

- breadboard
- clean dish towel
- pastry brush
- hot mitts

Ingredients
- cooking oil spray
- ¼ cup cooking oil
- 3½ cups all-purpose flour
- 1 package dry yeast
- 1 teaspoon sugar
- 1 teaspoon salt
- 1 cup water
- ½ cup kosher salt (optional)
- 1 slightly beaten egg (optional)
- ½ cup cinnamon and sugar mixture (optional)

Preheat the oven to 400°F, spray a cookie sheet with cooking oil spray, and rub oil on the insides of a large mixing bowl. In the greased bowl mix 1 cup of the flour, dry yeast, sugar, 1 teaspoon salt (regular, not kosher), and water.

Make a mound of the remaining 2½ cups all-purpose flour on a breadboard. Form a "well" in the middle of it (it should look like a volcano). Pour the ingredients from the first step into the center of the well and mix the whole thing together with those clean hands. Have your helpers knead the dough for 10 minutes. Kneading can be good exercise—push and pull the dough, punch it down, squeeze it with your fingers!

Put the dough in the large oiled bowl and cover it with a clean, *damp* dish towel. Set the bowl in a warm—but not hot—place to rise for 1 hour. It will not double in size, but it will grow.

Let the children punch the dough down with their fists (more exercise!) and then divide it into 12 pieces—adjust this to accommodate the number of children participating. You can now make traditional twisted pretzels, letters, numbers, triangles, or squares—any shapes you want. Put the pretzels on a greased cookie sheet one inch apart. You can leave the pretzels as is (plain), or you can brush them with a beaten egg and sprinkle the top with kosher salt. A "dessert pretzel" can be made by sprinkling the top of each one with a spoonful of the cinnamon and sugar mixture. Why not make a few of each? Bake for 12 minutes in the preheated oven. Serve warm. This recipe (from *Family Fun* magazine) makes a nice, low-fat school or special event snack.

Serves 6

Nutrition per serving: 350 calories; 10 g fat; 57 g carbohydrate; 2 g fiber; 8 g protein; 2% calcium; 20% iron

45 ✦ "Flattened Fruit" Treats

This treat, also known as fruit leather or fruit roll-ups, is a healthy alternative to the store-bought kind. Make it for a holiday gift, a school gathering, or a birthday party.

Materials
- blender
- cookie sheet
- pair of scissors
- plastic wrap

Ingredients
- 24-ounce jar applesauce
- 10 to 12 dried apricots or other dried fruit
- ½ cup dried cranberries (optional)
- ½ teaspoon cinnamon (optional)
- cooking oil spray

The dehydrating process for "flattened fruit" treats takes a *very* long time so don't make them the morning you plan to send them to school. They are, however, very simple to make. Preheat the oven to 150°F or slightly higher.

Place the applesauce in a blender. (You can try an unusual variety like raspberry applesauce.) Add dried apricots and a handful of dried cranberries if you have them. Add cinnamon. Puree in the blender until smooth. Spray a cookie sheet with cooking oil spray. Spread the mixture as thinly and evenly as possible. (A warped pan can make this a difficult task.) Bake (dehydrate) until done. (The flattened fruit treats should be bendable and not sticky.) This can take anywhere from 5 to 6 hours or as long as all night, depending on your oven. Cool completely. Cut into strips and roll up in plastic wrap. Since there are no preservatives in your flattened fruit treats they should be consumed within two to three days. (No refrigeration is needed.) Good stuff. **Serves 6**
Nutrition per serving: 120 calories; 0 g fat; 28 g carbohydrate;
3 g fiber; 1 g protein; 2% calcium; 4% iron

46 ✸ Vegetable Garden Bowl

This makes a great gift. Can you imagine having an entire garden without needing a big plot of land?

Read these directions from top to bottom before you begin the project. You will need to make a trip to the garden shop before you begin if you don't have the materials on hand.

Materials
- newspaper to keep working surface clean
- wide-mouthed ceramic, clay, or plastic pot or bowl with drainage holes

- small rocks, enough to cover bottom of container
- 1 bag "soilless" potting soil
- assorted seeds, vegetable or herbs
- 1 or 2 cups of water
- popsicle sticks, one for each type of seed
- marker
- ribbon, acrylic paint, brush to decorate container (optional)

Have the kids spread newspaper out on the working surface for this messy project. Find a wide-mouthed pot or bowl with drainage holes in the bottom. An adult will need to rinse the pot with boiling water to kill any bacteria or fungus that could harm the plants. Now the children can place a few small rocks on the bottom to help with the drainage. Next they fill the pot with "soilless" potting soil bought at the garden shop. (While you are there, buy the seeds. Try radish, cucumber, lettuce, carrots, peppers, and/or tomatoes.) The kids will enjoy poking holes in the soil (according to the directions on the packet) and then burying the seeds. Mark the location of each different plant by placing a popsicle stick with the name of the seed written on it. Water lightly and then place in a sunny window. Different vegetables grow at different rates. (Some may not grow at all.) Don't let your garden bowl dry out. When your salad plants are a couple of inches high you can present this beautiful, homemade gift. The plants will need to be transplanted to a larger patio container or an outside garden in the warm weather. Herbs also grow great, and they can remain in the bowl if your recipient has no room to transplant them. Frequent snippings of these plants actually help them thrive. Put a bright ribbon around the bowl, paint with acrylic (non-washable) paints, and let the kids present the botanical bounty.

47 ∗ Are You Getting All the Foods That You Need?

Materials
- food chart
  (1 for each
  family member)
- pen or pencil
- magazines
  (optional)

Fun Fact: A government study published in the journal *Pediatrics* said that less than 2 percent of children— ages 2 through 17—meet their daily nutritional requirements according to the food pyramid.

First, copy the food chart (shown on the next page) for each family member. (Refer to the food pyramid on page 61 for servings for children two to six years old.) Each person could provide color illustrations cut out from magazines for the columns on his chart. These charts can also be purchased in educational supply stores. Post each chart on the refrigerator.

Next, have each family member track how well (or poorly) he eats on a daily basis. Each day both the children and the adults need to check off or tally how many fruits, vegetables, bread servings, and so on they have eaten. (Each check is worth one point.) Write down how many junk foods were eaten that day. (Subtract two points for these "empty" foods.) How are the scores? Can the family do a little better tomorrow? Who eats the best in the family? Can the group design a better eating plan for all? Consider doing a family shopping list, menu planning, and taking turns preparing the new plan.

✷ Bobby ✷

DATE	6-11 Bread/Cereal	3-5 Vegetables	2-4 Fruits	2-3 Milk/Dairy	3-5 Meat/Fish	Fats/Oils/ Sweets

48 ✳ Bone Experiment That Would Make Frankenstein Shake

Materials
- chicken bone, scrubbed clean
- 1 cup of white or cider vinegar
- small glass jar with cover

Here is an experiment for your kids to try. This makes a great "show and tell" or science fair project! Place a chicken bone in a glass jar with vinegar in it. Tighten the cover and let the bone sit for four days. Take the bone out. How does it feel? Can you bend the bone in half? The bone has lost its strength because the vinegar leached the calcium out. This simple experiment teaches us that we need calcium in our bones to make our bones strong. Take this opportunity to talk to your kids about drinking milk and eating other dairy products and calcium sources such as dark green leafy vegetables. How about a simple lesson on osteoporosis? Some people think it is a disease of brittle bones that causes your bones to break when you get old. Actually osteoporosis is a young person's disease because it is in our youth that we build calcium into our bones. In fact, every two years children completely "replace" their skeletons with new bone mass. The Institute of Medicine reports that, "Girls build 92 percent of their bone mass by age 18, but if they don't consume enough calcium in their teenage years they cannot 'catch up' later."

As teens have doubled or tripled their consumption of soft drinks (soda or pop), they have cut their consumption of milk by more than 40 percent. Now *that* is scary!

49 * Make Your Own Peanut Butter from Scratch—Fresh Scratch

You can order jumbo Virginia peanut seeds from Gurney's Seed and Nursery Company. For about $1.50 you will receive 100 seeds. Plant them in the spring according to the directions. It will take all summer for the seeds to grow. At the end of the summer dig up your peanuts from underground. Shell them and then roast slowly following the directions for the sunflower seeds (see Activity 54). Write the company at:

110 Capital Street
Yankton, SD 57079
(605) 665-1930

Project Peanut Butter

Materials
- blender or food processor
- large spoon
- clean storing jar or plastic container

Ingredients
- ¼ to ½ cup peanut or corn oil
- 2 cups roasted peanuts
- salt and sugar to taste (optional)

Fun Facts: Will Keith Kellogg invented peanut butter in 1895 as a high-protein food for patients with bad teeth! Also, did you know that peanuts are a type of pea, not a nut? This information comes from L. Patricia Kite, author of *Garden Wizardry for Kids.*

Pour ¼ cup oil into the blender or food processor, then add roasted peanuts. Start by chopping the nuts coarsely, then gradually chop them finer, adding the additional oil (a little at a time) until you get a smooth blend. You can add a little salt and/or sugar to taste. Smoothness is largely trial and error according to the effectiveness of your blender. Spoon the mixture into a clean container and label your home-made product. Remember, choosy kids choose to make their own peanut butter! **Serves 12**

Nutrition per serving: 190 calories;
18 g fat; 5 g carbohydrate; 2 g fiber;
6 g protein; 2% calcium; 2% iron

50 ✴ Make Your Own Nutrition Folder

Materials
- pencil and paper
- pocket folder

Have your kids write to these organizations and request free information on nutrition or check out their websites:

American Cancer Society
1599 Clifton Road NE
Atlanta, GA 30329-4251
(800) ACS-2345
www.cancer.org

American Dietetic Association
216 West Jackson Boulevard, Suite 800
Chicago, IL 60606-6995
(312) 899-0040
www.eatright.org

American Heart Association
7272 Greenville Avenue
Dallas, TX 75231
(800) AHA-USA1
www.americanheart.org

Center for Science in the Public Interest
1875 Connecticut Avenue NW, Suite 300
Washington, DC 20009
(202) 332-9110
www.cspinet.org

Food and Drug Administration
5600 Fishers Lane
Rockville, MD 20857
(888) INFO-FDA
www.cfsanfda.gov

National Osteoporosis Foundation
1150 17th Street NW, Suite 500
Washington, DC 20036-4603
(800) 223-9994
www.nos.org

Before you contact these organizations, pick specific topics you want information on. Most of these groups have numerous publications available to the public, often for free or at minimal cost. Some topics you might be interested in are general nutrition for children, fast-food restaurants, school lunch programs, low-fat or low-cholesterol diets, recipes, shopping tips, or exercise and health. Have the kids read and then file the information in a special folder. Within the folder, make a section for favorite "good-for-you" recipes (ones you've invented as well as come across) and for coupons you've clipped to purchase healthful foods. Suggest the children share the folder with all of their friends, family members, and neighbors.

51 ✶ Pioneer Snack Food

Materials
- 3 to 4 apples
- peeler (optional)
- sharp knife for slicing
- 3-foot cotton string
- cotton sack, glass jar, or plastic bag for storing

Your family can make this delicious snack by slicing apples thinly—they do not need to be peeled first—then lacing them onto a string by pushing the string through a small hole in the core (no needle necessary!). Make sure there is plenty of space between the slices so the air can dry them on all sides. Hang the string in a sunny, sanitary window for about one week. Once they dry out you can place them in a bag or airtight container for an "anytime" treat.

Fun Fact: American pioneers frequently carried apples in their covered wagons. Apples stored well and were often the only fruit available on a long trip. Pioneers made a dried apple snack similar to what you can buy in the market today. First they had to peel, slice, and dry the apples in the sun. Next they put them in cotton sacks and hung them up in a dry area until they had the munchies!

52 ✶ Carmen Miranda Fruit Hat

Materials
- sturdy straw hat
- florist pins
- wide ribbon
- pair of scissors
- fresh, edible fruit

Here is a great way to make an impressive entrance at a party. Buy a sturdy straw hat, florist pins, and a wide ribbon at the craft store. Make two 1½-inch cuts on each side of the hat. This is where you will thread a

★ CAUTION ★ Make sure the recipient knows to remove all pins before eating the fruit.

broad and colorful ribbon through one side and over the top of the hat to the other side. It is OK that the ribbon goes straight over the hat to the other side because you will be covering it with fresh, edible fruit. Place an assortment of fruit around the brim and on the top, securing each piece of fruit with one or more clean florist pins (a regular pin won't provide enough support and could get lost in the fruit). Think color, weight, balance (don't use grapefruits or pineapples!), and variety as you place the fruit. Underripe fruit is better than overripe fruit. Now carefully place the hat on your head and tie the ribbon under your chin. This is a gift that you can give to the hosts. You will be remembered every time they take a snack from the hat!

53 ★ Appetizing Adornments

Materials
- grapes (all kinds)
- needle and thread

Thread green, red, and purple grapes onto a strong sewing thread with a needle. The children can decide the color pattern and length they would like. The jewelry you make with the children can be a "collaboration"—two or more people working together on a project. Try making necklaces, bracelets, and even earrings. Earrings are made by making a loop of thread that goes around your whole ear. The grape dangles at the bottom. (This doesn't require pierced ears!) After you are done waltzing around with your jewelry, you can snack on it! If you end up hanging up your grapes for a few days you may find that they have turned into raisins (or they may be moldy)! You can always hang them on a tree for the birds.

54 * Sunflower Snacks

Sunflowers grow like weeds. There are many varieties, and some grow very tall. Plant a few sunflower seeds from a packet bought at a garden shop (not the supermarket snack type). Plant according to the directions. When your flower grows, notice how the "face" follows the sun—this is why they are called "sunflowers"! After the stalk dies, remove the head. Lay it face up in the sun to dry out completely. If the birds don't make a buffet out of it, pull the seeds out once they have turned dark.

Super Sunflower Snack

Materials
- baking sheet
- hot mitts

Ingredients
- 1 cup sunflower seeds (shelled)
- cooking oil spray or 2 teaspoons oil
- salt or tamari sauce (optional)

Preheat oven to 250°F. Wash and dry the sunflower seeds. Either rub oil on the baking sheet or apply cooking oil spray to the surface. Now spread seeds out carefully on the sheet. Next, roast them in the oven. After the first 10 minutes, check seeds every 3 minutes. Open the oven door and pull out the tray to see if they are toasted to that perfect golden brown. Watch over your seeds carefully as they can burn quickly. Stir them every time you check them. The kids can help you judge how they are doing, but don't let them touch the baking sheet. Don't forget your hot mitts! Cool thoroughly before you eat them. You can sprinkle a little salt over them *after* they are roasted. Alternatively, try sprinkling them lightly with tamari sauce *before* you roast them. You can buy this sauce at a health-food store. Truly "delish and nutrish"! This is a healthful, natural snack food packed with vitamins. **Serves 8**

Nutrition per serving: 110 calories; 10 g fat; 3 g carbohydrate; 2 g fiber; 4 g protein; 2% calcium; 6% iron

55 ✷ A Grain of Truth

Experts believe it is healthier and more natural for us to eat more grains and other plant-based foods. The most nutritious types of rice are wild rice and brown rice. White rice is processed to remove the supernutritious covering (the "sheath") and as a result isn't as power-packed as wild and brown rice. Eat more brown rice!

Here is a great recipe for Rice-Sesame Crackers (adapted from *The Good Goodies* by Stan and Floss Dworkin).

Rice-Sesame Crackers

Materials
- quart pot with lid
- wooden spoon
- potato masher
- 2 baking sheets
- waxed paper
- rolling pin
- sharp knife

Fun Facts: Rice is a staple—a basic food—eaten by almost half the people of the world. Rice yields more food per acre than any other grain.

Ingredients
- 3 cups water
- 1 cup brown rice

- ½ teaspoon salt
- 3 tablespoons sesame seeds
- cooking oil spray or canola or corn oil

You can buy brown rice in bulk from the health-food store or in the natural-foods section of the grocery store. If you buy it in a package, follow the directions, if not, here are instructions for cooking brown rice. It takes longer to cook than white rice because of the sheath. Begin by bringing the water to a boil and then add the rice and salt. Bring it back to a full boil, cover and lower the heat, and let cook for 45 minutes. Remove from the heat and then stir in the sesame seeds. Mash with great energy using a potato masher! Set the oven to preheat at 325° F. When the mixture has cooled enough to handle it, divide it in half and squeeze in your hands to make two flat circles. Spray two baking sheets with cooking oil spray or rub with regular oil. Next, place one circle on each sheet—right in the center. Reshape the circle into a flat rectangle with tidy corners. Place a large piece of waxed paper over the mixture and roll it out as thin as you can with a rolling pin. You can patch any holes. Take off the waxed paper and cut out whatever cracker shapes you want: triangles, circles, squares. Gather the scraps, press the mixture flat, and cut out additional shapes. Bake at 325°F for 20 to 30 minutes. They should feel, look, and taste like crackers! **Serves 10**

Nutrition per serving: 80 calories; 2 g fat; 15 g carbohydrate; less than 1 g fiber; 2 g protein; 4% calcium; 4% iron

56 ✷ The Greatest Liquid Asset

Water does amazing things for our body, such as keeping our joints moving and helping us to digest our food. Water also keeps our body temperature normal. Sweating helps us cool down. When you exercise in the heat you lose a lot of water. If you wait until you are thirsty you are already dehydrated!

Materials

- scale

Here is an enlightening experiment for the kids: have them weigh themselves in the morning after breakfast and then have them go outside for vigorous play or a sports activity. Then have them weigh in once again at the end of the activity— before eating or drinking. Was there a change in weight? How much? Tell the children that they need to drink 2 cups of water for every pound of water lost. The American Dietetic Association advises that we drink a half cup of water every 10 to 15 minutes while exercising so that we do not get thirsty. Remember, our sense of thirst is not nearly as powerful as our sense of hunger.

57 ✷ Tree-House Banana Butter

Here is a recipe kids will think is yummy and grown-ups will think is yucky!

Materials

- small bowl
- fork
- zip-tight plastic bags

Ingredients
- 3 ripe bananas
- ¾ cup peanut butter
- 1 teaspoon shredded coconut (optional)
- ½ cup raisins (optional)
- 1 package of crackers
  (whole grain and low-fat)

Take bananas and mash them together with peanut butter. You can also add shredded coconut and raisins. Pack it into a zip-tight plastic bag. Grab a sleeve of crackers and scoot up a tree. Now poke a hole in the plastic bag and squeeze the "tree-house banana butter" mixture onto the crackers. Kid heaven! **Serves 5**

Nutrition per serving: 95 calories; 5 g fat; 12 g carbohydrate; 1 g fiber; 3 g protein; 1% calcium; 3% iron; 2% vitamin C

58 ✷ Summer Spurt Bars

Here is a delicious way to get a healthy boost during the growing months of spring and summer. Take your favorite cookie or bar recipe (peanut butter, oatmeal, or chocolate chip) and add any of the

Fun Fact: Did you know that children tend to grow more in the summer and spring than they do the rest of the year?

following: wheat germ, raisins, walnuts, oatmeal, honey, granola, diced dried fruit. You can even reduce the fat by replacing the butter with applesauce, apple butter, or prune butter (c'mon try it—prunes are just dried plums that have gotten a bad rap). Remember, sports and energy bars were invented by trial and error, so keep trying until you get it right!

59 ✦ Food Block Pyramid

Materials

- newspaper to keep working surface clean
- 15 to 26 wood, plastic, or cardboard blocks
- tempera paint—different colors
- paintbrushes
- water to rinse brushes
- paper towel for cleanup
- magazines with food pictures
- glue or paste
- pair of scissors
- food stickers

U.S. Department of Agriculture

This is a simple way to teach children to eat well by following the food pyramid and at the same time learn to count blocks. Below is the food pyramid designed for two- to six-year-olds. Take 15 to 26 plain wooden, cardboard, or plastic blocks. You can either paint the different foods onto the blocks, apply food stickers, or cut out small pictures of foods found in magazines and glue or paste them on the blocks. Each block represents one serving on the USDA Food Guide Pyramid. You will need blocks for fruits, vegetables, grains and breads, dairy products, meats and fish, and fats and sweets. Follow the guidelines in the illustration. After each meal or snack, have your child pick the blocks that represent what they have eaten. (One fruit block shows they have eaten one serving.) At the end of the day see how closely your "consumed" food pyramid matches the recommended guidelines. The children can count up their blocks and match them to the pyramid. (Three fruit blocks and three fruits in the pyramid—good job today!) As your children show improvement or a great effort in their eating habits, reward them with well-deserved praise!

60 * My Own Brand Baby Food

Make homemade baby food for a baby in your household or for a neighbor's or friend's baby.

Carla's 14K Carrots

Materials
- small jars with lids
- small pot
- tongs
- vegetable steamer
- food processor or potato masher
- clean dish towel or paper towel

- spoon
- white sticker labels and permanent marker

Ingredients
- 2 or more carrots, washed, peeled, and cubed
- ¾ cup water (or more if needed)

First thoroughly wash your hands, the jars, utensils, and ingredients. Take a clean jar and lid and submerge it in a pot of water. Place the pot on the burner on "high" setting and bring to a rolling boil. Keep the jar in the boiling water until you are ready to fill it. Have tongs ready to remove the jar. Steam two carrots in a vegetable steamer over ¾ cup of water. Let the carrots cool, and then puree them in a food processor or mash them by hand with a potato masher. Remove the jar from the boiling water and let it drain upside-down onto a clean dish towel or paper towel. Once dry, turn it over and spoon the carrot puree into the sterile jar and seal tightly by hand. Now you need to create your own label. Take a large white sticker and write the name of your baby food and the date it was made. Place the label on the food container. Refrigerate at once. Use the vegetable puree within 48 hours. These directions are *not* for long-term canning but rather for immediate use. Spoilage can occur if you leave jars unrefrigerated (for any length of time) *or* if they are refrigerated for longer than 48 hours. Try spinach, green bean, pea, or butternut squash purees. Can your crew help you think of clever names? **Serves 1**
Nutrition per serving: 35 calories; 0 g fat; 8 g carbohydrate; 3 g fiber; 1 g protein; 2% calcium; 2% iron; 380% vitamin A

61 ✳ Tour a Dairy, Cheese Manufacturer, or Pasta Factory

Materials

• telephone book

Look in the yellow pages for interesting field trip ideas. (You may need to look outside your area directory—check general categories such as "Food Prod-ucts: Manufacturers and Distributors," or specific categories such as "Cheese," "Pasta," "Dairies.") Call to see if a tour can be arranged. Children and adults can learn a lot about how food is processed, manufactured, packaged, marketed, and distributed. This is a wonderful way to spend time together and have an educational experience. The benefits include free samples!

62 ✳ Microtreats

Materials

• vegetable steamer
  (optional)
• sharp paring knife
• vegetable peeler
• clean serving towel
• small serving tray
• miniature silverware
• fancy cocktail napkins
• serving tongs

Fun Fact: Research done at the University of Illinois at Urbana-Champaign has shown that children who were introduced to vegetables and fruits daily for 10 days acquired a taste for these nutritious morsels.

Ingredients

• a variety of miniature fruits and vegetables

Try this approach to entice little ones to try minibites. Buy miniature vegetables and fruits at a grocery store or health-food store that carries a wide variety of produce. Some of these are seasonal or specialty items and not available everywhere. Cherry tomatoes, enoki mushrooms, mini-zucchini and mini–summer squash, spring asparagus, baby carrots, champagne grapes, seckel or forelle pears, baby bananas, and kumquats are fun choices. Wash and dry produce thoroughly. Some items your children will prefer steamed; others they'll like in their natural state (raw). Prepare by peeling, slicing, cubing, or shredding your selections. Arrange them on a doll-sized serving tray or mini–picnic dish

complete with miniature silverware, fancy cocktail napkins, and serving tongs. Pretend you are the waitperson. Throw a clean towel over your arm. Display the tray to the left side of each child. Allow the children to choose what they want to try and graciously serve your "guests." Remember, presentation is everything!

63 ✴ Safety Straw

Materials
- twirly straws
- melon scooper, sharp knife, cookie cutters, gourmet gadgets

Ingredients
- assorted fresh seasonal fruits

Kids love assorted fruits on a skewer. Instead of a sharp wood kabob stick, try threading the fruit on a twirly straw. Twirly straws are colorful, durable, and plastic—they are made up of unusual twists and turns. You can find these novelty items at dollar stores, party shops, and supermarkets. The fruits that are easiest to "impale" are watermelon, cantaloupe, banana, kiwi, star fruit, and strawberries. Use a round melon scooper, cookie cutters, and other gourmet gadgets to come up with some interesting shapes.

64 ✽ Very Funny, Ma

Take an apple, remove the core, and make a small horizontal hole all the way through the remaining apple using a thin vegetable peeler. Insert a gummy worm through the hole. Your little bird will eat the entire apple just to enjoy the gummy worm. Apples are a good source of fiber. Who said moms don't have a sense of humor!

Materials
- sharp knife
- thin vegetable peeler

Ingredients
- apple (1 per serving)
- gummy worm (1 per serving)

Nutrition per serving: 110 calories; 0 g fat; 29 g carbohydrate; 5 g fiber; 0 g protein; 0% calcium; 2% iron; 8% vitamin C

65 ✳ Zuke Population Explosion

In Sebastapol, California, people are careful to lock their car doors—not because of a high crime rate—but if they don't, they are likely to find a bunch of zucchini on their front seat in the morning! Celebrate the zucchini season by making this recipe.

Zuke Pickles

Materials
- knife and cutting board
- medium-sized bowl
- measuring cup
- mixing spoon

Ingredients
- 2 zucchini
- 1 cup vinegar (any kind)
- ½ cup canola oil
- dash of salt and pepper
- 1 tablespoon low-fat sour cream or yogurt (optional)
- 1 teaspoon sugar (optional)

These don't exactly taste like pickles because they do not have a lot of salt—they get their tangy flavor from the vinegar. Wash and dry the zucchini. Thinly slice the zucchini and place them in a bowl. Add the vinegar and oil. (Experiment with a "specialty" vinegar such as raspberry or tarragon if you have it.) Sprinkle salt and pepper over the zucchini and mix well but gently so they don't get bruised and mushy. Cover and refrigerate for 2 or more hours. The longer they marinate ("rest") the better they will taste. You can also add low-fat sour cream or yogurt and sugar to

Fun Fact: Did you know that August 8 is "Sneak Some Zucchini onto Your Neighbor's Porch Night"?

alter the taste. Create a zuke recipe that everyone in Sebastopol would love! **Serves 5**

Nutrition per serving: 170 calories; 18 g fat; 3 g carbohydrate; 0 g
fiber; 1 g protein; 2% calcium; 4% iron; 6% vitamin A; 10% vitamin C

66 ✦ Dial-a-Dietician

Materials
- telephone

Here is a "900" number you won't mind if your kids call. If you or your children have questions about nutrition, you can call the American Dietetic Association and have an immediate consultation with a registered dietician. This is helpful when your child is trying to convince you that if one bag of potato chips contains 2 percent of her daily vitamin C requirement, then 50 bags would be even better. There is a charge for this call. Call (900) 225-5267. For free brochures and referrals to registered dieticians in your area call (800) 366-1655.

67 ✦ Muffin Tin Snacks

Materials
- muffin tin
- serving spoon
- cups or bowls—
  1 per child

Ingredients

- dried fruit, cheese, fresh berries, raw vegetables, nuts, or your choice of other healthy bite-sized snacks

Put healthy snack choices into the little cubbyholes of a muffin tin. Let the kids make their own after-school "snack bar" by spooning out the servings they want into a bowl or cup. Offer them only healthy choices and they will be a captive audience . . . especially when they are hungry. Here are some good selections: raisins, cheese cubes, nuts, carrot sticks, cherry tomatoes, diced red and green peppers, cheddar fish crackers, raspberries, grapes, blueberries, cherries, strawberries, raw fresh peas, apple chunks, pineapple cubes, banana chips, dried apricots, etc. Your house will become instantly popular as an after-school hangout if you offer this treat!

68 ✳ Role Reversal

Let your child plan a meal, make the shopping list (using the Center for Science in the Public Interest [CSPI] best food choices for children), select the items from the grocery store, and prepare the dinner. Parents set the table, serve, and clean up! (The kids might want to present and serve any special creations they make.)

Materials

- CSPI's list of best foods
- pad of paper
- pen or pencil
- cookbook, family recipe, or "invented" recipe
- table setting—plates, cups, silverware, napkins, serving dishes, and utensils

Center for Science in the Public Interest List of "Ten of the Best Children's Foods":

1. Fresh fruits and vegetables—especially carrot sticks, cantaloupe, oranges, watermelon, and strawberries

2. Chicken breasts or drumsticks without skin or breading

3. Cheerios, Wheaties, or other whole-grain, low-sugar cereals

4. Skim or 1 percent milk

5. Extra-lean ground beef or vegetarian burgers

6. Low-fat hot dogs

7. Nonfat ice cream or frozen yogurt

8. Fat-free corn chips or potato chips

9. Seasoned air-popped popcorn

10. Whole wheat crackers or animal crackers

69 ✷ Salsa Sensation

You can grow almost all your ingredients in a windowbox . . . or at least start them off there. You will need the following seeds:

Fun Fact: May is National Salsa Month!

tomatoes, jalapeño peppers, onion seeds or sets, and cilantro (an herb that looks like flat parsley but has a much hotter flavor). Follow the directions on the seed packets carefully. Begin your project in March in order to have small plants by May. The directions on the seed packet will tell you how long each plant will take to grow. Some take longer than others. If this garden doesn't work out, go to the grocery store and buy the ingredients previously mentioned as well as garlic cloves, vinegar, salt, and pepper.

Materials
- paring knife
- food processor
- large spoon

Ingredients
- 2 peeled garlic cloves
- 3 jalapeño peppers
- 1 chopped medium onion
- ¼ cup fresh cilantro leaves
- 4 to 5 medium or 3 large tomatoes
- vinegar, salt, and pepper to taste

Here is what you do: In a food processor, pulse together garlic cloves, jalapeño peppers (sliced, diced, seeded, and veins removed), onion, and cilantro leaves. Add tomatoes, cored and quartered. Pulse again briefly—but don't turn this into ketchup! Add vinegar, salt, and pepper to taste (start with just a dash). Mix gently with a spoon after each addition of ingredients and then taste. Add more salt and pepper if you like and mix again. You should have about 3 cups of salsa. (You can use more or less jalapeño peppers to adjust the "zippiness.") Let the salsa rest in the refrigerator for 3 hours before serving. Olé!

Nutrition per serving: 35 calories; 0 g fat; 7 g carbohydrate; 2 g fiber; 1 g protein; 2% calcium; 4% iron; 10% vitamin A; 50% vitamin C

70 ✳ Carrot Head

Materials
- carrot
- sharp knife
- shallow dish
- water

Fun Fact: One carrot has more than an entire day's worth of vitamin A.

Here is a fun project—but don't expect a carrot to result from this activity. Place the top inch of a carrot (the part you usually throw away) on a shallow dish filled with water. (Adults should use a sharp knife to cut off the top.) Put the dish on a sunny windowsill and add water frequently because the water evaporates daily. In three to six days, the greens will start to sprout on the top. They will look like wispy ferns. Unfortunately, it is very difficult to regrow a full carrot this way—even if you transplant the top into soil. But you will end up with a nice decorative plant for your kitchen and enjoy watching the carrot top grow.

71 ✷ Epsicles

Try this delicious popsicle—it's a scream so let's call it a *screamsicle*!

Materials
- blender
- paper cups
- aluminum foil
- wooden sticks

Ingredients
- 2 cups of orange juice
- 1 cup low-fat or fat-free vanilla yogurt

Fun Fact: In 1905, an 11-year-old boy left his mixture of made-up powdered soda pop outside with the stirring stick still left in it. The temperature dropped overnight, and Frank Epperson found a delicious frozen treat in the morning. The "Epsicle" was born. Later it went on to be called a "popsicle."

Blend the orange juice with the yogurt. Pour the mixture into small paper cups. (You need to be able to peel the paper back.) Cover each cup with aluminum foil and pop wooden sticks through the center of the foil. (The foil will keep the sticks upright.) Put it in the freezer overnight. Yum! **Serves 6**

Nutrition per serving:

70 calories; 0 g fat;

15 g carbohydrate; 0 g fiber;

1 g protein; 6% calcium;

0% iron; 70% vitamin C

72 ✳ Bounce Berries

Cranberries have also been called "bounce berries" because when they are dropped they bounce like crazy! Call them by any name, but do try this healthy recipe for Thanksgiving or anytime—it is loaded with vitamin C and fiber.

Cranberry Relish—the Real Thing

Materials
- food processor or blender
- sharp knife
- large spoon

Ingredients
- 2 cups fresh cranberries
- 1 orange (peeled and seeds removed)
- ½ cup raisins, dried blueberries, dried apricots, or dried figs (choose any or all—this is optional)
- ¾ cup sugar

Fun Fact: Cranberries got their name from the Pilgrims who thought that their flowers looked like the beaks of cranes.

Chop the cranberries and the orange in a food processor or blender, or adults can chop the berries finely by hand with a sharp knife. The mixture should be coarse, not mushy. Add raisins, dried blueberries, apricots, or figs (all chopped up). Mix in sugar. Stir mixture up well and let it sit in the refrigerator for a day. Thank you, Pilgrims! **Serves 8**

Nutrition per serving: 120 calories; 0 g fat; 31 g carbohydrate; 2 g fiber; 1 g protein; 2% calcium; 2% iron; 20% vitamin C

73 ✦ Campfire Corn

Today besides eating corn we use it for oil, ketchup, paste, cough syrup, marshmallows, plastic, and even crayons!

Fun Fact: Corn has always been popular in the Americas. Corn fossils were found that dated back to about 5000 B.C. in Mexico. The corncobs were only a half inch long according to *Garden Wizardry for Kids!*

Materials
- bowl of water
- campfire or grill
- tongs

Ingredients
- corn (on the cob)

You can enjoy corn on a campfire or outdoor grill. First peel back the husks to remove the corn silk, then put the husk back up. Next soak the corn in water for 15 minutes. This way it won't burn when you grill it. Using tongs, put it on the grill or directly on the coals of the fire for 8 to 12 minutes—remember to turn it so it doesn't burn!

74 ✳ Rainbow Celery

Materials
- 3 (or more) tall glasses
- water
- food coloring
- 3 (or more) stalks of celery

Because celery contains so much water, you can try this fun experiment with your kids. Take three or more tall glasses of water and place 10 drops of food coloring in each glass. Use a different color for each glass. Then place one stalk of celery in each glass overnight. What do your kids see in the

Fun Fact: If you have ever put celery in the blender you know how much water this vegetable contains—it is about 94 percent water. This is why it isn't a very good energy source. It does contain some vitamin A, potassium, and phosphorus. You'd have to eat 35 pieces of celery (that's a lot!) to get the same amount of calories as one small piece of fudge (not much)—both have 200 calories. But celery will provide your kids with important dietary fiber and essential water.

morning? The kids can take the
colorful celery to school for a
lunch-box treat! (Because the
food coloring is diluted, the
colored celery won't stain
their mouths or teeth.)

75 * Grain Power

Here's a good grainy breakfast, made out of oats, to feed our
piggy brain! To be alert in school eat a good, hearty, low-fat
breakfast. The recipe below for "Oaty-Meal" is from *Kitchen Fun
for Kids* with some changes.

Oaty-Meal

Materials
- small pan with lid
- long-handled wooden
  spoon
- sharp knife

Fun Fact: The brain's weight
is only 2 percent of our total
body weight yet it consumes
20 percent of all our energy.

Ingredients
- ¾ cup water
- ⅓ cup old-fashioned oats
- ½ apple
- ¼ cup skim or low-fat milk
- 1 tablespoon dried fruit (raisins or
  currents, chopped dates or figs)
- ⅛ teaspoon cinnamon or
  apple pie spice

Place the water in a small pan and bring to a boil. Add the
oats and turn the heat down to low. If you are using 1-minute oatmeal follow the directions on the package, otherwise cook for 5
minutes, stirring occasionally. Cover the pan and remove from the

stove. Wash an apple and peel, core, and cut half of it into small chunks. Add the milk, apple, and dried fruit to the oatmeal. Add cinnamon or apple pie spice. Stir it up and chow it down!

Serves 1

Nutrition per serving: 190 calories; 2.5 g fat; 38 g carbohydrate; 6 g fiber; 6 g protein; 10% calcium; 10% iron; 8% vitamin A; 6% vitamin C

76 ✳ Totally Tasty Tortilla Chips

Try these homemade tortilla chips from *Kitchen Fun for Kids* as a healthier alternative to fried chips. They have half the fat of store-bought tortilla chips.

Materials
- large serrated knife
- cookie sheet
- paper towel or clean dish towel
- hot mitts

Ingredients
- 4 corn tortillas
- vegetable oil spray
- ⅛ teaspoon cayenne pepper or pizza spice mix to taste (optional)

Preheat the oven to 350°F. Stack the tortillas one on top of the other and then cut through them into eight pie-shaped pieces. Place wedges on the cookie sheet so that they do not overlap—do in batches if necessary. Spray the wedges lightly and evenly with the oil. Sprin-

Fun Fact: This is a story of disgruntled customers and an accommodating chef! Potato chips were invented in the late 1800s by George Crum, a Native American chef who worked in a large, fancy hotel. The customers complained about the fried potatoes being too thick (and probably too greasy!). The gracious chef tried slicing them paper-thin before he fried them—they were probably still greasy but they were a big hit!

kle cayenne or pizza spice over them, if desired. Place in the middle of the oven's center rack and bake for 15 minutes. Meanwhile, spread out the paper towels or dish towel. Take the chips out of the oven with hot mitts and cool them on the towel. Job well done! **Serves 4**

Nutrition per serving: 80 calories;

2.5 g fat; 13 g carbohydrate;

0 g fiber; 2 g protein;

4% calcium; 6% iron

77 ✴ Peanut Butter and Jelly Milk Shake

In a study cited in the "Liquid Candy" report from the Center for Science in the Public Interest, in the years 1994–1996, both boys and girls consumed two times as much soda pop as milk. Turn *off* the soda habit and turn *on* the milk habit by making this great PB and J shake!

Materials
- small microwave-proof bowl
- small blender
- tall drinking glass or cup
- straw

Ingredients
- 1 tablespoon peanut butter

- 1 cup skim or low-fat milk
- 1 cup nonfat or low-fat strawberry frozen yogurt
- 1 tablespoon strawberry jam

Put the peanut butter in the small bowl and microwave it until it has softened (this should take a few seconds). Place milk,

frozen yogurt, and strawberry jam in a blender. Run the blender until the mixture is well mixed and frothy. Pour into a tall glass and swirl in the peanut butter using the straw. When the kids drink it down, they will load up on calcium and protein! **Serves 1**
Nutrition per serving: 220 calories; 6 g fat; 33 g carbohydrate; 0 g fiber; 11 g protein; 30% calcium; 2% iron; 6% vitamin A; 6% vitamin C

78 * Colorful Dinosaur Eggs

Kids love hard-boiled eggs. Let them make this recipe and then eat the egg. They will get a dose of B-12, vitamin E, riboflavin, folic acid, calcium, zinc, iron, and essential fatty acids, and 6 grams of high-quality protein!

Materials
- medium-sized saucepan
- medium-sized bowls
- metal slotted spoon
- eggcup
- paper towels

Ingredients
- several eggs
- water
- 1 tablespoon of each food coloring
- alfalfa sprouts

Place eggs in a pan of water and bring to a boil, turn down the heat to medium and simmer for 10 minutes. Drain water and chill the eggs. Prepare several medium-

Fun Fact: While eggs are high in cholesterol, they actually qualify for the "low in saturated fat" label. It isn't the high cholesterol but rather the *type of fat* in foods that counts when it comes to being a factor in heart disease. "If the American Heart Association is not concerned about the cholesterol in eggs, neither should you be," according to *The Family Nutrition Book*. However, it is a good idea to limit your egg consumption to three a week.

sized bowls with 3 cups of water each
and stir in one color of the food
coloring into each bowl.
Hold one end of an egg in
one of the bowls for 2 to 3
minutes. Let it dry in the eggcup. Once dry, dip the uncolored
end in either the same color or a different colored water bowl for
2 to 3 minutes. Let it dry once again. Roll the egg on the paper
towel carefully to get cracks all over the shell. Be careful not to
tear the edible part of the egg. Place each end of the egg back in
the bowls for 5 minutes each. Peel away shell. If you dipped blue
and red, the middle will turn out purple! Serve your colorful
dinosaur egg on a "nest" of alfalfa sprouts.

79 ✻ Lime-Ade

Try this recipe as an alternative to
drinking soda, and you'll grin
instead of puckering!

Fun Fact: In the 18th
century, sailors used to get
a disease called scurvy. This
was caused by inadequate
vitamin C while on long
journeys. To correct this
problem, they would take
along cases of limes to eat.

Materials

- can opener (if necessary)
- medium-sized bowl
- large pitcher
- long-handled wooden spoon
- small knife
- tall glasses

Ingredients

- 1 small can (6 ounces) frozen
  pineapple juice concentrate
- ½ cup lime juice, bottled or
  fresh-squeezed
- 1½ cups water
- 1 tray of ice cubes

- 1 ½ cups sparkling water
- 1 lime

Defrost can of pineapple juice under warm running water. Combine the pineapple juice concentrate with the lime juice and water in a bowl. Stir with wooden spoon until there are no lumps of frozen juice. Put ice cubes in a pitcher, pour the juice mixture over the ice, and add the sparkling water. Slice the lime into five "wheels" and cut a nick into each wheel. Pour the lime-aid into glasses and slide a lime wheel onto the rim. **Serves 4**

Nutrition per serving: 120 calories; 0 g fat; 30 g carbohydrate; 0 g fiber; 1 g protein; 2% calcium; 2% iron; 40% vitamin C

80 ✴ Pick-a-Pepper

Let's make a delicious dip for our red peppers!

Materials
- knife
- small bowl
- mixing spoon

Ingredients
- 3 fresh red peppers (sweet)
- 1 cup nonfat or low-fat yogurt
- 1 cup nonfat or low-fat cottage cheese
- 1 package "ranch-style" powdered dressing

Fun Facts: Sweet red peppers have 10 times more vitamin C than green peppers. Cats and dogs don't need to eat vitamin C because their bodies make it—but you and I have to get it from food.

Wash and dry peppers. Cut peppers in quarters and remove the seeds and the membrane (white parts). Cut the quarters in half. Mix yogurt and cottage cheese together in a small bowl. Add ranch-style powdered dressing to taste. Stir in well. Put the bowl on the center of a plate. Arrange peppers around it. You can eat as much as you want because it is low in fat and high in nutrients. So pig out on peppers! **Serves 4**

Nutrition per serving: 170 calories; 9 g fat; 13 g carbohydrate; 2 g fiber; 11 g protein; 15% calcium; 2% iron; 90% vitamin A; 260% vitamin C

81 ✷ Snax Attack

When the munchies grab you, fight back with a handful of "snax attack"! This is a simple recipe that even the youngest child will enjoy making.

Materials
- measuring cups
- large bowl
- pair of scissors
- mixing spoon

Ingredients
- 3 cups popcorn
- ½ cup unsalted miniature pretzels or pretzel nuggets
- ½ cup dry roasted peanuts, almonds, or walnuts
- ¼ cup raisins or currants
- ¼ cup dried fruit (apples, peaches, pears, apricots)
- ½ cup dry cereal (Chex or Cheerios)

Start by cutting the dried fruit into small bite-sized shapes: circles, squares, and triangles. (Grown-ups should do this step for young children.) Let your child measure the ingredients with the measuring cup. (Don't worry—this recipe is easy to wipe up.) Put popcorn, pretzels, nuts, dried fruits, and cereal into the large bowl as it is being measured. Mix together with the spoon. Now fend off your hunger! **Serves 6**

Nutrition per serving: 270 calories; 10 g fat; 40 g carbohydrate;
4 g fiber; 8 g protein; 2% calcium; 10% iron; 6% vitamin A

82 ✴ Perfect Party Platter

What do you make that is different, healthful, and eye-catching for that special school party or event? Try this party platter and feel free to substitute items. Make sure the foods are healthful, easy to hold (finger foods) or serve, and not messy.

Materials
- disposable serving platter
- doilies
- paper muffin cups
- plastic wrap

Ingredients
- small boxes of raisins
- individually wrapped pieces of cheese

- strawberries, cherries, clementine oranges, or figs
- dried apricots or pineapple rings
- small bags of popcorn, pumpkin seeds, or sunflower seeds
- "flattened fruit" treats (fruit roll-ups wrapped in plastic and tied off with curly ribbon, see Activity 45)

Place doilies on the platter. Take one or two of the items listed and place them in the muffin cups—more hygienic this way—and then place the cups on the platters. Wrap the platter tightly with plastic wrap for a safe trip to school. Your child will feel very proud of his unique and colorful contribution!

83 ✳ Hold a Good-Bye Party

Materials
- box or bag
- pencil and paper

Here is the list of "Ten of the Worst Children's Foods" according to the Center for Science in the Public Interest's *What Are We Feeding Our Kids?* Scour your cabinets and refrigerator for these items, place them in a box or a bag, and haul them away to the dumpster or trash can. Wave good-bye as they depart. If you don't like wasting food, use them up and then try to avoid buying them in the future. Keep the list on the bulletin board or refrigerator and review it before you go shopping. Soon you'll have the list memorized, and you'll be saying good-bye to these bad guys forever!

The Terrible Ten

1. Soda pop

2. Hamburgers

3. Hot dogs

4. Whole milk

5. American cheese

6. French fries and tater tots

7. Pizza loaded with meat and cheese

8. Chocolate bars

9. Ice cream (other than nonfat or low-fat frozen yogurt)

10. Bologna

I've added to my family's list: doughnuts, potato chips and other high-fat chips, juice drinks that only have a small percentage of fruit juice, and those preassembled lunch meals. Discuss what foods your family thinks are the top 10 foods to avoid. Hold a family meeting to agree on your "healthy, *not*" shopping list.

III

Fun for One

You don't need a crowd in order to have a
grand ol' time! Start your child off on these
"solo" activities and watch him spend hours
playing and perfecting these skills.

84 * Aerobics Signing

Materials
• none

Gina Oliva teaches aerobics to deaf students. She wanted students all around the world to understand the signs for the movements, but people in France use French sign language; in Russia, they use Russian sign language; and in the United States and Canada, American Sign Language is used. Gina created the signs on the next page so that anyone in the world could take her class and understand the patterns. When she signs for her class, she uses her hands to show the movement of the feet, as well as the arm movements. Your child can learn this international skill. Participants in an aerobics class watch the instructor's face, so remind her to keep her hand movements near her face. It is fun to practice teaching in front of a big mirror . . . the child's reflection will always be so obedient!

"Watch Me" Start by getting everyone's attention. Bring index and middle finger to the eyes. (American Sign Language: Look at me.)

March in Place Hold hands out in front with palms down and elbows bent, mimic marching up and down with hands.

March in place

Step Touch Start with arms out wide at waist height, elbows slightly bent. Sweep one hand toward the other to show the drawing of the feet together in step touch. Do this on both sides, left and right.

Step Touch

Stay in Place

Stay in Place Hold arms out straight in front. Make fists with the pinky fingers and thumbs extending out. (American Sign Language: Stay.)

Lift the Heels (Hamstring Curl) Arms out wide with elbows slightly bent, palms facing behind you. Curl fingers up to show legs bending up behind you at the knees.

Lift the Heels

You can learn more about how Gina teaches aerobics to deaf students and what other aerobics signs are by writing to her at this address:

Dr. Gina Oliva
Department of Physical Education and Recreation
Kendall Green
800 Florida Avenue NE
Washington, DC 20002

85 ✻ Daily Health and Fitness Chart

Materials
• poster board
• markers
• ruler

This beats the chores and homework chart hands down! Make sure your child takes "ownership" of his health by using his own ideas in creating this chart. Here are some suggestions: list sport participation/lessons, dog walking, healthful foods such as five fruits and vegetables a day, teeth brushing and hygiene, daily meditation or relaxation, 10 to 12 hours of sleep, "aerobic floor vacuuming," or "speed table setting." Try to show him how many of his standard daily activities already "qualify." Together create an enticing and healthy reward system to look forward to at the end of each week. For example, eight stars might buy him a round of miniature golf. Soon healthy activities will become part of his lifestyle!

86 ✦ Sizing a Jump Rope to Order

Materials
- 12 feet of clothesline (rope)
- large pair of scissors
- cloth tape—any one color or
  a variety of colors

Remember how frustrating it was to have a jump rope that was either too long or too short for you? Now you can make your own! Have your child stand (with feet together) in the middle of a rope. Pull the rope up and tuck under her armpits (the rope should be taut). Cut off any excess rope that extends out and tape the ends of the rope so it doesn't fray. You could select several different colors of tape and create a design on the end of the rope for more pizzazz! Now your child has a special "customized" jump rope of her very own!

You can buy all types of jump ropes (and other home sports equipment) through

Sportime
One Sportime Way
Atlanta, GA 30340
(800) 283-5700
www.sportime.com

If you have purchased a rope that is too long for your child, have her wrap the rope around her hand(s) to shorten it while jumping.

87 ✦ Hip-Hop Funk Dancing

Materials
- cassette or CD player
- funky or hip-hop dance music

Put on some cool, hip-hop music and try these moves.

The Butterfly With feet in a wide stance, bring your knees in and out repeatedly. At the same time, with elbows bent, the arms follow the knees movement. This should look like a butterfly's wings opening and closing.

The Butterfly

Running Man

Running Man This is an in-place running step with knees lifting high up in front. Arms are held out to the side and lift up slightly with each step.

Snake With elbows bent, lead with your head to one side and follow the motion with the upper body (shoulders, chest, waist) return to the upright position. "Snake" to the other side.

Snake

88 ✦ Kite Flying Made Quick and Easy

Materials (to make one kite)
- 1 plastic grocery bag
- 14 feet of household string
- pair of scissors

Let's recycle some of those plastic grocery bags by making a kite. Cut a long piece of household string into two 12-inch lengths and one 12-foot length. The lengths do not have to be exact. Tie each of the 12-inch strings onto the bag handles (one string per handle). Tie the two strings together at the ends and then attach the long string where they join. Hold the string and run into the wind. Whoosh you luck!

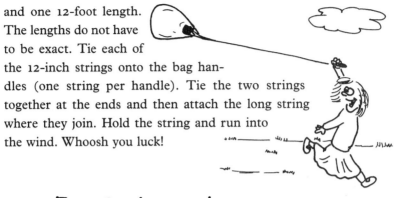

89 ⭑ Egg Carton and Ping-Pong Ball

Materials
- newspaper to spread on the floor
- 2 or 3 Ping-Pong balls
- *cardboard* egg carton
  (Styrofoam is difficult to paint)
- paints
- paintbrushes
- small bowl of water to clean brushes
- marker

This project will keep your child busy for a long while! It is part art project and part fitness skills training. Spread out a newspaper so that paint doesn't get on the floor. Tear off the top of the egg carton. Have the kids paint each egg pocket a different color. Wait until the carton is completely dry. Next assign number points to each "pocket" in the carton—write the number in the pocket with a marker. Consistency is helpful, yellow, for example, can always be worth 5 points while blue is always worth 10 points. Give the player 100 points for getting the ball in the one and only red pocket! Your child can create his own system. Stand back four feet and pitch the Ping-Pong ball into the pockets. Keep track of the points. Your child can compete against himself. This skill takes accuracy and hand-eye coordination, which is important in sports!

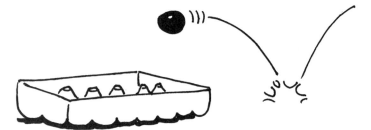

90 ✳ Swiss Ball

Materials
• strong beach ball or Swiss (resistance) ball

Many years ago, people in Switzerland exercised with large balls, and they are all the rage in health clubs once again! Here are some "Swiss ball" exercises you can do with a beach ball. The hardest part of this exercise is to blow up a beach ball. It will need to be very full of air—not soft and "squishy." You can exercise with your beach ball in many ways. Child and parent will equally enjoy doing these exercises together.

Stomach Curl-Ups Lie on your back with your heels resting on the ball. Slowly sit up, partway, and then lower back down. Try doing 10 curl-ups to start. Add on one more each session to strengthen your stomach muscles.

Stomach Curl-Ups

Wheelbarrow Push-Ups Put the ball
at your feet and lean forward so that you
lie on top of the ball. (The ball should be
under your hips.) Rock forward on the
ball until you can place your hands flat
on the floor in front of you. You are now

Wheelbarrow Push-Ups

in the push-up position . . . with a big ball underneath you!
Arms and body should be straight. Lower chest to the floor by
bending the elbows. Slowly do five counts down and up. Adjust
the position of the ball to give you more support if you need it.
As you get stronger, move the ball away from your hips and
(gradually) closer to your feet. Soon you'll be able to do a push-
up without the ball at all!

Back Bends Squat with the ball behind
you. Place your hands straight down next
to your hips. Hold the ball behind you,
next to your hips, so it doesn't sneak away.
Roll back slowly against and over the ball,
arching your back. Extend your arms
overhead and relax. Use your feet to gently
rock forward and back, stretching out your
spine. This feels terrific!

Back Bends

Hip Circles Sit on the ball with feet wide
apart. Rock the ball left and right and
forward and back to loosen your hip joint.
Try making full circles to the left and to the
right. Make sure you maintain good posture
as you sit on the ball.

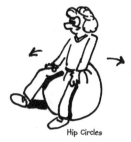
Hip Circles

Overhead Ball Toss with Feet Lie on
your back with feet up. Have your partner
toss the ball to your feet. Bend your knees

slightly and "toss" the ball back with your
feet. Have your partner try and catch the ball.
Switch places so each person gets a turn. This
improves coordination, strength, and timing!

Overhead Ball Toss with Feet

Feet Creepers Lie on your back with only
your heels resting on the ball. Lift your hips
off the floor and "walk" the ball toward your
hips. Now walk the ball back out. This strengthens your
hamstrings, glutes, and abdominals! (Make sure you tighten
those muscles as you "creep" the ball back and forth.) This
exercise can also be done sharing the ball between two people.
Lie opposite each other with feet
together. The ball should be under
both sets of feet. Now pass the ball
back and forth without losing control
of the ball. Pretty tricky!

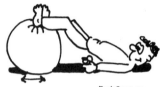

Feet Creepers

You can order a resistance ball from

Resist-A-Ball Inc.
4507 Furling Lane, Unit 202
Destin, FL 32541
(850) 837-9904
(850) 837-1089 fax
info@resistaball.com

91 ✻ Juggle with Scarves

Materials
• 3 brightly colored scarves, dish towels, or handkerchiefs

Juggling is a tricky skill. Practice is the key to success. Once
you get it, you'll never forget! Juggling with scarves is a good way

to learn the technique because they "float" in the air. This gives the novice more time to catch them. Once perfected, advance to beanbags and then to balls! Start by standing with your feet shoulder-width apart. Begin by using just one scarf. Elbows are by your side and the scarf is in one hand. Show your child how to toss the scarf in an arc slightly above the head and then catch it with the other hand. Now return the scarf to the "free" hand the same way. Once this is achieved try with two scarves. An "exchange" is done by tossing one up in the arc slightly after the other is released. Catch the scarves in the opposing hand! Ready for three? Place two scarves (scarf number 1 and number 2) in one hand and then one (scarf number 2) in the other. Throw scarf number 1 in the arc and when it starts to come down throw scarf number 2 and when it starts to descend immediately toss scarf number 3— immediately throw number 1 before scarf number 3 is caught! Your child can stuff the scarves in his pocket and practice at any time!

92 ✳ Man's Best Friend

Kids and dogs are a great combination for staying active. Take them both for a walk. If your child is old enough, she can do a "joint" workout with the dog: walk, run, lead him in a circle, and add in some tricks . . . even create a doggie obstacle course. Dogs and kids both need to exercise! All good dogs deserve a treat— so let your child reward your pup with a homemade dog bone.

Powerbones

Materials

- 2-quart saucepan
- large mixing bowl
- mixing spoon
- rolling pin
- breadboard or cutting board
- cookie cutter (bone-shaped if you can find one)
- cookie sheet
- cooking oil spray
- airtight container

Ingredients

- 1 pound beef liver chunks cut into 1-inch cubes
- 1 8-ounce can beef broth
- 1 stick of butter or margarine (substitute with low-fat margarine if your pooch is pudgy)
- 2 eggs
- 2 cups flour (either white or whole wheat)
- ½ cup wheat germ, cornmeal, or oatmeal (optional)
- ½ teaspoon salt
- 1 tablespoon garlic powder

Preheat the oven to 275°F. In a soucepan, cook the beef liver chunks in the beef broth until they are fully cooked. Remove from the heat. Put the liver in a large mixing bowl and cut the stick of butter or margarine into the bowl. Add the beef broth and mix everything together thoroughly. Add the eggs and mix again. Add in flour (white and/or whole wheat). To make the bones more nutritious, add wheat germ, cornmeal, or oatmeal. Add salt and garlic powder. Mix together until the dough is stiff. If you have a bone-shaped cookie cutter place the dough on a cutting board that has been sprinkled with flour so the dough won't stick to the board. Roll it out to about ½-inch thickness using a rolling pin (sprinkled with flour), and use the cookie cutter to make your treats. If you don't have a bone-shaped cookie cutter, you can hand mold the dough into bone or nugget shapes instead. Sprinkle them with cornmeal. Spray a cookie sheet with cooking oil spray, place the "bones" on the cookie sheet, and bake for 1¼ hours. Let them cool and harden outside the oven for 15 minutes. Store in an airtight container in the refrigerator. This is a great treat for your best friend!

93 ✳ The Balance Challenge

Materials
- none

A good time to work on balance is when you have a quiet space to practice all by yourself—this makes it a good skill for a child who has a few hours "solo." Can your child hold these acrobatic stunts for a full minute without falling over? Advise him to go slowly into these moves, find the point of balance, and focus his eyes on one spot. Balance is important in skiing, gymnastics, tennis, and, of course, the tightrope walk!

One Leg Stand

One Leg Stand Balance on one leg and hold the free leg behind you with knee bent, clutching the ankle in one hand. Hold for five seconds!

Tippy Stork Begin in the same position as above and bend all the way forward placing your free hand on the ground. Slowly return back to the starting position. Were you able to touch the floor without toppling over?

Tippy Stork

Knee Stand Start on all fours then lift one leg up, extending it straight behind you. Slowly lift the opposite arm off the ground and extend it

Knee Stand

straight in front of you, parallel to the ground. You should be supported by one knee and one hand. This is a good stretch for the back as well as a good exercise in balance!

Standing Arch Stand up straight with arms out to the side. Slowly arch back looking at the ceiling. Can you hold this position for 10 seconds without losing your balance? The key is to do this slowly and fix your gaze on a spot overhead.

Standing Arch

94 ✻ Hold Up the Wall Handstand

Materials
• an uncluttered wall

You can teach your child a handstand that she can do by herself (without a spotter). Find a wall where furniture and wall hangings (such as pictures and photos) are not in the way. Shoes should not be worn or the wall will get scuffed up. Place hands six inches away from the wall and lean shoulders and the back of your head against the wall. Slowly lift one leg up against the wall and quickly bring the other leg up next to it. The body needs to be stiff as a board and very straight or it is difficult to balance. The next step is to do a handstand against the wall with only one leg leaning against the wall for support. The other leg is straight up in a "free handstand" position. With time both legs will be able to be "free" from the wall. If balance is lost, the "hand-stander" simply leans back against the wall.

95 ⋆ Fitness Chain Letter

Materials
- pad of paper and pencil
- 3 envelopes
- 3 stamps (optional)
- 3 index cards ($3'' \times 5''$)

Here is a "combo" academic and fitness project for your child. Fitness chain letters are a fun way to interact with friends. Help your child make a list of three friends and their addresses. At the top of the list is your child's name and address—this way he will be the first one to receive back some exercises. (There are now a total of four names and addresses on the list.) Together write a cover letter that will tell the recipient about the project. The goal is to create a "Collection of the World's Best Exercises"! Your instructions should state that the person who gets the letter needs to send an explanation and a small drawing of one exercise on a $3'' \times 5''$ index card to *each* of the four persons on the list. The recipient will then add his name and address to the bottom of the list and cross off the first person on the list. (This way the list will always have only four names and addresses.) To start the chain copy the letter, list, and exercise card three times—one for each person on the list (excluding your child). Now have your child mail or hand deliver to each person on the list:

1. the explanation (cover) letter

2. the name and address list

3. your exercise card

In a few weeks your child should be receiving exercises in the mail. Hopefully no one will break the chain!

96 ✳ Silly Human Tricks

Materials

• none

Can you do this trick? Swing one arm straight up and down in front of you. With your other arm you need to reach over head, then out to the side (at shoulder level), and then straight down to your hip. Repeat to the side and then back up over head. Keep both arms in motion at the same time. It is very difficult because one arm has to count and move to two beats and the other one has to count and move to three beats. But this is not nearly as difficult as trying to do it switching arms! Your child will get a bang out of trying this.

97 ✶ Cartwheel with Hand and Feet Cards

Materials
- 4 pieces of stiff cardboard
- marker
- tape

One of the most basic acrobatic stunts is a cartwheel. When your child comes running to you eager to learn how to do one, try this activity! Trace your child's hands and feet onto four pieces of stiff cardboard. (One hand or foot for each separate piece of cardboard.) To learn a cartwheel, place the tracings on the floor as shown in the illustration and secure with tape. Start with the cardboard pieces close together. As your child learns to do the cartwheel better and can kick straight over the top, move the pieces farther apart. Encourage him to practice over and over. Learning a cartwheel takes a lot of practice. Give out a big holler when this skill is accomplished! Yahoo!

98 ✳ Recycled "Micro-Golf"

You've heard of miniature golf? Well this is miniature golf on an even smaller scale, so let's call it "micro-golf." *Micro* describes things that are very small—in some cases microscopic! This is a great way to recycle clean trash from your recycling bin.

Materials
- 1 old sneaker or shoe
- long cardboard tube or dryer venting tube
- cloth or electrical tape
- large square of aluminum foil
- objects to create golf "green," such as coffee cans, cardboard tubes and boxes, or chairs

Begin by making a golf putter from an old sneaker or shoe. Place the tube in the sneaker and tape it securely in place with strong cloth tape. Use as much tape as you need. More is better than less! Make a golf ball from crumpled-up foil. Next, work on the golf "green" (this is equivalent to a playing field in other sports). You can use any number of items to create this. Try coffee cans (with no top or bottom lid), paper towel or toilet paper tubes, shoe or cereal boxes, video or CD covers, juice boxes, or kitchen or lawn chairs (for big obstacles). Add your own ideas to this list! Help the kids cut holes out of the objects and create blind spots or ricochet shots. Add water hazards and sand traps if you are doing this outdoors. How about going uphill on a train-set ramp or under a building-block garage? Your kids will enjoy zigzagging around, through, and under these objects. Place some pinwheels, stuffed animals, and flags in the grass for added decorations. What will really keep them busy is changing around and adding to the "green." I think they'll *wow* you with their ideas!

99 ✴ "Tae Balloon" Kickboxing

Materials
- large balloon
- long string (as needed)

Kids love to kick and punch—here's a way for them to channel their energy safely! Hang a large balloon on a string either from the ceiling or from a tree limb. Make sure you are not near breakable objects or innocent bystanders. The balloon should hang down to eye level. Begin by standing in the "ready position"—one foot slightly in front of the other, feet shoulder-width apart, fists guarding the face, and elbows out wide. Here are some exercises you can do for the upper and lower body. Make sure you use both your left and right sides to increase strength and agility. "Tae balloon" kickboxing is for sports training, not for self-defense!

Straight Punch

Straight Punch From the ready position punch straight forward and immediately return to the starting position. This punch is simple, quick, and efficient.

Snap Kick You may want to lower the balloon to do this one. Hold the arms up in the ready position while you quickly lift the knee and extend the leg out (this is the "snap") and then return it to the bent-knee position. Lower your leg to keep your balance. Make this a quick, smooth, and all-in-one movement.

Snap Kick

Side Kick Face sideways to the (lowered)
balloon. Keep your arms in the ready
position through this whole kick. Tilt to
the far side (away from the balloon). Bring
your knee up toward your chest then
extend that same leg out to kick the
balloon. After you make contact with the
balloon, bring the leg back in toward the
chest before the leg returns to the floor.
This is done quickly in one movement.

Side Kick

100 ✵ Goal for It!

Materials
- pad of paper or poster board
- ruler
- pen or pencil
- stickers or stars (optional)

Children's National Goal Setting Week takes place the first
week in November. This is a good time to discuss health and fitness issues and to help your child formulate some goals for himself. (This is a good project for the whole family to do—it will
make a longer-lasting impression with the child if *everyone* joins
in!) Write down five fitness and health goals *with* your children
that they can work on for the month of November. You should
make a list for yourself as well! Make a chart and check off (or
place a sticker on) the successful attempts or accomplishments for
each day. At the end of the week review the charts and lists
together and see how everyone in the family did. Brainstorm an
appropriate reward that is in line with some of the tasks, such as
five consistent days of stickers qualify the child for an afternoon
of ice skating or three consistent days earns a frozen yogurt cone.
Remember that goals should be realistic, such as 20 jumping

jacks or 30 sit-ups, not something unachievable and frustrating. The purpose is to change long-term behavior in an easy-to-manage way . . . one step, hop, or bite at a time.

101 ✴ Backward Flip Out of Bed

Materials
- bed
- pillow

As a kid I don't think I ever got out of bed feet first like everyone else. Here is a "cool" acrobatic stunt your child can learn, and it may inspire your sleepyhead to get out of bed without a fuss! A favorite way to "dismount" is to have your child lie on her back on the bed, with back arched over to the floor. Have her place her hands on the floor. Now have her bend one leg, push off that foot and kick over, landing on her feet. It is important to keep the arms straight and place a pillow between the hands and head in case her form is less than a "perfect 10." Help guide your child through this exercise the first few times. Parents who don't have back problems can try this too when no one is looking!

IV

Me and My Shadow

You can help your baby's (and toddler's)
coordination and skill development as well as
share special moments as you playfully
"work out" together.

102 ✦ Create a Discovery Path

Materials
- towels
- ironing board
- car wash sponges
- paper bag
- stuffed animals
- bath rug or sofa cushion

Here is an Olympic-style obstacle course for babies and toddlers, and every participant is a winner! Add whatever household

objects you like that are rich in texture and color, just make sure they don't present a safety hazard. Roll up towels and place them 10 inches apart—these are the "high hurdles." Place a closed ironing board (covered with the pad) propped up on towels (approximately eight inches). This is your "balance beam." Take large sponges and place them at the end of the beam for a "soccer kick" into a paper bag that rests on its side. Place stuffed animals several feet apart so that your child can walk or crawl through the "S-pattern" for a "giant ski slalom." End with a rug or a sofa cushion on the floor for a "tumbleweed"—this is a somersault that your child does with your assistance. End with a gold medal hug!

103 ✳ One, Two, Three Roll

Materials
- couch and three cushions

The easiest way to teach your youngster a forward roll is by using your couch and the couch cushions. Place one cushion on the edge of the front of the couch tilting down to the floor. A second cushion joins the edge of the first cushion and lies flat on the floor. Your child lies on the couch (on the remaining cushion) and does a "tuck" roll forward down the first cushion "ramp" and finishes on the second cushion in a squat (more or less). You can help guide your child through these maneuvers. Gravity will assist with that rolling feeling you want your child to get. You can help your child stay centered and pass through the tucked position. Be prepared to yank those cushions off the couch frequently—this is a fun one for the small folk.

104 ✻ Pregnancy Exercises

Materials

• one mat for each participant

An expectant mother and her child(ren) can do these exercises together—these are good for all *three* of you!

Cat Stretch and Arch Both mother and child are in the all fours position with hands and knees on the floor. Lift the back up in an arch so that you look like a scared cat!

Cat Stretch & Arch

Hold for five seconds and then return to the starting position. Do this exercise five times. This stretches the lower back muscles and feels great to the pregnant mother. Kids like looking like a frightened cat—let them add a hiss!

Stir the Pot Sit on the floor with knees bent, heels together, and back straight. Hold ankles and rotate the upper body in circles so that you look like a spoon stirring in a pot. Do five slow

Stir the Pot

circles to the left and then five slow circles to the right. This loosens up the lower back and pelvic muscles.

Side-Lying Lifts Lie on your side with legs extended out. Rest up on your elbow or lie down with the supporting arm straight over your head. Lift the top leg

Side-Lying Lifts

up—no higher than a 45-degree angle from the floor—and lower it back down to the starting position. Try and do 10 repetitions to start. Do the same number on each leg.

Side-Lying Accordion Get into the same position as the side-lying lifts. Bring both knees into your chest by using your abdominal muscles. Pregnant women will

Side-Lying Accordion

find that this is a comfortable position and a good way to work those important stomach muscles. You will also find that while moms are limited by the size of their bellies, the youngsters are happy to show how easily they can do this—as they crunch up into a little ball!

105 ✳ Wagon Pull

Materials

• a wagon

Your child will love being in a little wagon, and you'll love the arm workout you will get!

Tricep Pull-Back Facing away from the wagon, hold the handle in one hand. Bend your elbow so your hand is near your hip and your elbow is straight behind. Push the

Tricep Pull-Back

wagon by extending your elbow and then release back to the starting arm position. Do five push-pull extensions on each arm.

Upright Row Facing the wagon hold the handle in both hands. Draw the wagon to you by pulling the handle up toward mid-chest. Elbows will bend out to the side as you do this. Then press the handle back down and the wagon will move away. Do 10 repetitions of this exercise.

Upright Row

Straight Arm Pull-Push This exercise can be done both facing and away from the wagon. Hold the handle in one hand and push and pull the wagon with a straight arm. By doing this exercise 10 times with each arm you will strengthen your shoulder.

Straight Arm Pull-Push

106 ✳ Fall Leaf Fun

Materials
- large armful of dried leaves
- blanket or towel
- broom and dustpan

Can you believe this is an *indoor* activity? Spread out a blanket on your kitchen floor and then place a large armful of dried fall leaves—gathered by you and the kids—onto the "mat." Find some nice music to accompany you and the kids as you dance over and through the leaves, toss the leaves in the air, throw one leaf up with one hand and catch it with the other. You can sit in the pile and lift the leaves up with your legs. Try to pass the leaves back and forth to each other—using just your feet. You can end with a log roll (straight body sideways rolls) through the leaves and finally pile the leaves on each other's backs. The cleanup should be easy and fun if you have kept your leaves in one area. Give a final sweep with the broom and dustpan. (Note: You don't need that many leaves to have fun!)

107 ✳ Butterfly Baby

Materials
- 2 yards of light fabric
- felt or cloth scraps, sequins, permanent markers, fabric paint, and brushes
- 7 feet of 1-inch sewing elastic
- needle and thread
- pair of scissors

It is so much fun to run through the wind with wings on your back! Cut out fabric into the shape of butterfly wings, decorating it with scraps of cloth, markers, or paint. When the wings are dry, sew on elastic wristbands (six inches long each) at the outer edges. Sew a small elastic loop at the center of the two wings, near the small of the back. For the chest straps, cut the remaining elastic in half. Sew one piece of elastic at the top of each wing, centered on the shoulders. Crisscross the two pieces of elastic across the chest and then run them through the loop in the back. Bring the two pieces of elastic around to the front and tie in a bow. Cut off any excess elastic. You can cut and hand sew the wings (you do not need a sewing machine unless you want a very "finished" product). You and your beautiful butterfly can run and dance outside together!

108 ✻ "Pair" Routine

Materials
• chair

Use your little one as your "weight." Do this only if you feel comfortable lifting your child. As the baby gets bigger, you will get stronger!

Thigh Strengthener* Sit in a chair with baby held securely (using both hands) on lower legs. Give the baby a ride as you lift your feet up off the floor and extend your legs from the bent-knee to straight-leg position. Do this slowly five times to work your quadricep muscles.

Thigh Strengthener

Baby Press* Lie on back holding baby in both arms. Press baby straight up and lower back down softly. Feel your arms strengthen as you do this exercise eight times.

Baby Press

Side-to-Side Twist

Side-to-Side Twist Hold the baby close to your body and stand with feet apart. Twist gently side to side and from left to right. This works the oblique muscles in the stomach. Try 10 repetitions each way. Baby will love the swinging motion.

Baby Bicep Curl* Standing with legs apart hold baby in your arms down in front of thighs. Lift baby to chest and lower back to thighs. Do 10 repetitions to strengthen bicep muscles in arms.

Baby Bicep Curl

*Exercises that can be done on a bed.

Safe Baby Lifting Guidelines for Exercises Above

1. Always use two hands to lift.

2. Hold on to baby, not baby's clothing.

3. Stand over mat or lie in the middle of a bed.

4. Keep baby close to your center of gravity.

5. Move slowly and carefully.

6. If you doubt your strength, balance, or grip, do not pursue the exercise.

109 ✳ Sponge Toss in Hot Weather

Materials

- plastic bucket or wash basin
- large towel
- tepid (not cold) water
- assorted washcloths, bath toys, and sponges

This game will help develop your child's dexterity and coordination as well as cool him off in the warm weather. Have your child sit on a towel on a grassy surface. Play toss and catch with wet washcloths and sponges. Show your child how to throw the washcloths, sponges, and soft tub toys back into the bucket of water you have placed on the grass. Your child will enjoy being splashed as the toys plop into the water. Move the bucket farther away as he gets more accurate. You can also have fun draping wet washcloths on each other.

110 ✻ Box o' Peanuts

Materials

- Styrofoam peanuts
- large cardboard box
- plastic containers
- shoe boxes
- plastic shovels and measuring scoops
- broom and dustpan for cleanup

Styrofoam peanuts can be fun! Place your child on top of a pile of Styrofoam peanuts or place your child in a box filled with the peanuts. Let him kick and throw the peanuts out of the box. Encourage him to walk and crawl through them and pour the pieces in and out of shoe boxes, plastic bowls, or buckets. Plastic shovels and scoops are fun to use. Be sure to promptly clean up when you're through with the activity. Sweep up whatever spills over and your cleanup is done!

✻ CAUTION ✻ Watch your child carefully to make sure she does not put the peanuts in her mouth. Skip this activity if your child is in this stage of development!

111 ✻ 76 Trombones

Materials

- oatmeal boxes
- uncooked beans
- disposable pie plates
- metal spoons and wooden spoons
- pots, pans, and covers

- paper plates and cardboard tubes
- "jingle bells"
- tape, glue, stapler, pair of scissors, colorful ribbons and yarn, pipe cleaners, crayons and markers

Gather the local playgroup and make musical instruments together! Next take a walk through the neighborhood, entertaining the residents with the joyous sound of your toddler and stroller marching band! Musical instruments can be made out of beans placed in a securely taped oatmeal box, two disposable pie plates banged together for cymbals (make handles), metal spoon and pot lid, two paper plates taped or stapled together with "jingle bells" inside. Kids aren't fussy—invent instruments with whatever you have around. If you can get hold of a recording of "76 Trombones," play it at an indoor concert! Did I mention bring cotton for your ears?

112 * Jingle Feet

Materials
- "jingle bells"
- pipe cleaners, shoelaces
- stuffed animals, beanbags, beanbag toys

Musical training at an early age is said to help the brain's development of math and logic. Here is a music and movement activity you can do together. String two "jingle bells" on the shoelaces of your toddler's or baby's shoes or string them on a pipe cleaner and strap them onto his ankles and/or wrists. While the child lies on his back teach him how to bicycle his legs. (This will help strengthen his upper thighs and work on coordination.) Place a stuffed animal between his ankles and help him bring his legs up over his head and then back down. (This exercise is good for the stomach muscles and inner thighs.) Tossing beanbags or beanbag toys is a good arm strengthener. This is a great opportunity to demonstrate and interact with your toddler—so join in the fun!

113 ✻ Hoop Dreams

Materials
- large pillow
- mat or bed mattress
- hula hoop

Try some baby sports conditioning! Many sports legends began their training in the crib . . . no kidding! This simple exercise helps develop the chest, arm, and tummy muscles as well as enhance grasp strength. Begin by having your infant lie on his back on a pillow. The pillow should be placed on a soft, safe surface such as a bed or mat. Encourage the baby to grasp the hula hoop you hold in front of him. You should hold the far side of the hoop with one hand and support his back with the other hand. Help him reach his hoop potential by doing a pull-up to either a sitting or standing position!

114 * Sheet Play

Materials
• small sheet or large pillowcase

Sometimes the simplest activities are the best—see if your child likes this one. Lie down with your baby or toddler on a carpet. Place a crib sheet or large pillowcase lightly over the two of you. Start by kicking the sheet off just using your legs. Will your baby join you? Encourage him to do so. Next try crawling on the floor while the sheet is over both of you—the baby can crawl under your body. For older toddlers, bunch up the sheet and have a gentle tug-of-war. You can also use the small sheet as a parachute. Sit up, each of you holding an edge, lift the sheet up overhead, and steal a kiss before it comes back down!

115 * Diaper Dash and Toddler Trot

Materials
• name tags with self-adhesive
• marker
• one roll of paper streamer
• animal crackers
• brown pipe cleaners
• green tissue paper
• pair of scissors
• small items or snacks for "prizes"
• juice

Another playgroup activity! Guaranteed to be more fun for the parents and caregivers than the kids! Create a crawl or "toddle" race by grouping the kids by age and similar developmental level. (Some babies walk earlier than others.) Each child needs a "number" to enter the race. Write large numbers on sticky name tags and attach to their diapers or T-shirts. Line up the kids at one end and the parents at the other. Call to your child—the first one

who crosses the paper-streamer finish line wins a box of animal crackers and gets to wear the olive branch wreath made of pipe cleaners and tissue-paper leaves. Every child is a winner and should get a "prize" and a "sports drink" (100 percent juice).

116 ✷ Playground Workout for Everyone

Materials
• playground

No one has to be idle at the playground. Here are a few exercises you can do with your child or while your child is playing. You are setting a great example by being active!

Bent-Knee Leg Lifts Hang on the pull-up bar and bring both bent knees up to chest. Try three repetitions to start. Also try bringing knees up as you twist to one side. Make sure you do the same number on the other side so you don't become "lopsided."

Bent-Knee Leg Lifts

Leaning Push-Ups

Leaning Push-Ups Place hands against a post or wall and position feet far behind. Do 10 push-ups in this vertical position. This is easier than doing them in the horizontal position.

Heel to Toe Rises
Standing on a log or balance beam rise up and down on toes 15 times to exercise the calves. Make sure legs are held straight.

Heel to Toe Rises

Railing Leg Extension

Railing Leg Extension
Hold on to the middle rung on the monkey bar ladder and keep weight on one leg. Lift the free leg into chest (bend knee) and then extend it straight behind and hold for five counts. Do five repetitions on each leg. Also work the outer and inner thigh by crossing the left knee in front of the chest to the right side and then extend it straight out to the left side. Repeat five times on this side and then five times with the right leg.

117 ✳ Teddy Bear Boogie

Materials
- cassette tape deck
- teddy bear music
- stuffed teddy bears

Pull out the Elvis Presley tape of "(Let Me Be Your) Teddy Bear" and a couple of teddy bears and dance to this rock 'n' roll number with each of you using a teddy bear as your dancing partner. You can jump and toss your bear around without worrying about hurting your partner. You can also string more than one teddy bear song together for a more aerobic workout. Some suggestions are "Teddy Bear Fever" or "Bears in Chairs" by Joan Oshansky or "Fuzzy Wuzzy Was a Bear" or "Teddy Bear Picnic." Make a collection to keep for future teddy bear parties.

118 ✺ No Bore Chore Workout

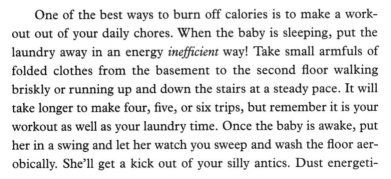

Materials
- rubber gloves, apron, and kerchief
- squirt bottle with water
- clean paintbrush
- rag or sponge
- clean mop head
- whisk broom and dustpan

One of the best ways to burn off calories is to make a workout out of your daily chores. When the baby is sleeping, put the laundry away in an energy *inefficient* way! Take small armfuls of folded clothes from the basement to the second floor walking briskly or running up and down the stairs at a steady pace. It will take longer to make four, five, or six trips, but remember it is your workout as well as your laundry time. Once the baby is awake, put her in a swing and let her watch you sweep and wash the floor aerobically. She'll get a kick out of your silly antics. Dust energetically to maintain a steady heart rate but don't get overly out of breath. Use your whole body as you wash windows or walls top to bottom and side to side. Start in a squat and rise all the way up on your tiptoes as one movement and then reverse. Do the same large movement side to side. Older toddlers will love to help you. Marja likes to play "Cinderella"—we dress her up in an apron and kerchief. She even likes to have her own pair of rubber gloves. Give your helper a squirt bottle with *plain water*, a rag or sponge, an unused paintbrush, a clean mop head, or a whisk broom and dustpan so she can "help" you!

119 ✻ Mirror Magic

Materials
- full-length mirror
- towel or mat

Babies (and toddlers) love to see themselves in a mirror. Pull out a full-length mirror and both of you stand, sit, or lie on your bellies facing the mirror. Help your baby learn the "swimming crawl" while looking into the mirror. Pretend to swim by moving your legs and/or arms while sitting or on tummy. Try arching your backs. Do peekaboo sit-ups where you help the baby up from a lying position. In the lying position the baby can't see his reflection; in the sitting position—peekaboo!—he can! Crawl up to the mirror and give the baby's reflection a kiss! Toddlers like to sit with their heels together and put their nose down to their toes watching themselves the entire time. Try watching while you do the same exercise with straight legs or sitting in a straddle. Parents can sit behind the child and practice stretching to the same side or in opposition to each other, all the while looking in the mirror. Try moving in slow motion in front of the mirror and then "quick like a bunny"!

120 ✻ Stroller Workout

Materials
- walking shoes or sneakers
- stroller
- towel
- water bottle

Accomplish two tasks at once and burn 321 calories an hour! For the aerobic portion of your workout, plan a strolling route that is free of potholes and traffic. Wear sturdy shoes and bring a towel and water bottle. Start walking at a comfortable pace to warm up; do this for 8 to 10 minutes. Pull off to the side of the pathway and do stretching exercises for hamstrings, calves, quadriceps, arms, chest, and shoulders. Now to get that heart going! Increase the speed and the length of your stride gradually and then maintain the pace for 15 or 20 minutes. You can add some "flavor" to your walk by doing lunge steps, walking on tip-toes, walking on heels, doing knee lifts, or skate walking with pushes out to the side and leg extensions behind you. Remember, the point of the activity is not to cover distance or to get home in a hurry. Bring down the pace of your walk for the last 10 minutes. On your way home look for a park or playground to do some conditioning exercises: push/pull the stroller as you squat, do lunges holding on to one handle (face sideways), follow with one-leg hip rotations while facing sideways, try 20 toe rises, and end with abdominal curls. Abdominal curls can be done by placing a towel on the ground in front of the baby. Lie on the towel facing the baby. Rest your feet on the stroller and talk to your baby as you do the crunches. Maybe the baby can keep count for you! Make sure to drink plenty of water along the way—especially nursing moms.

For information on a stroller that is great for walking and running, contact:

The Baby Jogger Company
P.O. Box 2189
Yakima, WA 98907-2189
(800) 241-1848
www.babyjogger.com

(Some of their jogger models can hold up to 150 pounds!)

121 ✻ Pool Laps

Materials
- swimming pool

Young babies have a reflex in their feet that causes your little one to draw his legs up when the bottom of his feet are touched.

Notice what happens if you take your baby in the pool. If the baby's feet touch the side of the pool he will "push off." Hold your baby "football" style (tucked safely under your arm, supporting the back and keeping the head above the water). Never let go of your baby or allow his head to go underwater. Let his feet make contact with the side of the pool and when he pushes off, help him glide through the water. Make sure you stay in the shallow end. Coax him along to the other end and turn around and try again. Repeat this over and over. You will be strengthening his legs and giving him a love for the water, and you will enjoy the close interaction with your baby. Water provides 12 times the resistance as air, so water walking is a great workout for you as well.

122 ✳ Nothing Like a Good Crawl

Materials
- big plastic or rubber ball
- rug or mat (if necessary)

Crawling is good exercise for both parent and baby. Lie on your stomach with your baby next to you, preferably on soft carpet. Place a big plastic or rubber ball near your baby's head. Crawl and push the ball with your nose and encourage your baby to do the same. Try peekaboo with the ball. Play like puppies, rolling the ball to the baby (just using your nose). Try to get the baby to imitate you and roll the ball back. The baby will think you are very funny!

123 ✳ Spider Leg Sit-Ups

Materials
- small toy (optional)

Sit with bent knees facing your toddler and have her do the same. Your legs should overlap each other's so that you look like a big spider with a jumble of legs (see illustration). Place your hands behind your head and slowly lift your upper body 45 degrees off the floor. Show and encourage your toddler to do the sit-ups with you—more for your benefit than hers! At the top of each sit-up give a kiss, wave, nose rub, or pass a toy back and forth. Slowly lower back down to the floor.

124 ✳ Jelly Belly

Materials
- none

Have your child sit on your stomach as you contract and flex your abdominal muscles to strengthen both your abdominals and respiratory muscles. Eventually you will break down in gales of laughter, which will be fun for both you and the baby—you'll also get a rock-hard stomach and deep laugh lines!

125 ✷ Super Parent

Materials

- chair
- mat or carpet

Here are a few exercises to do with your baby. You will need to hold on to your baby the entire time. Give these duo exercises a go:

Clippity, Cloppity! Parent sits on chair; baby sits on lap. Hold baby and do toe rises 25 to 50 times. (Build up to more repetitions daily.)

Clippity, Cloppity!

Upsy Daisy! Parent sits on chair with one leg extended; baby sits on lower leg and is held by parent. Do straight-leg extensions on each leg 10 to 15 times. Do not do this if you have knee problems.

Upsy Daisy!

Hi, Low, Off We Go! Parent sits on chair. Baby sits on one thigh and parent lifts that leg's knee to the chest. (Knee is bent.) Repeat on each leg 10 to 20 times.

Hi, Low, Off We Go!

Giddyap, Little Pony! Sit on a soft rug with legs straight out in front. Child sits on parent's thighs. Parent "walks" one hip forward at a time to go across the floor. This is a good gluteus strengthener, and kids love it!

Giddyap, Little Pony!

126 ✳ Laundry Basketball

Materials
- round plastic
  laundry basket
- pair of scissors or knife
- large piece of cardboard
- masking tape
- plastic or rubber ball

Play NBA (National Baby Association) basketball with an old laundry basket. Cut a large circle out of the bottom of a round plastic laundry basket. Attach a "return chute" out of cardboard fashioned in the shape of a chute (U-shaped). Set the "basketball hoop" on the floor. The child sits or stands a few feet away from the basket and throws a large plastic or rubber ball into the basket. The ball (hopefully) goes in and travels down the chute back to the happy hoopster!

127 ✳ Toddler Step Aerobics

Materials
- aerobics step or piece of wood (sanded) 2″ × 8″ × 18″
- full-length mirror

Small children can learn coordination by practicing step aerobics with you! Begin by placing an aerobics step (with no risers) on the floor in front of a mirror. (A piece of wood that is well sanded can be used instead.) Start by facing the step with legs apart in a straddle position, holding your child between your knees. Show her how to do a *basic lead*, which is easily cued (described) as "up, up, down, down." (Left foot on step, followed by right foot on step. Come off the step to the floor, left foot then right foot.) After she understands the basic feeling, stand next to her and do the same move, just holding her hand for guidance. The next step is to let her stand next to you and follow your pattern without holding hands. Finally, she can have her very own aerobics step to be just like mom or dad! Always count out the four beats and/or clap to each movement. After I taught my daughter, Grandma was my next student. Now the three of us perform our step routine together!

Here are some steps you can do with your child:

March in Place Stand on top of step and march.

Toe Taps Stand on floor in front of step and alternately tap toes on top of step.

Basic Lead Go up and come back down the step. Right foot up on step, left foot up on step, right foot down to floor, left foot down to floor.

V-Step This is a basic lead with the feet wide apart on top of the step and then brought together on the down steps that meet on the floor.

Over the Top Face the long way of the step and do a "step-together-step" onto and over the step. Come back "over-the-top" the other way.

128 ✳ Ladder Tricks

Materials
• ladder

Place a ladder, unopened, flat on the ground. Guide your child to walk on the edges (balance beam) all the way around the ladder. Next have him try walking and hopping through the open spaces or walking backward with a helping hand and stepping from one edge across the open space to the other edge (again with assistance). Can he walk along the letter *C* as outlined by the rungs and supports on the ladder? Try letters *S* and *L*. Can the child spell out his name? Mom and Dad—make sure *you* take a turn!

129 ✳ Rollercize

Materials
• rolling pin with two parts—roller and handles
  (not one piece)

That rolling pin you no longer need makes a perfect upper-body strengthener for your youngster. Place the rolling pin on the floor and have your child kneel and hold on to the handles. You guide her back and stomach as she rolls the pin forward and back.

Place a stuffed animal in front of her as a target. Parents can buy the adult version at a sporting goods store; this gadget is a wheel with handles on both sides. You'll feel your stomach, shoulders, and chest strengthen. Practice together!

130 ✻ Angel Circles

Materials
• none

You've probably done a variation of the "flying angel" with your child a dozen times. So try this to get a good abdominal and thigh workout. The parent lies on her back with knees drawn up to her chest. The child is held on the lower leg by the parent. First do repetitive leg extensions for your quadriceps muscles (bend and straighten your legs). Done? Try knee circles—same position but rotation occurs at the hip. End with shifting the baby side to side (same position) to tighten your abdominal oblique muscles. You'll feel this the next morning!

131 ✲ Youngster Yoga

Materials

- mat

Yoga is perfect for toddlers! It keeps them flexible and works on their balance, coordination, and concentration. Do these poses together. Can your child think of a new yoga pose to teach you? What will it be called? Can you two do it on both sides equally well?

Dog (Adho Mukha Svanasana)

Start in the "doggie" position on all fours—hands and knees. Breathe out and lift hips and stretch out your legs. This will look like a triangle. After several seconds return to the all fours position.

Dog

Hero (Virasana)

Start by kneeling on the mat, lower hips to sit on heels. Lift both arms straight over head and interlock fingers. Stretch upward with palms facing upward toward ceiling. Breathe out.

Hero

Sandwich (Paschimottanasana)

Sit on mat with both legs straight out in front with toes flexed. With spine straight, stretch forward and breathe out, placing chest on legs. Hold for several seconds.

Sandwich

132 ✳ Balloon Badminton

Materials
- heavy cardboard
- marker
- tongue depressor
- masking tape
- string
- balloon
- pair of scissors

Andre Agassi started practicing tennis by swinging a Ping-Pong racquet at a ball hanging in his crib. Start your future tennis star early! Trace your child's hand on a piece of stiff and thick cardboard, attach a tongue depressor stick or piece of cardboard for the handle. Blow up a balloon and hang it from a string in the doorway. Have your child practice his tennis or racquetball swing!

> ✳ **CAUTION** ✳ If any balloons pop, gather up the remains so that he doesn't put them in his mouth. You may not want to do this activity if your child is still in the stage of putting things in his mouth.

133 ✳ Bubbleflies

On a mildly windy day find a flat, clean, grassy area for your little one to chase a stream of "bubbleflies." "Bubbleflies" are bubbles (homemade or store-bought) that "fly away like butterflies." To make your own, follow the Special Bubblefly Mixture directions on the next page.

Special Bubblefly Mixture

Materials

- 3½ cups water
- ½ cup liquid dishwashing detergent
- 2 teaspoons liquid glycerin (optional)—purchase at pharmacy, herb and soap-making supply shop, or health-food store
- several drops of food coloring
- long-handled spoon
- bucket with handle
- pint-sized plastic container with screw-on lid (optional but recommended)
- bubble wand, plastic bubble pipe, or any bubble blower

Place water, liquid detergent, liquid glycerin (optional), and food coloring in a plastic bucket with handles. Stir with spoon until it is mixed. You can use the mixture directly from the bucket or transfer it into a smaller container. Use a wand or any other bubble-making device to create your stream of bubbles.

Don't just sit and blow the bubbles, stand and run to get your toddler (and you) exercising! This exercise enhances coordination as he grasps at passing bubbles and tries to catch them with two hands together. Stand next to him and blow the bubbles slightly above his head height. Move your arm in circles and waves, high and low; spin in a circle; or run and make a trail for him to catch behind you. Together try to catch the bubbles before they pop or land on the ground.

134 ✳ Yarn Ball, Yarn Doll

Yarn is a great material for young children's exercise activities because it is safe, soft, and easy to hold. Making yarn balls and yarn dolls is a good quiet-time activity. Pull them out for some innovative exercise playtimes.

Yarn Balls

Materials
- 2 pieces of shirt cardboard
- pair of scissors
- 1 colorful skein of yarn or several balls of "scrap" yarn (left over from a previous project)

These are made by cutting two five-inch-diameter cardboard circles. Adults should use sharp scissors to do this. Cut out a three-inch-diameter hole in the center of each circle. Put the circles together and wrap the yarn around them by going through the center and looping around the outside and then going back through the center again. Do this until the inside circle is almost completely filled and you've used up a lot of the yarn. Separate the circles a bit and cut between them with the scissors. Wrap a piece of yarn several times around the center and pull it firmly to cinch up the ball. Fluff and trim the ball as needed. Practice playing catch, rolling the ball back and forth, and tossing the ball into an empty trash basket, or just enjoy squeezing it to strengthen hands. Let the child explore the interesting texture.

Yarn Dolls

Materials
- ball of yarn
- pair of scissors

These are great to use instead of beanbags. Each one can have its own character, color, and adornments. Simple ones are just as much fun as fancy ones. Wrap a ball of yarn around your open hand (fingers spread) 20 times. The wider your hand, the bigger the doll. Carefully take this yarn loop off your hand and set aside. Make two more yarn loops this way. One of these loops will be the body, one the arms, and the other the legs. For the arms use a short piece of yarn to tie off the loop a half inch from each end. This will give the effect of hands. You can do the same for the legs. Now thread the two loops through the body. Thread the arms one and a half inches down from the top (leaving room for a head) and the legs at the base. Tie off a head with a short piece of yarn and make a waist between the arms and the legs by tying off at the belly. If you want to make a skirt, omit the legs and tie off the waist and cut open the loops at the bottom. Spread the yarn out so it looks like a broom and you will have a skirt. You might also add braids made from three strands of yarn and then tied onto the top of the head. Play toss and catch the doll with two hands. Then try one hand. Can you catch sitting down? Can you dance with the doll 'round and 'round? Put the doll on your head and walk without dropping the doll. How many things can you and your child think to do with this special exercise-mate?

V

Magnificent Me!

Our human bodies are truly unique and talented. The more we learn, the greater our desire to appreciate and take good care of ourselves.

135 ❋ Eye Can See You

Materials

• none

This is the "dominant eye" trick! Your child probably knows if he is right-handed or left-handed—but does he know which of his eyes is stronger? Have him look at a small object across the room with both eyes open. Next he places his thumb one foot away from his nose so it is in front of the object. Now close the right eye. Close the left. Does his thumb seem to jump to one side when the right eye is closed? If so, his dominant eye is the left one. If it works the other way around, his right eye is dominant.

136 ✻ Steering and Veering

Materials
- large field or yard
- blindfold

Keeping on "the straight and narrow" is tough when you're walking with your eyes closed! Take your child into the schoolyard or the middle of a large flat field. A helper (adult or older child) should stand next to the child for safety purposes and alert her to any hazards as she does this "veering" experiment. The helper will blindfold her eyes. The child should then try to walk straight ahead. Do not let the helper guide or coach her in any direction. She will find the results surprising. She will end up walking in a huge circle either left or right—not a straight line. This is called "veering"!

137 ✷ Lub-Dub, Lub-Dub

Materials

ONE, TWO, THREE...

- clock or wristwatch with second hand or stopwatch
- pen or pencil
- paper

Finding one's heart rate is educational: it tells you what kind of fitness shape you are in. It is also easy to do. The best time to take a heart rate, or pulse, is first thing in the morning—while still lying in bed. The child places his index and middle fingers against his throat or on the underside of his wrist. Can he feel his pulse? Once he does, he looks at a nearby clock or wristwatch and counts the number of times the heart beats, or pulses, in one minute. Write it down to keep track. This should be done three days in a row in order to find the average. Help him out if he has a hard time finding his pulse or counting the beats. The lower the heart rate, the better the fitness condition of the person. Top "aerobically conditioned" athletes have heart rates in the 40s while the average person's heart beats 70 to 80 times per minute. A healthy kid's heart rate hovers around 70. Athletes also can pump out twice the amount of blood per beat because their hearts are so strong. This means their bodies can deliver a lot of oxygen and nutrients to wherever they are needed. Very efficient and useful! Of course they need to train in aerobic sports such as running, swimming, or bicycle riding to make their hearts stronger. A healthy, powerful heart doesn't have to beat as often to pump oxygen around. Have your child test the entire family!

Fun Fact: Lumbering elephants have a heart rate of 25 beats per minute. Skittish little mice have quick heart rates that beat 500 times per minute.

138 ✳ Put on That Happy Face

Materials
- clock or wristwatch with second hand or stopwatch

Gather the kids in your neighborhood and ask them all to hold a big grin. Time it with a watch. Next, have everyone frown. Did they hold the frown face for less time? Probably, because it takes more muscles to frown than to smile. Grumpy kids must have stronger face muscles!

Fun Fact: It takes 17 muscles to smile and 43 muscles to frown.

139 ✳ There Is an Ocean in My Head

Materials
- large shell or paper cup

Cover your ear with a large shell or a paper cup. Do you hear the ocean? Actually, what you are listening to is the blood rushing through your ears as it goes through your entire body.

Fun Fact: It takes less than a minute for all the blood to completely travel through your entire body.

140 ✶ Can You Outrun a Sneeze?

Materials
- running track
- wristwatch with second hand or stopwatch

Fun Fact: Snails travel at a rate of three feet per hour. Chickens run at 9 miles an hour. Horses run at 35 miles an hour. Cheetahs run at 70 miles per hour. A sneeze can travel up to 100 miles per hour!

Go to a school track with a stopwatch or wristwatch with a second hand. Ask the gym teacher or track coach how many laps need to be run to cover a one-mile distance. (Usually it takes four laps to equal one mile.) Run one lap as fast as you can. If it took you two and a half minutes to run a quarter-mile lap, you will need to multiply that time by four. Because 2.5 × 4 = 10 . . . you ran a 10-minute mile! In 60 minutes (one hour) you would run six miles per hour. Help your child calculate the math. So . . . did the child outrun the sneeze?

141 * Announcing the New, Instant Weight-Loss Program

Materials

- none

> **Fun Fact:** If you weigh 100 pounds on earth you would weigh 16.6 pounds on the moon.

Yes, you too can weigh one-sixth of your current weight! No exercise or dieting involved . . . just a short trip to the moon!

Here on earth the only safe way to lose weight is through a balanced, sound diet and a regular exercise program. Do you or your kids want to lose some weight or have a friend who does? Encourage your kids to be good friends and go on daily walks with the person who wants to lose weight. (Adults may want to join them for safety and fitness reasons.) Begin by walking to the third telephone pole or any spot not too far away. Next day go to a stop sign or fire hydrant. The next day go to a flashing yellow traffic light. Spot your landmark for the next day before you return home. Each day you will walk a little farther, become a bit more fit, and get to know your friends *and* family better!

142 ✶ How Are You Like a Giraffe?

Fun Fact: The giraffe has the longest neck in the world.

Materials

• mirror

People don't have long necks—so how are we the same as a giraffe? Despite the variance in length, both humans and giraffes have only seven vertebrae. Vertebrae are the small bones in your spine. In your neck they make it possible for your head to move. Let's see how many different ways your child's neck moves. Do these moves gently and slowly. Have your child look straight ahead in a mirror—then tip her head to the right without lifting up her shoulder. Then try it to the left. How close to her shoulder can she go? Next have her try looking behind her without twisting her shoulders. How far can she see? Can she see farther over the other shoulder? (Owls can turn their heads around very far!) Last test—as she looks straight ahead, have her relax her shoulders and drop her chin down to her chest. Can she touch her chin to her chest without slouching forward?

143 ✴ You Have Two Faces

Materials

- large mirror (bathroom or closet-door mirror)
- small mirror (12″ × 12″)

You will need two mirrors, a large mirror such as in your bathroom and a small hand-held one. Have your child look into the big mirror; hold the small mirror in the middle of his face and tilt it back so that he can see the reflection in the big mirror. Now flip it over the other way so that he can see his other face. Can he see a difference? Some people say they have a "good side" and always turn their face in a particular direction for the camera. Love both faces equally!

Fun Fact: Did you ever notice how your face is not symmetrical? This means that the right side of your face isn't exactly the same as the left side.

144 ✴ Talented Ears

Materials

- paper
- pen or pencil

Is anyone in your family an ear wiggler or a tongue curler? Not everyone in the same family has the same skills or attributes. Sometimes one child can curl his tongue into a straw shape while another cannot. Perhaps a parent can wiggle her ears up and down—without using her hands or facial muscles to help. At the next family gathering have the children, parents, cousins, aunts, uncles, and grandparents try and see if they can do either trick. Have the children draw out a family tree with everyone's name and how they are related. Next circle all the people's names who can curl their tongue. Make a square around the names of all the people who can wiggle their ears. Did you find any interesting results? Are there any other special skills in the family? This activity can liven up any family get-together!

Fun Fact: Did you know that everyone has the muscles in their ears to make them wiggle—but not everybody knows how to use those muscles?

145 ✳ Strange but True

Materials
- acid-free paper
- pens or markers
- pair of scissors
- string
- metal coat hanger

While babies grow inside their mothers they grow a tremendous amount each day. Remember, we each start out as one cell. If babies were to continue that pace until their 10th birthday, they would be 50 feet long! Let's measure your child's growth in a new, memorable way. On a large piece of paper, trace your child's hands and feet. Label each tracing with her name, age, and the current date. Cut out the tracings, carefully store them in a box, and then put the box away in a safe place (such as the top shelf of a closet). One year later make another tracing. Label and cut out this second set. Place the first year's set over the second year's drawing for comparison. Show your child. She will be delighted to see how she has grown in the past year. After you have viewed the results, place all of the tracings in the storage box. Do this for five years. After you have five sets, you can make a mobile. This is done by poking a hole through the hands and feet and threading a piece of string through each hole. Vary the length of the strings from 8 to 18 inches. Knot the end of each string. Attach the opposite end to different parts of the hanger. Hang the hanger anywhere! This will make a great memory mobile!

Fun Fact: Babies increase in size 8.2 million times.

146 ✳ Maybe I'll Pass

Materials
- clock or watch

If you eat a double cheeseburger with bacon and an extra large order of fries and top it off with a chocolate milk shake, you have eaten 1,840 calories and have consumed 96 grams of fat. This is more fat than is found in a stick of butter! To burn off all these calories you would need to run at a speed of 5.0 miles per hour for 2 hours and 10 minutes. Or you could walk at 3.5 miles per hour for 3 hours and 40 minutes. How about washing dishes for 8 hours? Prefer to sleep it off? Stay in bed an extra 30 hours. As you are telling your kids this information they may be tempted to say, "Oh, that would be easy!" or "I could do that!" Put them to the test. See how long your kids can jog in place. Most children will stop from boredom long before they actually get tired! Ask them whether they would prefer to eat a low-fat, lower-calorie meal or exercise hard for a long time. This will help your child think about good choices.

147 ✳ Muscle Metabolism

Materials
- video camera and tape
- barbell, dumbbells, mats

> **Fun Fact:** Muscle weighs four times as much as fat.

Did you ever see a person who *weighs more* than another person, yet the person who *weighs less* is bigger in overall size? Very muscular people often weigh more than you would guess. Often they stump the carnival hawkers who run the "guess-your-weight" booths. Muscles in your body need energy to work. That means muscular people use, or "burn," more calories. If two people look the same but one has more body fat and less muscle, that person will not burn as many calories throughout the day. Weight training is important for people who want to burn more calories (and body fat). Even children should weight train to become stronger and more fit, according to children's resistance training researcher Dr. Wayne Wescott. Before starting, be sure you and your child have each consulted with a doctor. Schedule an appointment for both you and your child with either a certified personal trainer or gym teacher. Have the instructor design a home program that you can do *together*. Often it is hard to understand written notes, so ask if you can bring a video camera into the gym to record the correct form for the suggested exercises, the order of the work-out, and the instructor's words of advice (including number of repetitions for each exercise and safety information). This way when you go home you will do the routine the right way. If your trainer suggests equipment, ask about the cost and best type to buy. (You may be able to find equipment at a yard sale.) Avoid buying fitness equipment that appears to be trendy. Stick with the tried and true (dumbbells, barbells, and mats). Lift weights together every *other* day—muscles grow bigger on their rest day, not on their workout day! Every few months schedule a "tune-up" appointment with the instructor.

148 ✻ Grandma and Grandpa Pump Iron

Fun Fact: All muscles get stronger at any age as long as you exercise them.

Materials
• none

The good news is that muscles don't know how old they are. They don't know if they are 10 years old or 100 years old. That means even Grandma and Grandpa *who never exercised before* can begin a program for the first time in their lives and get results! National Senior Health and Fitness Day is in May. How about taking senior citizens for a supervised workout? This could include swimming, walking, or using Nautilus weight-training machines. First they need a doctor's OK. Call different senior centers and health clubs to see if they have a fitness program specifically designed for seniors. Can guests come for a day? This might be the perfect introduction to exercise that your loved one needs. Don't forget to go with them and work out, too!

149 ✳ Thumbbody Is Flexible

Materials
• mat

> **Fun Fact:** There is no such thing as being double-jointed (having two joints). Some people's ligaments are just more flexible than others.

Can you touch your thumb to your forearm? (Your other hand can help with this exercise.) *Everyone* can work on their flexibility and become more "stretchy." Many people don't think being flexible is important—but it is. It helps you with all your daily activities, prevents sports injuries, and can even help you maintain good posture. Spend 10 minutes every day stretching with a partner after you are both properly warmed up. Try *passive stretching*. Here are some examples of passive partner stretches.

Breathe deeply and relax to gain the best results. The person stretching should go very easy and slowly. Switch places!

Hamstring Stretch Have one person sit on the floor with his legs straight out in front. The second person stands behind him and gently leans on his back with slow and even pressure. The person being stretched should try to relax by exhaling as he feels the weight on his back. Repeat the stretch three times and then switch positions.

Hamstring Stretch

Shoulder Stretch One person sits on the floor with his legs extending straight out in front and hands locked behind his neck. The other person stands behind the first and holds his elbows, stretching them back very gently. Remember, this should be done gently and evenly. Count to three as you hold the position, then release. Try it five times and then switch places.

Shoulder Stretch

Straddle Stretch Both people should sit in a straddle (legs wide apart in a V formation) facing each other. Hold each other's hands and rock side to side and forward and back. Stretch slowly and gently, feeling your legs loosen up over the 30 seconds that you do this exercise.

Straddle Stretch

150 ✳ High Expectations

Materials

- marker
- yardstick
- thin book

Fun Fact: Did you know that at age two you are approximately half the height you'll be as a full-grown adult?

Let's see if the Fun Fact is true. Parents and siblings who are fully grown can look up their height by either searching in their personal medical records or by contacting their childhood pediatrician. Ask for a copy of your medical records—the secret lies within! Younger children love tracking their height and will enjoy this "long-term study." Have your child stand inside a closet with his back against the wall. Heels, hips, shoulders, and head also need to make contact with the wall. Place a thin book on top of the child's head and check to make sure that his chin isn't jutting upward—you know, trying to get that extra inch in! The child should step away with the parent still holding the book against the wall. Make a line with the marker and then remove the book and write in the child's name, age, and the date. Use the yardstick to tell the child how tall he is. You are probably wondering why this should be done in the closet. This is because you can probably avoid painting over this area for a long time. My grandparents kept the height of all eight grandchildren marked until we had children of our own. Then, one day the painters came . . . and you can figure out the sad ending to this story!

151 ✶ Funny Face

Materials
- pencil, marker, or crayons
- paper
- cup or mug
- pair of scissors
- mirror
- tongue depressors or popsicle sticks
- tape

Fun Fact: Thirty small muscles run from our skin to our skull, which allow our face to create a whole range of expressions.

Can your child exercise these muscles and come up with some unique looks? Trace the opening of a cup onto paper 20 times. Cut the circles out. Have your child look into the mirror and experiment with making faces. When he finds one particularly amusing he should draw it onto a circle. Try to accumulate 20 different expressions on the round circles. This high number will allow the child to stretch his imagination as well as his facial muscles! Take the finished circles and turn them over—backside up. Place a tongue depressor (flat wooden stick from the doctor's office) or a popsicle stick on the back and tape it down. Your child will enjoy showing off his many faces and moods to everyone he meets!

152 ✷ Cold Hands, Warm Heart

Materials
• none

Show your child how quickly blood can rush into an area by having her squeeze her hand tightly until it turns white. Tell her that she has squeezed a lot of the blood out of the area. Now both of you should watch closely and have her open her hand very fast and see how her hand turns red again. This is the blood rushing through the vessels to where it is needed. Discuss how in the winter your hands often turn white from the cold. By pumping your fist open and closed or shaking your hands you can help the blood warm up the area. Another trick is to make huge, fast arm circles to get the blood down to the hand quickly. Remember this for next winter!

Fun Fact: Blood circulates through blood vessels (little tubes) to keep us warm and provide oxygen and nutrients to every part of our body.

153 ✷ Squirmy Sleeper

Materials
• pencil and paper

Do you think you can stay still and sleep at the same time? Do you think you could make it through the whole night without turning over?

Ask permission to observe one of your family members taking a nap. Watch quietly and record the number of times that he changes position in 20 minutes. Shhh—quietly leave the room without making a peep.

Fun Fact: You can't sleep without moving or you would be very sore and stiff the next day.

When he wakes up you can tell him how many times he changed position and what his favorite sleeping pose was.

154 ✳ Up, Down, Up, Down, Exercise That "Levator Labii Superioris Alaeque Nasi"

Materials
- clock, wristwatch, or stopwatch

Do you know what muscle you are exercising?

Can you sneer for five minutes? Can you raise your eyebrows 100 times using the 30 muscles that are required? Can you crinkle up your nose for two minutes? These are fun contests you can do during a long car ride. You may end up holding the world record for "Levator Labii Superioris Alaeque Nasi" lifts.

Fun Fact: This muscle with the longest name actually is very small and controls a very tiny movement. It is located beside your nose and raises your upper lip. It allows you to "sneer" like a villain.

155 ✻ Two Hundred Muscles Go for a Walk

Materials

• none

Walking is a great way to be out in the fresh air and simultaneously exercise one-third of all

Fun Fact: Most of the 200 muscles walking requires are located in the lower body— the legs, hips, buttocks, calves, and feet.

your muscles. You and your child can make this workout even better by adding in arm movements. Bringing your arms above chest level makes your heart beat faster and harder. Keep your walking stride as natural as possible as you incorporate these arm movements. Try these:

Chest Press Place both hands on your shoulders. While taking a step press both hands forward so that your arms are straight in front of you. As you take your next step return your hands to your shoulders. Do 20 shoulder presses and then lower your arms and walk with a regular arm swing. After one minute do another set of shoulder presses. Do five sets (20 shoulder presses and one minute of rest is one set). Now go on to the next exercise below.

Chest Press

Alternating Overhead Press Begin with your hands on your shoulders and press up overhead with the first step, return to the shoulder position on the second step. Do this 20 times and then return to a natural arm swing as you continue to walk. Do five sets (as described above) and then try the next exercise below.

Alternating Overhead Press

Side-to-Side Pump Place one hand on your shoulder with elbow bent. The other arm is extended straight out to the side. Switch positions with each step. Your arms will look like windshield wipers!

Side-to-Side Pump

156 ✷ Are You a Gazelle, Polar Bear, or Dolphin?

Materials
• apple

Could a gazelle swim in the ocean? Could a polar bear leap through the desert? Could a dolphin survive in the Arctic? Probably not. Each animal is built for certain conditions and abilities. So are we—after all, we are animals, too! Some athletes are better at sprinting while others are better at marathons. Part of this is determined by our natural build. Part of our athletic success is determined by our training. The location of our center of gravity is important. Sprinters have lower centers, and high jumpers have higher ones. To help your child find her center of gravity, have her kneel on the floor with her buttocks on her heels and her hands behind her back. Have her bend all the way forward at the waist while still sitting with her buttocks on her heels. Her nose should be several inches from the ground. Place an apple under her nose. Now have her change to a kneeling position so that she is upright and not sitting on her heels. Once again, tell her to bend forward as far as she can and try to pick up the apple in her mouth. If her center of gravity is high, she will topple over more quickly than someone with a lower center of gravity who may be able to successfully bite into the apple. This is a good challenge for any gathering of kids (or adults)!

157 ✴ Have Some Heart

Materials
• none

Extend some gratitude to your heart! If you were to squeeze a tennis ball 100,000 times you would appreciate how hard your heart has to work. How can we help our heart to cope with this huge task? We can make our hearts stronger and bigger by working out. This will allow the heart to accomplish its huge job with less effort. Here is a running game that gives everyone in the family a "cardio" (heart) workout. Form a line with all your family members. Go out for an easy jog. Let the littlest runner set the pace. The person at the back of the line has to run to the front of the pack and take over the lead. The new leader now heads up the group for two minutes or until three telephone poles are passed. Then the pattern repeats with the person in the back becoming the new leader. This is a fun distraction and a great way to have your whole family become "heart healthy." Make sure you do this three to four times a week. Start easy by just practicing the "caterpillar relay race" for 10 minutes. Gradually increase the workout time to half an hour. Your heart will thank you!

Fun Fact: Your cardiac muscle (also known as your heart) has to work 24 hours a day pumping more than 100,000 times. It pumps out enough blood to fill 150 bathtubs in one day!

158 ✳ Eagle Eyes

Materials
- chalk
- yardstick or straight board
- beanbags, small blocks, or other "non-bouncy" objects

Did you know athletes often have better peripheral vision than nonathletes? Peripheral vision allows athletes to see more out to the sides while looking straight ahead. It can give them that extra edge! They can see the ball while watching where they are running. Have your kids test their vision by drawing a protractor on the sidewalk with chalk. This is a measuring device similar to a ruler. It looks like a half circle with a straight line connecting the half circle at each end. Sit in the middle of the straight line, facing the semicircle. Look at an object straight ahead and hold both arms out straight to your sides—at shoulder height. Hold a beanbag or small block (anything that won't bounce) in each hand. Gradually bring your arms in front of you, still keeping them straight. Stop as soon as you can see both of your hands. Now drop the beanbags and see where they land. Let someone else have a turn and see whose beanbags are closer to the straight line. Peripheral vision can be developed by participating in sports. So if your peripheral vision needs some work, play sports and develop your "eagle eyes"!

159 ⁕ Spin Like a Top

Materials
- piano stool or stool with seat that freely spins

Skaters and gymnasts need to be able to spin or twist quickly. It could make a difference when it comes to landing on their feet after a flip or, perhaps, getting that "perfect 10" score. For the gymnast, a lower center of gravity helps a flip turn over more quickly and often—this is how some are able to do double or triple somersaults. (Successful gymnasts are often short in stature for this reason.) Arm positions help a skater or gymnast spin, twist, or somersault faster. Watch these athletes in action! Usually they start with their arms outstretched wide and then they draw their arms in to spin or rotate faster. Sometimes it looks as if they are giving themselves a big bear hug. You and your child can try this on a stool in which the seat spins freely—such as a piano stool. Take turns sitting on the stool with arms out wide. Start the spin by pushing off with your feet. To spin faster, draw your arms in more tightly to your chest. Make sure your feet don't drag on the ground—that will slow you down. Did you spin faster or more often when you brought your arms in? Open your arms wide to slow the spin down. If you "spot," try to focus on an object several feet away; it will help you be less dizzy!

160 ✻ Kangaroo Jump Training

Materials

- yardstick or measuring tape
- removable tape
- chalk or talcum powder
- rag or paper towel for cleanup

Successful basketball players or high jumpers have strong powerful legs. They "explode" into their jumps. You can train your legs to become more powerful and "explosive" by jumping every day. Measure one yard up from the floor on a wall or doorway. Place the yardstick vertically at the top of that point and tape it securely in place. Rub chalk or talcum powder on the top of all participants' fingers. Face sideways to the yardstick, crouch down, and jump up as high and quickly as you can, gently tapping your chalk-covered fingers on or next to the measuring stick. Make sure you tap the hand that is closest to the wall or doorway. Always land with bent knees back into the crouch position. Turn and practice it on the other side. Try five jumps in a row. Practice jumps from a deeper knee bend or just pushing off with your feet. What works best? Have others try, too. Be sure to wipe off marks when you're done. Jumping requires a strong back, buttocks, and lower-leg as well as upper-thigh strength!

161 ✦ Walk This Way

Materials

• none

Do we need our arms when we walk? Our arms actually are important even though we walk with our legs. Put your arms on your head—does it make it easier or harder to walk? Try walking the "wrong way"—left arm swings forward as left leg swings forward, right arm swings forward while right leg swings forward. Do you feel like a clumsy monster? "Power walking" involves really pumping your arms to get a more vigorous stride and a better workout. Bring your arms up to shoulder height and keep your elbows bent at a 90-degree angle. Do not make your stride too long or too short—this is not good for your hips. Walk as naturally as you can. Notice how good arm action really helps your walking pace!

162 ✴ Handy to Have

Materials

- adhesive (first-aid) tape
- tray
- orange or banana
- paper and pencil
- several pennies
- wallet or change purse
- lip balm stick

Fun Fact: There are 19 joints in the fingers and hands, which allow our hands to work like tools.

See how many of these joints your children can locate. Tape around the joints using adhesive tape so that their fingers can't bend. Assemble a few items on a tray and see if the children can do these ordinary tasks without being able to bend their fingers. Place the items listed above on the tray. Can your kids peel the orange or banana? Write their name using pencil and paper? Pick up the pennies and put them in a change purse or wallet? For the grand finale, put lip balm on lips without a mirror! Pretty difficult! Joints do make our hands "handy."

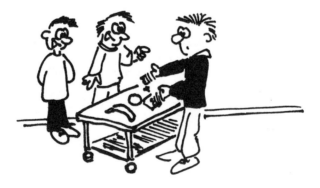

VI

Here Comes Super Kid!

Strength training, done correctly and safely, is
beneficial for all ages, from children to seniors.
Strong children are less prone to athletic
injuries and feel more confident and capable.

163 ✳ Bicycle Bands

Materials
- bicycle inner tube
- pair of scissors

Resistance bands or exercise tubes are frequently used in strength-conditioning classes at fitness centers and health clubs. Here is how you can make your own resistance bands at no cost. Go to your local bicycle shop and ask if they have any inner tubes from road bike tires that they are discarding. (You do not want the mountain bike type unless you are Arnold Schwarzenegger.)

Cut through the tube on both sides of the valve and throw the valve away. Now you have an excellent resistance band. At this price you can get one for each member of the family! Give shorter ones to the younger kids. Here are some exercises the whole family can do standing in a circle. Work together to correct form, count repetitions, and give kind words of encouragement!

Bicep Curls Stand with both feet together on the middle of the bicycle band. Hold an end in each hand with arms fully extended, hands by your hips, and palms facing forward. Keeping your elbows to your sides, slowly bring your hands to your shoulders and then slowly return to the starting position.

Bicep Curls

Upright Rows Use the same starting position as the bicep curls but with palms facing backward. Bring your hands straight up to midchest position with your elbows bent out to your sides. (When explaining this to little children, call it the "bow tie" exercise!)

Sitting Overhead Press Sit on a chair with the middle of the band under your upper thighs. Hold the ends of the band—one in each hand—with elbows bent, at shoulder height. Extend your arms slowly overhead and then return your hands to the starting position.

Upright Rows

Note: Count slowly to four to get to each position and then count to four again to return to the starting position. Take your time to enjoy the stretch of the band!

Sitting Overhead Press

164 ✷ Simple Incline Bench

Materials
- 3 or 4 pillows
- 1 ladder-back chair
- small rug, mat, or 2 thick towels
- 2 dumbbells (3 to 5 pounds)

This will help to strengthen the chest and the front of the shoulders. Give each member of the family a chair. Children can use their own small chairs. Tip back a ladder-back chair onto the floor and elevate the top end of the chair one to two feet off the ground by placing it on a mound of pillows. Use wide pillows for greater stability. Lay a small mat or several thick towels over the back of the chair for comfort. Grab a set of dumbbells (three to five pounds) and do one full set of each exercise below. (A set is a group of 8 to 12 repetitions.)

Shoulder Press Lie back in the chair (as if you were sitting on it). Place a dumbbell in each hand and then place your hands by your shoulders. Press the weights straight up over your chest until your arms are extended. Return to the starting position. Count slowly to four as you press up and slowly to four as you return.

Chest Flye Begin in the same sitting position as above. Hold a dumbbell weight in each hand directly over your chest with arms extended. To the count of four, slowly open your arms out to the side and then slowly return to the beginning position. (Think of holding a beach ball over your chest, open your arms out to the sides, and then squeezing the beach ball once again.)

If you can't do eight repetitions easily and with good form, decrease the amount of weight you're using. Begin with one set. Work up to three sets of each exercise. Breathe out as you press up or together with the weights. (Holding your breath can cause your blood pressure to increase.) Watch and help each other. Little ones can count for the adults, and the adults can help the children move their arms fluidly. Now instead of having to lug a heavy weight-lifting bench back down to the basement, lift the chair upright and slide it back to the kitchen table. How convenient!

165 ✳ Water Bottle Weights

Materials
- 12- or 24-ounce water bottles
- sand or water
- moleskin fabric (with adhesive)
- pair of scissors

Fill water bottles with sand or water for quick and easy hand weights! Remember when you fill your bottles that the more sand or water in the bottle, the heavier they will be. Tired? Drink some water and lighten your load! (I would suggest you empty the sand out!) Choose bottles with ridges for a built-in handgrip or make your own ridges with strips of moleskin. You can buy moleskin at the pharmacy in the foot-care section. Purchase the kind that has adhesive on one side. Remember, water bottles come in different sizes. Which size works best for you—12 ounces or 24 ounces? Once your handy hand weights are ready, the family can play "Mother, May I?" with the exercises below. You can also add exercises that you have learned in other sections of this book. Start the game by having the children line up across the starting line. Teach your children the correct standing position. You will say, "You may stand with feet shoulder-width apart and knees slightly bent." The children must respond, "Mother, may I?" and then get into the proper position. The one who says, "Mother, may I?" and gets into the right stance the fastest will be the first leader ("Mother"). Mother presents the first exercise to the first person in line by saying, "You may do eight tricep presses." The children must respond, "Mother, may I?" Mother then says, "Yes, you may." Then they do the exercise. Mother then instructs the next person in line with a new exercise and/or a different number of repetitions. If any player forgets to say "Mother, may I?," he or she must go back to the starting line and start over. The first one to the finish line wins. Work with the children to help them with their form and to make sure the exercises are done slowly. Make sure the children do not do more than 12 repetitions for each exercise. By playing "Mother, may I?," your children will learn the proper names of the exercises and get a great low-weight, high-repetition workout, which is ideal for children. Make your children's day—play with them!

Tricep Presses Hold the bottle in both hands over your head. Bend your elbows so the weight rests between your shoulder blades, behind your head. Press the weight slowly overhead and then return back to the original position. (This works the back of the upper arm.)

Tricep Presses

Front Raises Hold a bottle in each hand. Arms are straight and the bottles are by your hips. Raise the left arm in front of you to eye level and then return to your hip. Do the same with the right arm. After you have done both the left and the right arms,

Front Raises

you have completed one repetition. (This works
the front of the shoulders.)

Lateral Raises Hold a bottle in each hand
and begin with your hands resting by your hips.
Slowly raise the bottles out to the sides up to
shoulder height. Return to the hips for one
repetition. (This works the sides of the
shoulders.)

Lateral Raises

166 ✸ Beetle Back

Materials
• a bed

I learned this Fun Fact in
1,000 Facts About People by
Dee Turner. Humans aren't
like beetles, however. But you
can strengthen your back. Lie

Fun Fact: Rhinoceros
beetles can carry 850 times
their own weight on their
backs.

facedown with your lower half on a bed and your upper half off
the bed, then lift your torso. You will definitely need a helper to
hold down your ankles so that you don't end up doing a headstand
on the floor. If your helper doesn't put a lot of weight on your
ankles, you will tip forward! Start with a few repetitions and then
gradually increase the number. Return the favor to your helper!
(Adults will probably need
two children to hold down
their ankles—one child
per leg.)

167 ✳ Concentration Curls

Materials
- 1 dumbbell
- chair or bench

This is a funny name for a biceps exercise that makes you look like you are really thinking hard in order to do it. Put a serious look on your face, and passersby will think you are really concentrating!

"C" Curls Sit on a bench to do this biceps exercise. Knees should be comfortably apart. Place your left hand on midthigh of the left leg. With the right hand pick up a dumbbell. The right forearm rests on the right thigh (you will be leaning forward). Bring the dumbbell up to your chin by "curling" (bending at the elbow) your arm. Slowly extend your arm back down. Repeat 8 to 12 times for one set. At each practice session add another rep. After you can easily do 12 repetitions, you can work on adding a second set of 8 repetitions. Take a two-minute break between sets and let your workout partner (another child or adult) do a set. Who has the better concentration face?

I68 * Perfectly Plain (and Fancy!) Push-Ups

Materials
- mat, towel, or rug
- full-length mirror
- chair or couch

Every kid knows how to do a push-up! Do you know how to make this basic exercise harder and more interesting? Make sure your basic push-up has perfect form before you try these advanced ones. That means you need a straight back and when you go down to the floor, just bend your elbows—nothing else should wiggle, sway, or dip! Check to see that your backside doesn't look like a mountain!

1. Put one foot over the other and balance on the supporting foot while doing your push-ups. Switch feet!

2. Put your arms farther out in front of your shoulders. Did you feel the difference in your upper abdominals?

3. Now try putting your hands together making a diamond shape with your fingers and thumb. Elbows bend out to the side. It's hard to balance on this one!

4. Can you do a push-up with your hands on a wall? Can you do a push-up with your feet on the floor and your hands on a chair? Can you

reverse this and put your feet on the chair and your hands on the floor? This is hard because there is more weight on your arms.

169 ✶ Chin-Up Bar Exercises for Your Stomach

Fun Fact: Abdominal exercises can be done every day unlike other strength-training exercises, which should be done every other day.

Materials
• chin-up bar

Stomach muscles are "endurance" muscles—we use them every day to get out of bed, stand up straight (they support our spine), twist around, and even to breathe! You need strong stomach (or abdominal) muscles for every sport. Next time you are at the playground try these exercises while hanging on a chin-up bar:

Leg Lifts Hang on the bar and bring your legs straight up so that you look like the letter L. Have two people hang on the bar and see who can hold the L the longest! Is there room for three people? If so, try with three! Can the whole family fit on one bar? Who has the strongest abdominal muscles in your family?

Leg Lifts

Bent Knee Twists Hang on the bar, bend your knees, and bring them up to your chest. Hold for three counts and then lower your legs straight down. Try a trickier variation: twist your body as you bring your bent knees up to your chest. This works the oblique abdominal muscles—the muscles used for twisting! Hold

Bent Knee Twists

on each side for three counts before you lower your legs back down. How's that for a challenge?

Thread the Needle Hang on the bar and bring your legs up straight. Try to pull (or thread) your legs between your arms (the needle). This takes both strong shoulders and abdominals. It also takes flexibility. Have a contest with the children against the adults. I'd put my money on the flexible children!

Thread the Needle

I70 ✴ Beach Ball Fun with No Sand, Salt, Wind . . . or Beach

Materials
- mat
- beach ball
  (pick a size to match
  the participant's size
  and make sure ball is
  fully inflated)

> **Fun Fact:** Many years ago in the second century, a Greek physician named Galen invented exercises with a large ball.

Not only are these exercises fun and different because you have a great prop, but you will also find that the ball assists you with certain exercises that are usually difficult. Here are some ways you and your family can use a beach ball to get stronger:

Stomach Strengtheners

Stomach Strengtheners
Lie on your back and put your heels up on the middle of the ball. Interlock your fingers behind your head and lift your

chin halfway up to your knees. Don't try to sit all the way up—just do this "crunch." Start with five repetitions and add one each day. See how many each person can do. Compete against your own record, not each other, on this one!

Rocking Push-Ups Do a push-up with your belly on the ball, rocking forward and back using the ball for support. As you rock forward, bend your elbows, and as you rock back, straighten them. These "assisted" push-ups will help strengthen your arms. Keep the lower body tight with legs straight out behind you. Start with 10 and add one each session! See how many you can work up to!

Rocking Push-Ups

Hamstring Roll-Ups

Hamstring Roll-Ups You'll feel this exercise working! Lie on your back and bend your knees, placing your feet on the middle of the ball. "Walk" the ball forward (rolling it away from you) taking "baby steps." Then, using both feet together, roll the ball back to your hips. You will feel the muscles on the back of your legs working. Do 10 repetitions and build up from there, adding one per session. Show the kids where the hamstring muscles are (large muscles in the back of the thighs).

Leg Lifters This exercise works your stomach and your inner-thigh muscles. Lie on your back and hold the beach ball between your legs. With straight legs, squeeze your thighs together, lifting the ball off the ground until it is directly over your stomach. Slowly lower the ball back down. Repeat 10 times to start, then add one each workout.

Leg Lifters

171 ✻ Plyometrics— What's That?

Materials

- long rope (10 to 15 feet)
- 2 cinder blocks, tree stumps, or heavy chairs

Fun Fact: Plyometrics is a new training technique to build power as well as strength.

Start your training by placing a rope stretched out on the floor. Begin at one end and do zigzag jumps as quickly and as powerfully as you can, hopping back and forth over the rope with feet together. This takes a bit of coordination! If you are really good at this, try the super-plyometric exercise! Take two heavy chairs, cinder blocks, or tree trunks. Wrap the rope around the chair legs, cinder blocks, or tree trunks so that the rope is tightly secured and stretched out taut. You should start with a low rope height and perfect your plyometric zigzag jumping before you make it higher.

Note: Children under 12 should not jump down repeatedly from any height greater than 18 inches. This is because their bones are not fully developed, and they are at higher risk for growth plate injury.

172 ✦ Fondasize!

Materials

- mat or rug
- sealable plastic baggies (sandwich size), 2 per person
- sand
- 2- or 3-inch-wide ace (first-aid) bandage
- first-aid tape
- pair of scissors

Jane Fonda created a whole series of great exercises using leg weights. You can make your own "disposable" leg weights at home! Fill two sealable plastic baggies with sand and wrap each one around your ankle with a first-aid ace bandage. Secure the ace bandage in place with first-aid tape. Cut the bandage to the best length for you, so that your ankles don't feel too bulky. Don't wrap it so tightly that your foot goes numb! These are easy and inexpensive enough to make extras for everyone in the family. Gather the gang, put on some great music with a strong beat, and lead a conditioning class! (Ankle weights can make you a little clumsy, so don't try doing aerobics with them—just do the "floor work" conditioning exercises.) Count 10 repetitions of each exercise and then switch legs. Make up some of your own conditioning exercises as well!

Side Leg Lifts Lie on your side, leaning on your elbow. Lift the top leg up and then lower it slowly. Make sure you do not lift higher than a 45-degree angle from the floor. Do an equal number on both legs. This works the outer thigh.

Side Leg Lifts

Inner-Thigh Lifts Lie on your
side, leaning on your elbow. Bend
the top leg and place your foot in
front of the "resting" knee. Lift
the bottom leg off the ground as
many times as you can plus one!
(Now that leg is no longer resting!)
Repeat with other leg.

Inner-Thigh Lifts

Donkey Kicks For this exercise
your hands and knees are on the
ground, doggy-style. Bring your
knee into your chest and then
slowly extend it straight behind
you. Bring the knee back in and
repeat this exercise on each leg 10
times—and then add one for good luck!

Donkey Kicks

173 ✷ Giant Steps

Materials
- pen or pencil
- paper

Have the kids and the grown-ups try doing these all the way
across a field, yard, or long hallway or room and everyone will definitely find that their legs are getting a gigantic workout! Watch
form and make sure to stop when the steps become sloppy or
careless—you don't want to overdo it or get an injury! How many
giant steps does it take to cross the field or yard? How many
"baby steps" does it take to get back? (Baby steps are done by putting the front foot's heel against the back foot's toe.) Do long side
steps: face sideways and take a big step forward and then slide legs

together toward the lead (front) leg. Repeat all the way up the field. Walk backward doing baby steps. Who can do this without losing their balance? Each person can make a list of the different steps on a piece of paper. Next to each one write how many steps it took for each trip up the field. Compare the results and discuss the findings! Do the taller people take fewer or more steps? Do the shorter folks take more baby steps? Why?

174 ✳ Good Morning, Broom!

Materials
- broom
- towel (optional)
- 2 quart bottles (optional)
- sand or water to fill bottles as needed (optional)

No, this is not a trick you can use to get your children to clean up the house. It is a great strengthener for some major muscle groups—the back, hamstrings, and the gluteus maximus (the rear end)! Serious weight trainers use this exercise.

Place the broom handle across the back of your shoulders. Place the towel around the broomstick to help cushion your upper back if the pressure bothers you. Wrap your arms over the broom.

Bend forward at the waist with a straight back and then come back to the upright position. Do 8 to 10 repetitions. If you have a strong back you can hook on some plastic quart milk bottles filled with a little sand or water. Remember to keep the weight light for the kids. Seal the bottles up tight!

175 ✦ Air Jacks

Materials

• none

Can you easily do a lot of regular jumping jacks? Here is a jumping jack challenge that is guaranteed to give you Superman-strength legs! First try this with your hands on hips. (Later add the arms, swinging them up overhead and back down by your sides with each jump.) Start with your feet together. As you jump into the straddle position flare your feet out before you land. This means open them wider than the straddle position in midair. Then you pull them back in to land in the straddle. To return to the starting position, flare them out first and then quickly pull your legs together. This exercise takes speed, endurance, and strength in your outer- and inner-thigh muscles as well as your calves and quadriceps. Now this is an efficient exercise!

176 ✴ Minitramp— Cheap and Safe!

Materials
- 8- to 12-inch-deep piece of foam rubber
  (4' × 4' minimum size)

The kids (and you!) will have a blast by jumping on a thick piece of foam rubber and at the same time strengthening legs, heart, and lungs! Place the foam rubber (your "minitrampoline") in the middle of a wide-open space. Practice tuck jumps, straddle jumps, pike jumps (bend in half at the waist) jumps with a turn, zigzag jumps to the corners—you name it! You can buy foam rubber inexpensively at salvage stores or some bedding stores. Jumping is a great overall conditioner, and it burns calories, too. Kids love the wobbly feeling they get in their legs from muscle fatigue. Best of all, they won't be wearing out the mattress springs!

177 ✷ Hula Hoopla

Materials
- 1 hula hoop per participant
  (try to match the size to the person)
- '50s music
- cassette or CD player

Making hip circles with a hula hoop works a very important group of muscles in your stomach called the obliques. The oblique muscles lie in an X shape on the sides of your abdomen. You need these muscles to twist and turn . . . and what is a better way of strengthening them than hula hooping! Here we go. Feet apart, hold the hoop at hip height, bring it way back to one side as a wind up, and let it go and rotate your hips in a circle. See how many circles you can do. Do it on the other side so that you don't walk around lopsided! Who in the family can hula hoop the longest? The fastest? The fanciest? Can this be done with two hoops? Put on some '50s music and videotape the sock-hop event!

178 ✴ Power-Up!

Materials
- plastic milk crate or bottom step of a stairway

You can use either a bottom step in your house or a sturdy milk crate to add power to your jumps. Face sideways and stand close to the step or the crate. Put one foot up on the step and push down on that leg quickly, thrusting the free leg's knee up in the air. It looks like a hop with power. Do it several times. Now turn around and do it on the other side. You can also do two-legged power-ups on a step—a crate isn't big enough or sturdy enough. Push off the ground with two feet and land on the step with two feet. Hop back down and repeat. Keep a mental record of how many hops or jumps are done at each practice session. Add one a day to increase your fitness level!

179 ✴ Big Arms

Materials
- chair, bed, desk, or sofa (your choice)

Triceps, not biceps, are what give arms their big size. (Girls can't get as bulky as boys because they have different hormones. However, girls can get strong and toned doing these triceps exercises regularly.) A simple and effective triceps exercise that can be done almost anywhere is the "triceps dip." It can be done on the edge of a sofa, a bed railing, an airplane or train seat, or an office desk . . . so you don't need any equipment. You don't even need to change into workout clothes!

Triceps Dip Place your hands, with thumbs in, on the sides of a chair or railing. Scoot your rear end forward, so the weight is on your arms. Lower your rear end down and the push back up using the tricep muscles in the back of your arms. Do 10 to 12 repetitions.

Cross Leg Dip Try the same exercise but make it harder by crossing one leg over the other. Now more weight is being supported on the arms. Try doing five to start.

VII

Games from Long Ago and Far Away

Many of the games we play today are variations of ones from long ago. Despite the differences and similarities—the fun remains!

180 ✶ Ta Galagala

Materials
- chalk
- small stone

If you like a challenge you'll like this game from Nigeria. Take a piece of chalk and draw eight circles (*kurtus*) in a row. Stand at the end of the circles and throw a stone (*kwalo*— "KEWHL loh") into the first circle. Jump over it and into all the circles up and back except the one the stone is in. Pick up the stone and throw it into the second circle, jumping into every circle except the one with the stone in it. Continue with this pattern until you have thrown the stone into each circle. Try not to fall out of the circles or miss a circle—if you do, your turn ends!

181 ✳ Scratch

Materials
- paper squares or chalk
- tape (optional)
- small pebble

You can use either newspaper squares or sheets from an old magazine to make the

Fun Fact: The *scotch* in hopscotch is from the old English word "scratch." In Poland it is called "klassa," and in Trinidad it is called "jumpy."

hopscotch pattern indoors or if you don't have a sidewalk or driveway to draw on. If you use paper, secure the paper to the floor with a few pieces of tape. If you have a sidewalk or driveway available, use a piece of chalk to draw this pattern. You will also need a small pebble to toss. Start by throwing the pebble onto the first square. Balancing on one foot, hop over that square and hop all the way up and back down the pattern, bending to pick up the pebble on the way back. Remember to stay on one foot! When you come to two squares side by side put one foot in each square (as long as there isn't a pebble in it). Continue on to the second square and then the third. Keep going until you've played on all the squares. Make sure everyone takes turns after each pass. This game requires a good sense of balance!

182 ✳ Chunky

Materials
- 10 sticks, 6 to 8 inches long
- flat round stone

Try this Cherokee Indian game called "Chunky." Players begin by placing two sticks into the ground (one foot apart) and then rolling a flat round stone between the two sticks. Then they quickly throw more sticks at the ground where they think the rolling stone will land. (This has to be done as soon as the stone is rolled.) The player who throws the stick closest to the fallen stone wins! (Be careful never to throw the sticks near anyone.)

183 ✹ Yogasize

Materials

- exercise mat
  or rug

Yoga means "union" in Sanskrit, an Indian language. See if you and the children can do the "warrior" pose. It takes balance, strength, and concentration! Stand with one foot in front of the other with both arms held straight over your head. Tilt your body forward at the hips and lift one leg up directly behind you. Keep tilting forward until your chest and leg are parallel to the ground. You should look like the letter T. Hold the pose for 10 seconds and return to the starting position. More yoga exercises are listed in Chapter 9.

184 ✹ Thread the Needle

Materials

- hula hoop

Here is a challenging group game using hula hoops called "Thread the Needle." Have everyone join hands in a big circle—

keep holding hands through the whole game! One person in the circle has a hula hoop that he is continuously spinning on his arm. That person passes the spinning hoop to the person next to him who has to climb through it while trying to keep the hoop in motion and still holding on to the first person's hand. The hoop goes from the second person's arm, over her head, and then down to her other arm. Then the neighbor next to her has to try to do the same thing. This is a good game for a party—it is simple and a guaranteed "giggle maker"!

185 ✳ Brinca

Materials

• chalk or string for starting and finish lines

Here is a great game from Spain! The goal of this game is to get to the finish line with the *least* amount of steps, jumps, and hops. The actual (long version) name of the game is *Brinca* ("hop"), *da un paso* ("take a step"), *salta* ("jump"). You will need to mark a starting line and a finish line 15 to 30 feet away. The players line up behind the starting line, and an announcer calls out any combination of the three Spanish words to instruct the players on what to do. For example, *salta, brinca, salta, da un paso* would be "jump, hop, jump, take a step." Here is a hint to pass on: make the movements big so that the longest distance is covered with the fewest steps. Be careful to keep your balance. Not only is this game a strength, balance, and coordination builder, but if they don't know them already, your kids will also learn a few words of Spanish!

l86 ✳ Pokean

Materials
- 3 to 4 tamale wrappers or corn husks (partially dried)
- 6 to 12 feathers
- 12-inch length of wire or string
- pair of scissors

Zuni Indians are Native Americans who enjoy this game called "Pokean." To make a pokean you take two strips of tamale wrappers or corn husks and lay them across each other to make an X. Take a third piece and fold it into a small square to be placed on top of the X. Bring the long ends up so they meet over the small square and tie them with a thin piece of corn husk (use scissors to cut a thin piece). You may need to use a piece of wire or string to hold it together firmly. It needs to be tight for the next step, which is to tuck feathers into the opening. Any number of feathers is acceptable. This will look like a funny badminton shuttlecock. The goal is to keep this homemade toy in the air with the *greatest* number of hand taps. It is similar to "hacky sack" except you use your hands. It is important to keep your hand as flat as possible and be sure to count the number of taps out loud.

187 * Lame Hen

Materials
• 20 18-inch sticks

How about a relay race from China? Gather up 20 sticks. Make two rows of 10 sticks—each about a foot and a half apart. (They should lie flat on the ground and look like hurdles from above.) The sticks on the left and the sticks on the right should be in line with each other. Both teams need to be 15 or 20 feet behind the first stick. At the word "go" one player from each team hops on one foot clucking like a hen up and over all the sticks, picks up the last stick, turns around at the end, and comes back with that stick. The player places that last stick in front of the first stick and hops back to the end of the line. When the first player is back in line, the next person goes and does the same thing. (Note how all the sticks are being moved closer to the line.) After all the sticks have been moved once, the game is over. Whichever team moved all the sticks first is the winner!

188 * Japanese Horseshoes

Materials
- 1 12-inch stick
- 1 6- to 8-inch stick for each player

This is a game of horseshoes that doesn't require anything more than a few sticks. You will need a one-foot target stick called a *nekki*, which is firmly pushed vertically into the ground several feet in front of the thrower. Each player needs a smaller (six to eight inches) throwing stick, which they propel at the nekki target stick as if they were skipping rocks. (It is a sideways throw . . . if possible!) Each child takes a turn and then lets the next child in line try. Whoever knocks the target stick down wins. You can see that this game requires skill and a little practice, but very few materials!

189 ✷ Inuit Games

Materials

• none

The Inuit people live in the Arctic and have invented many games to keep up their hunting skills all year round—and to keep warm! One trick is called the "toe jump." All players line up side by side and squat, holding on to their big toes. At the count of three, everyone jumps forward as far as they can. The tricky part is to keep holding on the entire time. Another fun game is the "knee walk." This really works on balance skills! Have kids kneel on a soft grass surface or rug. (Be sure they are wearing long pants to prevent rug or grass burns.) Instruct (or show!) the kids how to place kneecaps on the ground and clasp ankles in their hands behind them so that their feet are close to their rear ends. Now try walking around without letting go of the feet or falling over!

190 ✴ Hide-and-Seek Aboriginal

Materials

• none

The children in Papua, New Guinea, play a form of hide-and-seek in the moonlight called "Pao Poo." Translated this means "who will hide." They begin the game in the center of the village. (You can adapt this to be limited to your neighborhood or backyard.) One child is called the "seeker" and kneels down and covers her eyes. A second child is the "tapper" and gently taps the seeker on the back while singing out this song:

Tontoku pai poa pio
Simolomo Tama Toki Tong
Pao Poo

When the tapper sings out the last line ("who will hide") the seeker names a child out loud. The child whose name is called goes and hides. The song is repeated until all the children are named. (The tapper can help the seeker with all the names.) While the seeker is still covering her eyes, the tapper then goes and hides. Once he is in his hiding spot he makes a loud "Whoo!" sound. All the other hiders do as well and then they remain quiet. The seeker then looks for the children. The "found" children can help look for the others. After everyone is found the game is over and the kids are exhausted—after all, they had a whole village to hide in! You may want to play this game only during daylight hours. Adapt the rules to fit your needs.

191 ⋆ Dodge Shells

Materials

• rubber ball

Make a large circle with as many children as you have available. One child is chosen to be in the center (he or she is "it"). A rubber ball is thrown at the child in the center by one of the children in the circle. The child in the center dodges the ball to avoid being hit. If the child is hit, the thrower joins the child in the center. There are now two targets to aim for! If there is a "miss," the person who catches the ball is now the "thrower." The game continues until all the children are "it"—in the center of the circle.

> **Fun Fact:** Many years ago, the ancient Greeks thought it was fun to throw shells at their opposing team. The goal of the defending team was to try to avoid being hit by a sharp shell. Ouch! This was the original (and more painful) version of dodgeball.

192 ⁎ Deer in the Lord's Park

Materials

• none

The goal of this game is to capture the "deer"! Begin by making a circle and having everyone hold hands. Designate one person to be the "deer." The deer has to weave

Fun Fact: This is a game from Old England brought to New England by the Pilgrims. Back home in Old England all the deer that roamed around were owned by lords. In the new country, everyone could freely capture any deer at any time.

in and out of the closed circle doing different movements (spinning, hopping, dipping, jumping, or leaping—whatever movements she likes). The deer quickly and unexpectedly taps a person to be the hunter. Now the hunter must try to catch the deer, weaving in and out and doing the *same moves* as the deer. If the deer leaps, so must the hunter. If the deer crawls, the hunter must do the same. If the hunter is lucky enough to capture the deer, the deer goes in the center of the ring and is "out." She must wait until the game is over to be released. If the deer can get safely back to her starting place without being tagged, the hunter becomes the new deer. Eventually you will have too many people in the center to continue the game and the game is over!

193 ✳ Blindman's Bluff

Materials
- blindfold
  (handkerchief
  or bandana)

> **Fun Fact:** "Blindman's Bluff" is a game from the 1800s. The blind player was called Buff.

This is a small group game where Buff is blindfolded and spun around three times. The rest of the players run or walk around Buff. Buff tries to catch one of the players by listening to their footsteps or their giggles! When Buff catches a player, that player becomes the new Buff.

194 ✳ Graces

Materials
- 4 wooden dowels, ½-inch thick and 18 to 24 inches long (check hardware or craft stores for these), or ordinary straight sticks with no bark on them (same dimensions)

> **Fun Fact:** "Graces" was played in the 1800s by girls in long skirts and boys in breeches.

- 1 large plastic coffee can lid or small
  (6 to 8 inches) wooden hoop
- pair of scissors

We don't have a modern version of "Graces" nowadays. This is a long-forgotten game that your family can bring back! Players should pair up. Each player needs two long and narrow two-foot sticks. Each pair needs a hoop that is about six to eight inches in diameter. You can make the hoop out of the plastic lid of a coffee can. Use scissors to cut a large circle out of the center of the lid, leaving a one-inch ring of plastic. The players should stand several feet away from each other. One player places her sticks in the center of the hoop and holds it in front. She criss-crosses her sticks and then draws the sticks away from each other, making the hoop fly across the room to the other player. The harder the pull, the farther the hoop will fly! Each player tries to catch the other one's hoop on his or her sticks and fling it back. How far can the hoop sail and still be caught? How long can the volley continue?

195 ✷ Christopher Columbus Discovered Soccer

Materials
- rubber bands
- 1-inch Styrofoam ball (optional)

Fun Fact: In the late 1400s, Christopher Columbus saw native Haitians kicking a gummy ball made from the sap of a rubber tree.

Your kids can make an old-fashioned soccer ball by collecting rubber bands and wrapping them around each other until the ball is big enough to kick. You could also start with a small Styrofoam ball as the core to make this project go faster. (Don't try to make one as big as a regular soccer ball—that would take a long time and require huge rubber bands.) Test the ball on friends, neighbors, and family. Gather folks who are sitting on the porch after dinner and engage them in a lively game of neighborhood soccer! Set up two goals at either end of a field or on a dead-end street. Now practice dribbling the ball (short, repeated kicks to move the ball up the field) and shooting it into the net. Encourage passing between players of all sizes, ages, and abilities. It is very tricky with a small ball! You don't need to have all the formal rules of a real soccer game . . . just have fun and thank Chris for discovering soccer as well as America (as rumor has it)!

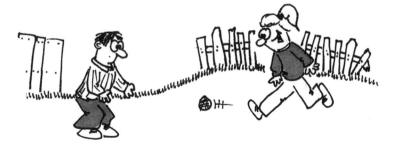

196 ✳ Flip Sticks

Materials

- felt, glue, paint, glitter, yarn
- pair of scissors
- 3 ¾-inch-thick dowels, 2 cut to 18 inches and 1 cut to 24 inches (or find sticks of approximately these lengths and remove any bark, for each player)

Fun Fact: "Flip sticks" have been traced back 2,000 years to Asia.

Kids can make a modern version of flip sticks by first decorating the sticks and then flipping them (a form of juggling). Give the kids felt cut into assorted shapes to glue onto the longer sticks. Also give them pretty pieces of colored yarn to wrap around the sticks. Make the flip sticks bright and festive! Show the players how to hold the two short batons, one in each hand, and then flip the longest stick (the wand) with the smaller batons. Try to keep the wand from falling on the ground. You can tap the near and far ends. You can bring the sticks up high or way down low. Try flipping the wand a full 360 degrees and then catching it again . . . keep it moving! Show the kids how to pass them back and forth to a friend. See what cool moves they can invent.

197 ✷ Hawaiian-Italian Lawn Bowling

Materials

- several candlepin (small) bowling balls or bocce balls
- target, almost any object would be suitable

> **Fun Fact:** Two thousand years ago Roman soldiers played an outdoor bowling game called bocce. Some people say that lawn bowling actually comes from England. In France, bocce is called *jeu de boules* or *petanque*.

We played a game of lawn bowling in Hawaii that was really fun and really hard! You will need small bowling balls. Ask a bowling alley for old balls that they no longer use and find something for a target (such as a flattened paper bag, a hula hoop, or a crate that you place on its side). You also need a hill. Stand at the top of the hill and try rolling the balls down to the center of the target. The tricky part is you can't roll the balls straight down the hill. To make it more of a challenge, try rolling the ball in a loop—that's the way we did it in Hawaii!

198 ⋆ Old-Fashioned Hockey

Materials

- two large brown paper bags
- 2 inches of newspaper
- stapler
- old brooms or hockey sticks (one for each player)
- tennis ball, softball, or Wiffle ball

Fun Facts: Hockey has been around a long time. In different countries, it had different names: Hockey in England was called *shinty* in Scotland. In Ireland it was called either *bandy* or *hurley*. Long ago in America it was called *shinny*. Shinny was played with curved sticks and a leather-covered ball.

Begin by making homemade bases out of two large brown paper bags. Fill each one with one inch of neatly stacked newspaper. Staple the open end shut. Flatten bags out and you will have two bases. Next you are ready to set up your "Shinny" game. You can use either hockey sticks or old brooms and a softball, tennis ball, or Wiffle ball. Divide your players into two teams. Set up two bases, one at each end of the field. (These are the goals—early players didn't use nets.) Choose one person to be the "mounter" for each team. For the first round, one mounter places the ball at his base and whacks it to the opposite side trying to get it to the base for a "win." The other players "shinny" the ball up the field with their sticks to get it to the opposite side's base. If someone succeeded, just once, this was considered a victory!

199 ✽ Pok-Ta-Pok

Materials

- peach, apple, laundry, or trash basket
- pair of scissors or sharp knife
- hammer and nails or rope
- ball

Fun Facts: Many years ago, in Central America, the Mayan and Toltec natives played a game with a rubber ball and stone "hoops" that were placed 25 feet up on a stone wall. This was a form of basketball, except you could not use your hands, just your hips, elbows, and knees. Captains hated losing because it might mean they would be beheaded! Dr. James Naismith invented modern-day basketball in 1891. He used a peach basket for the hoop.

Make a "hoop" from the basket. Use scissors or a knife to cut out a hole at the bottom of the basket large enough for the ball to drop through. Secure the basket on a wall or a tree with hammer and nails, or tie securely with a rope. (Make sure the basket is hung at a doable height. It is important that the children experience success!) Have the children line up in front of the hoop and shoot the ball, standing four feet away from the basket. (Adjust the distance forward or backward depending on the child's age or skill level.) Next let them try it with their eyes closed. Try again facing backward. As they become more successful, they can move the starting line farther from the basket and try these skills again. They can keep moving farther and farther away until no one can make a basket. This is a good way to build hand-eye coordination and upper-body strength and to develop ball-throwing skills.

200 ✳ Baggataway

Materials

- empty, clean half-gallon plastic milk or water jug (1 per player)
- 2-foot wooden dowel, with the same width as the opening of the plastic jug (1 per player)
- pair of scissors or sharp knife
- heavy-duty tape
- ball

Your kids can play lacrosse without expensive equipment. Help them cut a plastic jug according to the picture below. Place the spout end over a wooden dowel stick so that it fits snugly into the jug's opening. Wrap the spout end securely with heavy-duty tape. Practice tossing and catching the ball between two or more players. Kids who are playing by themselves can practice throwing the ball at a target, such as empty plastic soda bottles or milk jugs.

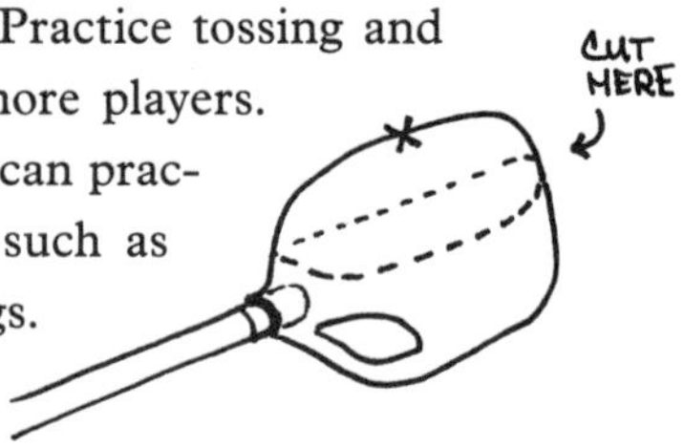

Fun Fact: "Baggataway" is the name that French settlers in America gave to a popular Native American game. A stick with a net was used to fling a ball around an open space. Sometimes up to 500 people played in a game. Having so many people chasing one ball resulted in many injuries and even some deaths. In 1876, a dentist named Dr. George W. Beers invented the rules of the modern version of this game that we call lacrosse.

CUT HERE

201 ✳ Cork and Feathers

Materials

- pin
- cork
- pushpin thumbtack
- 12 to 16 feathers

The kids can make their own shuttlecock and try passing it back and forth with their friends—using just their feet! Make a circle of pinholes at one end of the cork. Carefully glide the feathers into the holes and turn the feathers so they form a closed circle. Try a few test runs. Your shuttlecock should land on the cork end without feathers. Nowadays a weight is added to the "nose" of the shuttlecock to help the aerodynamics—it balances the "birdie" during flight. You can experiment with this by using a pushpin-style thumbtack to secure a "weight" into the cork. Have the kids try different small objects as weights. The kids can tuck this little toy into their pocket and bring it wherever they go. This way the gang can play old-fashioned badminton without having to haul out a net and racquets.

Fun Fact: Back in ancient China, a form of badminton was played without a net or even racquets. Players formed a circle and would kick a "shuttlecock" back and forth to each other. This funny-looking piece of cork with feathers stuck into it would never fly straight, so they called it "the wobbler."

202 ✳ Pickwick Club

Materials

- 1 roll crepe paper streamer
- 1 plastic grocery bag
- pair of scissors
- strong tape (electrician's, duct, or cloth)
- chalk
- ½-gallon milk or water jugs filled with sand or dirt
- lawn chairs (or empty cardboard boxes)
- jump rope

Fun Fact: Bicycles were invented in the mid-1800s. Bicycling became very popular right away. One could get fresh air, a view of the countryside, exercise, and a fast way to get somewhere! Clubs were formed and races were created. One of the first races took place in Paris in 1868. A bicycle club was formed in England called "The Pickwick Cycle Club of London."

Have the children form their own "Pickwick Club" (choose any name) and create a bicycle safety day in your neighborhood. Arrange a safety course or participate in one provided by your town's police department. Practice hand signals. Discuss good safety practices such as wearing a helmet all the time. Let the children decorate the bicycles with streamers woven through the spokes. They can cut crepe paper or plastic grocery bags into half-inch-wide strips that are one foot long and put the strips together and tape to the handles. Next create an obstacle course where everyone can practice steering and braking skills. Create chalk-line patterns (long S lines) for lanes, put out sand-filled plastic jugs for bikers to weave around, place lawn chairs or upside-down boxes for circling, and stretch a jump rope 10 to 15 feet from the end of the course to mark a line for braking. Enhance and modify the course to accommodate the different ages and skill levels of the kids. With a bit of creativity the obstacle course can last all spring, summer, and fall!

203 ✶ Bob and Weave the Needle

Materials

• none

A minimum of six players is needed to play this game. Set the participants up in two straight lines facing each other (three players per side). "Line one" holds hands with the person across from them in "line two." The couple at the beginning of the line holds their hands up high to form an arch; everyone else in the line goes through one at a time in order and says the following:

The needle's eye
That doth supply
The thread that
Runs so true;
Ah! Many a lass
Have I let past
Because I wanted you.

The game continues until everyone has a chance to be the

Fun Fact: Back in time—before television was around—sewing was a favorite (and necessary) pastime. This game originated in England in the 1600s and was brought over to America. It is based around the importance of sewing skills.

archway. Unlike "London Bridge Is Falling Down," no one gets caught in the archway! Try the game again; this time sing faster and move more quickly through the pattern!

204 ✦ Tennis Anyone?

Materials
- dress-up clothes and shoes
- tennis racquets and balls
- old-fashioned lemonade
- parasols or umbrellas

In the early days of tennis, women wore long skirts. Can your child imagine running after a fast tennis ball in this heavy and cumbersome attire? Have whichever kids want to pretend they are women tennis players from "long ago" dig through the costume box and pull out long dresses, long-sleeved blouses, and uncomfortable shoes. (Make sure

Fun Fact: History buffs have traced tennis back to the time of the Crusades in France where tennis was played inside palaces with bare hands. People later played tennis with gloved hands and then a bat or paddle. In the 16th century, these royal folks began using a strung racquet. In 1877, Major Walter Wingfield invented tennis as we know it today, in Wimbledon, England—sound familiar?

the shoes don't present a hazard such as twisting an ankle and the skirts aren't so long as to trip on them.) Tie long hair up in a bun and attempt a game of tennis! Afterward serve ice-cold lemonade to the parasoled, refined ladies from the 1800s on the "veranda" (porch, stoop, or deck).

205 ∗ Jump over a "Horse"

Materials
- 2 plastic milk crates
- 3 feet of strong rope
- bath mat (3' × 4')
- thick rug (4' × 6')
- cardboard
- pair of scissors
- crayons or markers
- string mop
- tape

You can make a vaulting horse by placing two plastic crates side by side on ground that is flat and free of holes and debris. (Do not double up the crates to make the horse taller—this could cause a serious injury.) Tie them together securely (in more than

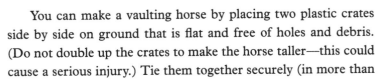

one place) with a rope. Lay a bath rug or small carpet over the horse. Find a second thick rug to place on the other side of the horse for a landing mat. Draw a cardboard horse head and use a string mop for a tail. Attach to each end of the horse with tape or extra rope. Take a few steps to get a running start and jump over the horse. Smaller children can do a squat jump or straddle jump over the horse by placing their hands on his back.

Fun Fact: In 1811, Friedrich Ludwig Jahn was credited with creating modern gymnastics. He filled an open-air gymnasium with gymnastics equipment such as rings, parallel bars, and the "horse." Gymnasts would run down a runway and do flips and stunts over a leather-covered bench that was made to look like a horse, complete with head and tail. Today's vaulting horse doesn't have the head or the tail.

206 ✳ Puss in the Corner

Materials

- none

You will need a total of five players; four will stand in the make-believe corners of an imaginary box and one will be in the center. The one player in the center is "Poor ol' puss" and she calls out, "Poor puss wants a corner!" The other players try to coax puss into their corners. When puss calls out, "Go!," everyone (including puss) quickly rushes to trade places. Everyone must leave his or her corner and seek a new "home." Only one player can be in each corner. Whoever can't find a corner becomes the new puss. Both young and old can enjoy this simple game.

Fun Fact: This is a fun party game that the Pilgrims brought over.

207 ✱ Merlin's Mirror

Materials
- roller skates, helmets, protective pads
- 2 cardboard boxes
- jump rope
- heavy-duty tape
- 8 large plastic drinking cups
- 4 stuffed animals
- cardboard and markers for sign
- 2 garden hoses

Fun Fact: Joseph Merlin was an inventor from Belgium. He may have had some great ideas, but he wasn't very coordinated. While he was demonstrating his roller-skating apparatus in a ballroom in 1759, he crashed into a mirror and broke the violin he was playing!

Your family can practice their roller-skating coordination by placing obstacles on a driveway. Give these obstacles creative names. For example, cardboard boxes stacked up with a jump rope stretched across for skating under could be the George Washington Bridge. Large plastic drinking cups placed upside down make road hazard cones. Stuffed animals need a sign that says, "Caution: Animal Crossing!" Two hoses parallel to each other to form a chute can be a "lovers tunnel." No one will dawdle at that obstacle! Practice will help the children feel comfortable and in control when skating—just have them leave the violin at home!

208 ✷ Crooked Croquet

Materials

- 9 wire hangers
- wire cutters
- 2 wooden dowels, 18 inches long and 1½ inches thick, or same size sticks (with no bark)
- golf putter or sponge mop (wood handle cut to 3-foot length), or 3-foot length of 2 by 4 and 6-inch length of 2 by 4 and hammer and nails to make your own mallet
- tennis ball, baseball, or other small ball

> **Fun Fact:** Back in the 1700s in France a game was invented to be played on the lawn, which involved wooden mallets (hammers), wooden balls, and curved hoops. It was called croquet.

You can still find croquet sets for sale in sporting goods stores and some toy stores. Here is how you can make your own set, which is really a lot more fun! Cut wire for hoops from hangers.

You'll need 9 wires in 20-inch lengths. Bend the wire into half circles for the hoops ("wickets"). Stick the dowel rods ("stakes") into the ground for starting and ending points. Use a golf putter or sponge mop, or make your own croquet mallet with two pieces of wood nailed together in the shape of a T. Use any small ball. Now have some fun setting the hoops into the ground. You can follow the standard lawn croquet course or make any pattern you like. Just remember to leave enough room between hoops to fit a person swinging a mallet. Each player takes a shot, and if he gets it through the first hoop he can go on to the next. If he misses, the next person in line goes. The first person to get through the whole set wins. Redesign the hoop pattern and play again!

VIII

Healthy Hullabaloos—
Big Parties, Gatherings,
and Events

If you enjoy organizing a big to-do you'll love
these special fitness and health-driven
activities. Add your creativity and special twist
to make these happenings your own.

209 ✳ Neighborhood
Sports Newsletter

Materials
- pencils or pens
- paper

- computer
- access to photocopier
- stapler
- camera and film

Are a lot of the neighborhood kids active in sports? Does the gang get together after dinner for a pick-up game of Frisbee, softball, or kickball? Here is an activity that is half fitness and half academics. Create a newsletter for the entire neighborhood. It will be informative, great for boosting self-esteem, and helpful in fostering the spirit of teamwork and cooperation. The kids are the authors and illustrators as well as the center of attention on this project. In addition, each participant can have an important job such as typing the stories into the computer, editing, copying, and distributing the weekly, biweekly, or monthly publication. Here are some topics you can include: competition results, practice and game schedules (for Little League, American Youth Soccer Organization, etc.), fund-raising information, classified section for outgrown or unused equipment, carpool requests and schedules, training tips, special recipes, and a paragraph highlighting the "Athlete of the Week." Everyone should be included at some point. After the publication is printed and copied, the kids can walk around the neighborhood together distributing the free publication. A parent should accompany the delivery crew through the neighborhood for safety's sake.

210 ✳ Hoedown Family Night

Materials
- telephone book
- large room or open space outdoors
- music system (if needed by instructor)
- microphone (if needed by instructor)

Gather neighbors and friends for a "healthy family night out" at your house. Locate a dance teacher who is willing to volunteer time or have everyone pitch in and hire an instructor. Look in the yellow pages under "dance instruction" or seek out talented leaders among the participants you invite. Try something new! Russian folk, Spanish flamenco, Israeli circle, Latin samba, Appalachian clogging, Polish polka, swing, country line, or ballroom dancing are great styles! Some forms of dance are easier to learn than others, and a good instructor will make all the difference. If your evening is a success, try a second gathering at someone else's house. Do this weekly, biweekly, or monthly. Dancing is a wonderful way to exercise without feeling like you are working out. All ages can participate. What a great way to meet new people, gather old friends, and burn off a few calories!

211 ✳ All Children Exercise Simultaneously Day

Materials
• none

This is a special day in May when children from all over the world will exercise at the *exact same time*. The purpose is to promote health, nutrition, peace, and unity. Have your child ask his gym teacher if the school is planning to participate. If not, this is a great chance to introduce the idea. What special way can the school or class observe this day? Come up with an ace idea!

All Children Exercise Simultaneously (ACES) has a website: www.projectaces .com.

2|2 ✴ Sports Tag Sale

Materials
- poster board and pushpins or masking tape for signs
- card tables or picnic tables
- price stickers, price tags, and markers
- money box with change
- receipt book (optional)
- calculator
- paper or plastic bags, cardboard boxes, newspaper, bubble wrap, rope (to make hauling away easier for your customers)

How about selling off any unused sporting equipment you own and using the proceeds to buy a new piece of equipment the whole family can enjoy? This will provide some new motivation for everyone! Two weeks prior to the planned date (select a rain date as well), have the family collect and clean the items they want to sell. Together figure out a fair price, and label each item with stickers or paper tags. This is a good opportunity to rid your garage or basement of outgrown skates, plastic sports toys that are too "babyish," card collections, exercise equipment that is gathering dust, and memorabilia you no longer enjoy. Brainstorm with your kids on ways to publicize the sale. Place ads in local newspapers; send announcements to friends, family, and neighbors; or place notices in local shops (ask permission first) and on community bulletin boards. Three to seven days before the tag sale, place posters up around the neighborhood. The night before the big event put out the picnic tables. Early the next morning arrange your items by sport or size. Large, expensive items such as bicycles and sleds can be grouped together, all skiing equipment should be together, and weight-lifting bench, barbells, dumbbells, and weights should be next to each other. You can price them as a set (with a discount) as well as individually. Be flexible on your price; remember, this is stuff you no longer want. Assign each child a job or an area. Have that change box ready . . . and hope for good weather! When you're done, add up the proceeds and hold a family meeting to decide how to spend it. Buy a volleyball set, a standing basketball hoop, or snowshoes or inline skates for each family member. Did you make a huge amount? Consider taking a ski or camping trip, karate classes for all, or tickets to a professional hockey game.

2|3 ✶ Power-Walking Club

Materials
- sturdy walking shoes
- water bottles
- reflective vest or clothing
- flashlight
- wristwatch

Who doesn't like to go for a walk after dinner or on a weekend morning? Gather friends and family for exercise, conversation, and fresh air. This activity is suitable for everyone from babies in backpacks to toddlers in strollers, to teenage best buddies, to grandfolks. Everyone will need comfortable walking shoes and a water bottle. If you are walking at dusk, it would be wise to wear reflective clothing and carry a flashlight. Try charting out a one- to two-mile course on safe, well-lit streets. (Later on, as the group gets into better shape, you can extend the mileage.) This way you will know the mileage as well as potential hazards: potholes, exposed roots, or areas of heavy traffic. Begin with an easy warm-up walk of 5 to 10 minutes. This will warm up the muscles and gradually increase the heart rate. Next, take a short break and stretch the muscles in the legs, arms, shoulders, back, and neck. This should take about 5 minutes. (You can alternate "leaders.") Now your power walk can begin! Start with a brisk 10- to 15-minute walk and then slow the pace down for the last 5 minutes. End with a cool-down stretch. Here are some helpful hints: All participants should select a comfortable stride that they can maintain. Steps shouldn't be too long or too short. Faster walkers can walk together and slower walkers can form a group as well. Arms should swing freely up to shoulder height with elbows slightly bent (no more than at a 90-degree angle), and hands should stay relaxed. Make sure walkers drink plenty of water along the way. If the participants are chatting while they walk, this is good! This means they are exercising their heart and lungs at the right pace. Remember to plan your next meeting before the group goes home. Make this a habit you can't break!

214 ✳ "You're a Real Smoothie" Stand

Materials
- poster board
- pens and paint
- thumbtacks
- blender
- extension cords
- ice
- plastic or paper cups
- straws, garnish, and drink umbrellas
- fruit juice
- knife
- fresh fruit
- paper towels
- sponges
- napkins
- tablecloth
- plastic containers with lids
- cooler
- money box and change
- festive clothes and hats

Kids love setting up a lemonade stand. Lemonade stands were a longstanding American tradition in the 1900s. Try a smoothie stand in the new millennium! Adults should supervise this project. Several days before the planned date have the kids make roadside signs to advertise the stand. They can also put signs up around town for the event. Make sure you have a blender, one or more extension cords if needed, plenty of ice, plastic or paper cups, straws, drink umbrellas, a variety of fruit juices (orange, apple, peach, or blends), cut up or small pieces of fruit (strawberries, bananas, pineapple, blueberries), paper towels and sponges for cleanup, and napkins to give out. Set up the table with a pretty tablecloth. Store all your ingredients in clean, covered containers—perishables should be kept in a cooler filled with ice when not in use. Have a money box ready with extra change in it. Before the kids start experimenting with smoothie combinations, make sure their hands are very clean. Have them create recipes and give them interesting names: Patty's Powerful Potion, Mango Mocktails, Jamaican Me Crazy Jivin' Juice, etc. Post a sign listing the drinks and their prices. Throw on some festive clothes and have a blast!

2l5 ✷ Health-Spa Birthday Party

Materials

- 2 chaise longue chairs
  (for the manicure and pedicure stations)
- 2 stools or chairs (for the facial and hair stations)
- 4 small tables
- 4 small wastepaper baskets or paper bags
- wash basin with warm water and soap
- hand towels (1 per person per station)
- Assortment of nail files, orange sticks, nail brush, nail scissors, nail polish, polish remover, cotton balls, hand and foot lotions, alcohol for sterilizing scissors and nail brush (1 complete set for manicure and pedicure stations)

- Assortment of combs or
  brushes, elastic bands,
  ribbons, barrettes,
  headbands, hair spray
- Mild facial cleaners and
  astringents, facial
  masks, cotton balls,
  washcloths (1 per
  person), hypoallergenic
  face cream, and clip-on
  combs to hold hair back
  from face
- antibacterial cleanser
  for the "professional" at
  each station to use between customers
- goody bags for personal products
- cassette tape player and relaxation music
- healthy refreshments and beverages

For my daughter Marja's seventh birthday I didn't hire a clown or magician, I hired a masseuse! We had several stations set up for manicures, pedicures (with footbaths), facials, hair fashions, massage chair, and a healthful snack bar. Each station had a chaise longue or stool and a small table set up with cotton balls, cotton swabs, cleansers, creams, lotions, and potions! The girls' goody bags contained a comb, nail file, nail polish, lotion, and different hair bands. The boys received manicure sets in pouches. (These kits were used *during* the party so that the kids would not be sharing implements and germs!) Our masseuse did chair massages while three high-school girls manned the beauty and "spiffing-up" stations. The kids rotated among the stations. In the background we had soft relaxation music. Our refreshments included organic popcorn, vegetable chips, fruit skewers, and granola bars dipped in chocolate. You've never seen a quieter party! The kids talked about it for weeks—it was really fun and different.

216 ✷ National Backyard-Games Day

Materials—*any assortment*
- balloons
- volleyball net and ball
- soccer ball
- football
- Frisbees
- burlap sacks
- softball and bat
- badminton racquets and birdies
- chess or checkers
- game guidebook (optional)
- refreshments and beverages

There is one designated day in May (the date changes each year) when neighbors and friends gather together to play games in a park or large backyard. Each family brings an activity. One group can bring a volleyball net, another a set of horseshoes, and someone else can provide the burlap bags for a sack race. Quiet board and card games are also nice. Here are some group games you can play:

Nose Balloon Race Have a row of adults stand opposite a row of children. The players put their hands behind their backs and place a balloon between each pair of noses. The balloon must stay in place as the pairs go up the field and back. First couple back wins!

Push-Up Contest How many push-ups can each participant do with a clap in the middle? For youngsters, let them do push-ups with their knees down. How many can you do? How many push-ups can a dad do with a child straddling his back?

Snake Slither Once again the child is on the parent's back. Parents lie flat with a child lying on top of them. They must slither up to a line and cross it without losing their "guest."

Foot Fun Ride Children stand on their parents' feet and hold their hands. Parents must walk or travel as quickly as they can to the finish line without losing their rider. If the child falls off, the couple must start again.

Neighborhood Log Roll No this isn't a dessert—it's a game. You will need a wide-open space. Adults and children alternately lie down head-to-toe until a huge log is made. Everyone grabs the feet of the person above them and holds on tight. On the count of three, the whole group rolls together . . . or tries to!

Lap Circle Tired? Have a seat in your neighbor's lap. Start by making a *tight* circle with all participants standing as close together as possible facing sideways, so you see the back of the person in front of you. On the count of three, everyone sits down on the lap of the person behind them. If everyone does this simultaneously, and you are close enough together, then this works without the entire circle collapsing. If it is done like a game of dominoes—one at a time—it doesn't work and everyone falls over!

217 ✸ Ballet School Party

Materials

- ballet (or sports theme) invitations
- medium-sized room, cleared of furnishings
- cassette tape deck and music, if needed
- combs and elastic bands for dancer
- hair spray or gel
- instant camera and film
- ballet- or sports-themed paper goods—tablecloth, cups, napkins, plates
- ballet- or sports-themed cake

Hire a ballet instructor to come to your house and teach the children a class. Clear a room of furniture and other hazards. A wood or vinyl floor is best, but wall-to-wall carpet is also acceptable. Provide a tape deck for the instructor to use. Recommend that the kids arrive in their ballet attire—leotards, tights, tutus, and ballet shoes for girls and T-shirts, sweatpants, and bare feet for boys. You can help the girls pull back their hair into a tight bun and slick the boys' hair back with gel. Take an "instant" picture of each child with the teacher and have the teacher autograph each one—send it home with the child. You may prefer to hire a soccer coach, swim instructor for a pool party, or trampoline teacher if you have a home trampoline. Contact the local gyms, public schools, and the YMCA and YWCA for instructors-for-hire and facility rentals. Party stores may have themed paper goods to enhance your party. Local bakeries often have sports figures for their custom-ordered cakes. Don't be limited by convention, choose *any* sport, instructors of aerobics to tai chi are easy to find!

For theme party items contact:

Paradise Products, Inc.—"Fling Decorating Kits"
P.O. Box 568
El Cerrito, CA 94530
(800) 227-1092, to order catalog

Websites for party products:

www.kidsparties.com
www.mallpark.com/party
www.partymakers.com
www.partypaks.com

218 ✷ Ytrap Drawkcab (Backward Party)

Materials
- invitations
- goody bags (turned inside out)
- inside-out balloons, small puzzles (completed), plastic horse and rider, and other goodies for bag that can be reversed or placed inside out
- chairs
- cassette tape player and music
- "Pin the Tail on the Donkey" game (optional)
- refreshments and beverages

This is fun because you are not restricted by what you do—just how you do it. The fun comes from the host's creativity, not extravagance and labor. To set the stage, send out upside-down and inside-out invitations that begin with "thank you for coming!"

Even the stamp can be upside-down. To read the invitation, invitees will need to face it into a mirror—all the writing is backward. Suggest the attendees wear their clothes inside out and backward. Greet the kids at your backdoor, "Thanks for the neat gift, hope you had fun, thanks for coming, good-bye!" Give them their goody bags with inside-out items. For example, older children can have inside-out balloons, completed puzzles to undo, a backward rider on a plastic horse. Here is the best part (especially for your birthday child)—begin with the birthday cake before pizza and salad and then immediately open presents! Thank them enthusiastically before gifts are opened. Play musical chairs in reverse—choose the winner first, then add chairs instead of taking them away. The kids sit when they hear the music and roam about at the silence. What other movement games and activities can you play in reverse? Try backward relay races or *remove the tail* from the donkey (the child will need to locate the tail with his correct number). When the kids leave, welcome them, thank them for coming, and say, "Hello!"

219 ∗ Family Fun Run

Materials

- oak tag paper or number cards and safety pins
- markers
- crepe paper (streamers)
- microwave meal covers
- colorful ribbon (1 inch wide)
- pair of scissors
- stapler
- beverages and refreshments

This is great way to get to meet neighbors. You will need a few items that can either be homemade, ordered through a catalog or website, or found at an athletic store. Make or buy race numbers to pin on with safety pins, award ribbons, and a starting gate. You can order professional-looking number cards and starting gates by calling Spring Co. at (800) 383-0305. If you prefer you can make the runners' numbers with a marker and oak tag paper. Look in the yellow pages to find an award company that sells ribbons and trophies. You can purchase your awards or easily make ribbons from the metallic covers of microwave meals. To make awards, cut out round disks from the microwave covers and staple a loop of wide blue, red, or white satin ribbon. This ribbon can be purchased at a sewing and novelty store.

Check the weather forecast to make sure your event can be held. If the weather is favorable take a run, bike, or drive along your chosen path to confirm that it is safe and free of fallen or strewn debris and other hazards. Keep the fun run to a mile or less or the nonrunners will find it less than fun! When race day arrives, line up your friends and give out their numbers. Have someone start the "walk, run, stroller race." The finish line can be made out of banner flags or just a piece of crepe paper stretched out marking the end. Next, pass out beverages, fresh fruit, and energy bars. The awards can be given for *any* reason in *whatever* categories you have decided. You can be serious or outrageous! "First, second, and third place finishers," "slowest to cross the line," "nicest sunglasses," "cleanest baby in stroller," "wildest shoelaces"—give everyone an award!

220 ✳ Boot Camp Party

Materials
- army fatigues and hat or dark clothing
- clipboard
- whistle
- 1 or more old tires
- 2 10- to 12-foot ropes
- cardboard box
- pair of strong scissors to cut cardboard
- mats, small rugs, or towels
- camera and film

G.I. Janes and G.I. Joes will love being challenged at this birthday party filled with physical fitness tasks. Invite guests to wear army fatigues or dark clothing and sneakers. No party dresses today! Plan out a circuit-training course complete with obstacles that already exist or ones that you have placed. If you live near a playground, have the kids run to the playground with an adult (the "drill sergeant"). Give the "squad leader" a clipboard with prewritten instructions for each station. (The birthday child can be the squad leader.) At home you can put out tires for an agility run, a rope for climbing, cardboard-box hurdles, mats for push-ups and sit-ups, and a stretched out rope to crawl under, belly down. The drill sergeant or squad leader will need a whistle and a stern look! Plan the entire circuit ahead of time and keep your young recruits running or marching in line from site to site. Praise, encourage, and make allowances for different fitness levels—after all, this is supposed to be fun fitness! Grab a camera and take some great candid shots of your little troopers struggling through their first day of basic training! Put a photo in each thank-you note.

221 ✷ Make Your Own Kid and Baby Buffet

Materials
- low table
- serving spoons and bowls
- plastic wrap
- plastic plates (these are sturdier than paper ones) and utensils (no knives)
- cellophane tape

- antibacterial, individually wrapped hand wipes or several bottles of cleansing gel
- drink boxes
- baskets
- beach towels or blankets
- paper towels
- basic assortment: lettuce; tomato slices (not cherry tomatoes, which could cause choking); green, red, and yellow sweet pepper slices; baby carrots; cucumber slices
- specialty food assortment: hardboiled egg halves, seeds and nuts, raisin boxes and dried fruit, different types of sprouts, gherkin pickles, celery stuffed with peanut butter and raisins, individually wrapped string cheese and foil-wrapped cheese triangles, watermelon cubes, and gourmet popcorn
- entrée assortment: minipizzas, tiny bagels with different fillings (cream cheese or peanut butter), small yogurt containers, and chicken legs with a "flat side" so they won't roll (cut out a wedge)
- baby bar: baby-food jars, paper bibs, baby bottles, applesauce, yogurts, animal crackers, or teething bagels
- several small waste containers

Kids enjoy choices, and they love to be treated the same as grown-ups at a party. Set up a low table with small, cut-up items for the "Kid's Salad Bar." You can include any or all the basics, specialty items, and entrées listed . Each item should have its own serving spoon or be individually wrapped to discourage little fingers! Make sure the food bowls are close to the center of the table so that the kids can slide their plates along the edge—cafeteria-style. Tape plastic spoons and forks, and antibacterial hand wipes to the bottom of each plate. (Be sure to tape loosely or be available to help the kids remove the utensils.) Drink boxes can be set out in a basket on the picnic blankets. The best blankets are old beach towels placed edge to edge. They are easier to throw in the wash than bulky, cumbersome blankets. Also set out a roll of paper towels on the blankets in lieu of paper napkins, which fly away and are too small for big kid-sized cleanup jobs! These steps will make it easier for the kids to carry (and focus) on their plates! You can also make a "baby bar" for babies and toddlers. Set out an assortment of handy items as a convenience to parents and a treat for baby! Include many strategically placed wastebaskets to encourage kids to clean up after themselves. The parents will appreciate the convenience and thoughtfulness of your buffet and setup as much as the kids!

222 ✷ Milk Shake Saloon

Materials
- checkered tablecloth
- table
- 1 or more blenders or milk shake machines
- extension cords, if needed
- cooler
- several bags of ice
- low-fat ice cream (any flavors)—
  1 scoop per serving
- low-fat or skim milk—4 to 6 ounces per serving

- tall cups
- bendable straws
- extra-long plastic spoons
- syrups (any flavors)
- hose or bucket of water for cleaning up and washing out blenders
- paper towels and sponges
- plastic containers for leftover milk shakes

What's better than a tall, cold bubbly after a hard day of pony rides? If you're renting a pony for your party, or having any kind of Old West party, this saloon goes hand in hand with the theme. At this party, a "tall, cold bubbly" is a frothy milk shake. To set up the "bar," place a checkered cloth on the table. Put out one or more blenders or electric milk shake machines. Have extension cords available if needed. In a cooler, place ice and plastic containers of low-fat ice cream (plastic containers hold up better than paper ones) and jugs of low-fat milk. On the table put tall cups, bendable straws, extra-long plastic spoons, and an assortment of syrups. Keep a hose nearby to rinse out the blender containers. Have paper towels and sponges on the table for spills and washing up. It is also a good idea to have plastic quart-sized containers available to store any extra mixtures. Children choose their own blend of ice cream and syrups for a special shake. Happy (and full) cowboys and cowgirls one and all!

At www.partypaks.com they have a "country line-dancing party" that comes with cowboy hats, party goods, decorations, and even a videotape to learn some dances!

223 ✸ Hula Happening

Materials
- wide crepe paper, green or any preferred color
- pair of scissors
- yardstick
- pencil
- cloth tape to match color of crepe paper
- 1 package of tissue paper (assorted colors), cut into 6″ × 6″ squares
- needle and strong thread
- Hawaiian music
- luau dinner
- video camera

This tropical theme works any time of the year! Kids can make their own hula skirts out of wide, stretchy crepe paper cut partway up into strips. Measure each child from hip to midcalf. Determine the length of the skirt needed, and cut the sheet of crepe paper accordingly. Lay the paper out flat and use the yardstick and a pencil to outline the strips running vertically all the way around the skirt. Leave a border of six inches at the top of the skirt. Do not cut the strips higher than the border or the skirt will fall apart. Put the skirt around the dancer's waist and tape into place using strong cloth tape. Leis are easily made by stringing tissue-paper balls together. Cut tissue paper into 6″ × 6″ squares before your guests arrive (this will save time). Use a variety of colors to enhance this project. Have the kids choose their color squares and then "scrunch" the paper into tight balls. String the tissue-paper balls together using a needle and strong thread.

Make the leis long enough to freely come off over the head. Knot the ends of the string together. Put on some Hawaiian music and learn the hula! You don't know how? You can order this tape and have a quick lesson!

Hula for Children
Island Heritage
99-880 Iwaena Street
Aiea, Hawaii 96701-3202
(800) 487-7299

If you can't get a tape, let the kids invent their own hula dance. Hula dancing is storytelling told expressively with hand, facial, and body movements. Have the children create a story line to "dance out." Hawaiian music in the background is inspiring. Serve a luau dinner indoors or out. Grab your video camera and record this party for your collection of great family memories. Aloha!

For luau paper goods, menus, recipes, and decorations, check this website: www.partypaks.com.

224 ✱ Old-Fashioned Olympics

Materials
- running track, field, or yard for 191-yard race
- broom handle
- Frisbee
- art supplies (paint, markers, or crayons and paper)
- paper and pencils for writing poetry
- toga sheets—guests can bring their own
- greenery and twist ties for olive branch wreathes

Here is a party idea dating back to 776 B.C. The location was Ancient Greece. The scene was the Temple of Zeus in Olympia.

The event—the first Olympic Games! Back then the Olympics included the sharing of art and poetry as well as the first sporting event: a 191-yard footrace. This is roughly halfway around a football field. Later on other sports were added: wrestling, chariot races, javelin and discus throwing, horse racing, and the pentathlon. If you can't seem to get your chariot tuned up for the event, stick with the 191-yard run, and add a javelin throw using a broom handle and a discus toss with a Frisbee. Make sure there is plenty of room and that the other guests are free from danger. By adding a poetry or art contest you will round out the activities and give your less athletically inclined guests a chance to shine. Guests can wear togas (a sheet loosely draped over the body and tied at one shoulder). The contest winners receive olive branch wreaths to wear on their heads. These can be made by fastening any greenery together with plastic bag ties. To top off the festivities, Greek food can be served at mealtime—stuffed grape leaves, Greek salads, and gyros!

225 ✻ Jogging Treasure Hunt

Materials

- paper and pencil to write clues
- tape and pushpins to attach clues
- pirate loot bags
- small clue rewards wrapped in colorful paper (1 per pirate): small boxes of raisins,  sunflower seed packets, homemade fruit roll-ups, plastic bags with popcorn and/or nuts, packages of carrots, sugar-free gum, or little toys such as erasers, pencils, and bookmarks
- treasure box (shoe box covered with wrapping paper is fine)
- "big" treasure (1 per pirate): jump rope, sweat headband, sweat socks, iron-on sports patch, Frisbee, Wiffle ball, or sports biography paperback

Aye, aye, mate! Here is a fun activity to get your pirates panting! This is an aerobic treasure hunt! At the starting point everyone begins by jogging in place. The first clue is read to them. For example:

Roses are red, violets are blue,
You'll find a tire near this next clue.

Once solved, all the pirates need to *jog* or *run* to the next clue—including the reader! The clues should be spaced out enough to get a bit of a jog in. At each clue is a small trinket or treat that the kids can stuff into their pirate loot bags. The jogging pirates continue from clue to clue until they find the final treasure box, which holds the "big" gift.

226 ✱ Wok 'n' Roll Party

Materials

- rice paper, envelopes, pen, and stamps for invitations
- bathrobes and sandals (guests can bring their own)
- low table or floor mat and cushions
- chopsticks
- moist, warm washcloths and wooden tongs
- fortune cookies
- paper goods for table settings
- paper lanterns (optional)

Hire an Asian chef to prepare a delicious meal in front of your guests! The kids will enjoy seeing the way Asian food is made, watching the chef use her utensils, and learning the names of different ingredients. Send a rice paper invitation to each child. You may be lucky enough to find someone who can write the guests' names in Chinese, Korean, or Vietnamese—depending on the country you are choosing. Children can wear bathrobes tied with wide, colorful bands. Sandals can be brought or worn, depending on the weather. Each child can make an egg roll that the chef can then custom cook. Certain types of egg rolls or dumplings are steamed in a bamboo steamer instead of fried—this makes them more healthful. Next the chef can show off her lightning-fast technique as she slices and dices a stir-fry for the wok. Woks maintain the food's nutrients by quickly sautéing vegetables at a high heat. What is the secret to perfect rice? The chef can show you! Once the meal is prepared the guests can remove their shoes, sit on cushions on the floor, and eat at a low table using chopsticks. Use wooden tongs to pass out warm, moist washcloths to cleanse hands before the meal. Enjoy the meal and then end with custom fortune cookies. You can create and personalize the fortunes based on what you know about each guest. They will be so surprised! To find a chef, call Asian restaurants listed in the phone directory. Plan the menu in advance with the chef. Ask the chef to bring all ingredients, cookery, and utensils. The host can supply the table settings.

For custom fortune cookies:

e-fortunecookie.com
2737 Minnehaha Avenue South
Minneapolis, MN 55406
(800) 808-3678

227 ✷ Big-Top Party for the Big Day

Materials
- poster board and markers
- tickets, homemade or purchased at party goods store
- costumes—guests can bring their own or host can supply
- animal masks or makeup
- hoops
- cardboard boxes
- top hat, cloak, and whistle
- chairs or benches
- cardboard box and ribbon for concession vendor
- popcorn in cups or paper bags
- fruit juice boxes
- peanuts in small bags

- low-fat hot dogs and hot dog buns
- packets of relish, ketchup, and mustard
- paper hot dog holders (homemade or from party store) or paper towels
- watermelon
- napkins
- fortune-teller's tent
- table for face painting

Send out a circus announcement poster as the invitation and include several small tickets for your guests to use at the event. Suggest that they plan a short circus act to demonstrate and they should wear the appropriate outfit. Children can work in groups or do a solo performance. How about a lion tamer, two-person acrobatic team, tightrope walker, clown, juggler, or magician? If someone doesn't have an act planned, have plenty of props available to inspire the imagination. Animal masks, hoops, and overturned sturdy cardboard boxes are useful to a small group wanting to put on a wild-animal act. Makeup, costumes, and silly props are fun for even your youngest guest to clown around in. The birthday child can be the Master of Ceremonies—just supply top hat, cloak, and whistle.

Arrange chairs or benches in a large semicircle for your tent. Have a helper serve food and beverages up and down the aisles. The serving tray can be made from a two- or three-inch high cardboard box with a ribbon threaded through the farthest ends and then placed around the neck. Serve popcorn in paper bags; juice boxes; peanuts in small bags; healthful, low-fat hot dogs in buns; and watermelon slices for dessert. Don't forget condiments and napkins. If you want to be extravagant, you can buy a roll of tickets, paper hot dog holders, and popcorn circus boxes at a party shop. You can even rent a full-sized popcorn maker at an equipment rental store. Set up a table for clown makeup and a tent for fortune-telling. (You'll need to enlist friends who like to dress up and play the part for this!) The kids can use the tickets they have received in their invitation to "purchase" food, beverages, and the special activities.

You can order circus supplies, including rings, juggling balls, spinning plates, and juggling scarves, from Circus Smirkus (a circus camp for kids).

Circus Smirkus
One Circus Road
Greensboro, VT 05841
(802) 533-7443
Fax: (802) 533-2480
E-mail: Smirkus@Together.net

228 * Sundae, Mondae, Tuesdae, Anydae Treat

Materials
- ice cream scoop
- blender (optional)
- small bowls for dessert
- bowls and spoons for toppings
- napkins, paper towels, and sponges for cleanup
- bowl of hot water to rinse off scoop after each use

Ingredients

- low-fat frozen yogurt or ice cream
- fresh fruit, either whole, sliced, or blended into a puree (strawberries, blueberries, bananas, raspberries)
- toppings such as granola, toasted wheat-germ, ground or chopped nuts, raisins, dried cranberries, or blueberries

These sundaes are so good for you—how can they even be considered a special treat? They contain plenty of vitamins and minerals including calcium. Most children only get a part of the calcium they need each day. Here is a way to sneak in the needed nutrient!

Scoop your ice cream or frozen yogurt and add the fruit and toppings of your choice. Try to be a "purist" and avoid goopy, syrupy, high-fat toppings—stick to natural and fresh ingredients.

229 ✳ Community Walking Map

Materials

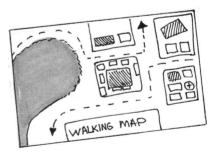

- poster board and markers
- water bottles and refreshments (donated)
- balloons and banners (donated)

Contribute to your community by introducing a town walking guide! First contact the appropriate town officials (council members, mayor, chief of police, or public safety department) to get permission. Next, contact area organizations and businesses who could back this project financially (if needed) and, more importantly, "in spirit." Contact the American Heart Association, American Lung Association, American Cancer Society, Lions Club, Junior League, Jaycees, Scouts, and other organizations to lend their support and assistance. Map out three to five walks that differ in length and that are in various locations around town. Make sure the routes are free of danger (potholes, roots, traffic, unlit or isolated areas). Next, work on getting your maps printed. The easiest way to handle this is to use maps that already exist and highlight the routes you have devised. Label the routes and provide a description (mileage, parking availability, start/finish location, type of turf—stroller friendly, wheelchair accessible). If you need to raise money to cover the printing costs, hold a fund-raiser, solicit area businesses, or ask for funding from town officials. Area businesses could pay a small fee and be listed as a sponsor of the project and have their business card printed on the edge or the reverse side of the map. Enlist supporters to donate services for printing, advertising (local newspaper and cable television), promoting, and distributing the maps.

Get the word out! How about holding a community walk for the "Grand Kickoff"? Find a central location as the starting point. Have a town official introduce the program and kick off the walk. Make sure you have volunteers to guide people along and to pass out the maps. Vendors can donate bottled water and refreshments. The town can donate police and ambulance services. The police car can lead the "parade," and officers can stop traffic to cross walkers. The ambulance service can provide on-site medical care if needed. Sponsors can decorate the starting gate with balloons or banners. The American Heart Association and other organizations may be able to donate pamphlets and even set up a table for blood-pressure screenings and general information. Walking is one of the most enjoyable and healthiest forms of exercises—share the joy!

230 ✻ Indoor Beach Party Is a Shore Thing

Materials

- swimsuits, hats, sunglasses, towels (guests can bring their own)
- lotion
- snorkel mask and flippers
- sandbox-quality sand
- sandbox or baby swimming pool (optional)
- plastic tarp
- bright light
- umbrella
- beach chairs
- shovels and buckets
- tape deck
- ocean sounds on tape
- cooler, ice, and fruit drinks
- Beach Boys music and other 1960s-era dance music
- healthful "beach" food or grilling food

Do you own a good vacuum cleaner? Do you have a basement playroom? Throw a beach party . . . indoors! Beach activities can be fun and fitness-oriented. Invite your guests to wear swimsuits, hats, and sunglasses and bring towels. (You can coat the kids' noses with zinc oxide and give them small bottles of regular lotion as pretend sunblock.) Greet the kids at the door wearing a snorkel mask and flippers. Purchase a bag or two of sandbox-quality sand and a large sheet of plastic tarp. Place the tarp under a sandbox and fill the box with the sand. If you don't have a sandbox you can purchase an inexpensive baby swimming pool instead, or just go without and pour the sand directly on the tarp. Keep the kids under control and your sand will stay in the sandbox or on the tarp. A bright light in the corner can be the sun. Put up an umbrella and place beach chairs around the sand. Supply shovels and buckets. Don't forget to play ocean sounds in the background and serve drinks from a cooler to really set the mood. When it is activity time, put on a Beach Boys tape and have a dance party. Do "the limbo," "the swim," "the pony," "the mashed potato," and "the twist"! For dinner, cook outside on a grill—even if it is cold out. Your guests will leave feeling a little warmer and the winter will seem a little farther away!

231 ✻ Longest Leapfrog

Materials
- field or large yard
- cassette tape player
- music
- cooler
- green-colored fruit punch or limeade

Widen your social circle by holding the longest leapfrog train that you can. Everyone—short and tall, young and less young—can be invited. Invite neighbors, friends, and family. Have the guests bring guests, and their guests can bring guests! Find a wide-open field or large backyard. Start with one person squatting down as another person leaps over her back and squats three or four feet in front of her. The next person leaps over the first two and squats in front of them. A helper or spotter can assist the little ones. Establish ground rules at the beginning—such as, this is a teamwork project and jumpers need to be gentle on the person squatting. Lay out the route in advance. Play some frog-themed music and supply a large cooler of frog fluid (any green beverage—lemon-lime combos work well). Have a hoppy day!

232 ✴ The Iron Family

Materials (your choice)
- in-line skates or roller skates
- bicycles, tricycles, wagons
- swimming pool
- kickboards and any needed safety equipment
- minitrampoline
- jump ropes
- hula hoops

Create a family quadathalon day! Yes, this is a *four-event* challenge. Everyone has a personal goal instead of competing against different family members (after all, that wouldn't be quite fair!). Select four activities or sports that all the family members enjoy: walking or jogging, in-line skating or biking, swimming or water-walking, minitramp or "jump rope jump-a-thon." The younger ones can vary or modify an activity to make it doable. For example, they can use a kickboard and swim three laps. The older children or adults can do the crawl for three laps without using their legs! Rest if needed between events. Take the time to use necessary safety equipment. End with an event where everyone can participate together, such as hula hooping. Did everybody reach his or her personal goals? Try again next weekend. Is there an improvement? Did everyone have fun? That is the number one goal!

IX

Cool as a Cucumber

Everyone needs ways to relax, slow down, and unwind. Try these out with your kids, and enjoy the tranquility that follows.

233 ✶ Koala Bears Are Sleepyheads

Materials
- 1 cup dried chamomile
- ½ cup dried rose petals
- 1 cup dried lavender
- ½ cup dried peppermint
- 1 cup dried lemon verbena

Fun Fact: Koala bears look sleepy because they really are. Koalas eat only eucalyptus leaves. These leaves contain a natural chemical that makes the koala sleepy and relaxed.

- large bowl (big enough to hold
  4 cups of dried herbs)
- measuring cup
- several small gauze bags (find at a herb shop),
  lacy handkerchiefs, or silk pouches (find at a
  yard sale or vintage clothing store), silk or
  lace ribbon, needle and thread (all optional
  items)
- small basket (optional)

Tell your kids they are not koala bears so they shouldn't eat eucalyptus leaves (they could become ill)—instead they can make herbal sachets. The herbs in this recipe are thought to help people relax and feel calm. The sachets can be placed on a pillow. The beautiful smell of these herbs may even help your kids fall asleep! You can find the dried herbs in an herb specialty shop or some health-food stores, or you can even grow these herbs yourself from seed or by purchasing small herb plants at a nursery. Dry them by hanging cuttings upside down in small bunches until they are brittle. Discard the stems. Kids can mix the ingredients by digging their hands right into a large bowl filled with fragrant herbs. This provides maximum enjoyment! Put the herbs in homemade lace pouches or handkerchiefs. Tie with pretty ribbon or sew the pouches closed. As an alternative you can put the herbs into inexpensive gauze bags sold at herb shops. Baskets can also be used. Give the gifts away or use them in the kids' rooms . . . and have a good night!

234 ✶ Rub My Feet, Please!

Materials
- pillows to sit on
- massage oil, baby oil, or hand lotion (optional)

Fun Fact: Ancient Asian medicine connected each part of the foot to a corresponding organ. Traditional wisdom said that if you rubbed that part of your foot it would help the organ that ailed you.

Ahhh, there's nothing like having your aching feet rubbed at the end of the day to help relieve tension and stress. You can trade foot rubs by sitting across from another person on a soft pillow and placing a foot in each other's lap.

The best time to get a foot rub is after a bath when feet are squeaky-clean. Begin by gently but firmly holding both feet so that the person doesn't feel too ticklish. Hold for a minute or two until she is relaxed and calm. Next take a little oil or lotion, warm it in the palm of your hands, and rub it slowly on her feet and ankles. Start your massage at the heel; make long, even strokes; and then try using your thumb in circular motions. Try new things that you think would feel good. Work your way up to the toes. Use one hand to rotate the ankle and the other to massage the foot. Kids not only love massages, they also make great masseuses—teach them early on!

235 ✳ Watch the Clouds Go By

Materials

- none

My daughter Marja finds it very relaxing to stretch out a blanket and watch the clouds overhead. After a long day at school, just resting and enjoying the beautiful blue sky and the puffy clouds helps her to unwind. I like to lie down with her and listen to the birds and feel the warmth of the sunshine and the coolness of a gentle wind. It is also nice to try this in the early evening when the night sky is filled with stars. Try it with your children.

236 ✳ Breathing Class

Materials

- none

My friend earns her living teaching people how to breathe! She says if we learn at a young age how to breathe the right way, we can help control our stress when we are older. Start by sitting up nice and straight in a cross-legged or lotus yoga position (which is more "pretzely"). Place your hands, palm side up, on your knees. Close your eyes. Now take a deep breath through your mouth and breathe from your belly so that your ribs go out to the sides (you should feel as if you were filling up a balloon in your stomach). Next *slowly* let your breath come out your nose—it should take twice as long to breathe out as in. Relax your face, forehead, and shoulders. Let all the tension go. Breathe slowly in and out until you get a comfortable rhythm and deep breathing becomes second nature. Listen to your breath. You only need to practice a few minutes a day. Encourage the children to remember this very relaxed feeling so they can use it when they feel tense. It is a handy tool for parents as well!

237 ✳ The Ultimate Bath

Materials
- 2 large towels and 1 midsized towel
- bubble bath or bath oils (optional)
- cassette player and relaxing music on tape
- pj's
- soaps and sponges in basket (optional)

Children love water—after all, we began life in a pool of water! Make sure your tub is nice and clean. Place two large, fluffy, soft towels in the dryer so they are nice and toasty when the children get out of the tub. Fill the bath with water that it is not too hot or too cold. Add bubbles or bath oil if your children like these. Put on some soft, relaxing music—how about Bach, folk music, harp duets, or Peruvian Andes music? Before the kids climb into this peaceful paradise make sure they have cozy pajamas ready for when they get out. Gather soaps and soft sponges and place them in a basket on the rim of the tub. Roll up a mid-sized towel for the back of the neck to be used while reclining in the tub. Have the bather climb in and lie all the way back, and put the rolled-up towel in place. The chin should rest on the water's surface. Arms should float in front of the body. When the bath is over, double wrap her in the towels that were warming in the dryer. (Never leave a young child in the tub alone; have someone watch her while you get the warm towels.) Put on lotion and pj's, and have her climb straight into bed. Now *you* will have a restful night!

238 ⁕ Special Sandman Spritzer

Materials
- plastic spray bottle
- 10 drops lavender essential oil
- 8 ounces purified water

Our favorite relaxation potion works like a charm to lull our son Noah into a sleepy state. Even though lavender is known for its relaxation qualities, it works all the better because Noah associates it with a nice, peaceful, quiet feeling. We use it *only* when he needs to calm himself, and we don't use it as a perfume! For example, when he is tossing and turning in his crib, we'll "spritz" him with lavender water. The scent helps him to relax and drift off to sleep. This is called "aromatherapy." *Aroma* means "pleasant odor" and *therapy* means "treatment." Lavender can be purchased as an essential oil from an herb shop or natural-food store. Only adults should handle the essential oils because they are full strength and can cause a skin reaction. Pour eight ounces of water (purified if you can get it) into a clean spray bottle that you have saved or purchased. If you are recycling a bottle from home, make sure it is not one that had toxic cleaning chemicals in it. Place several drops of the essential lavender oil into the bottle. Tighten the top and shake gently. Place it near the bed so the "Sandman" can find it easily!

239 ✹ My Peaceful Room

Materials

- 3 soft pillows and pillowcases (clouds, stars, planets, or cow-jumping-over-the-moon designs are available at bedding and linen specialty shops, in catalogs, or at department stores)
- 1 set of flannel or cotton sheets (same design)
- 1 fluffy comforter (old "worn-in" ones can be more snuggly than new ones)
- string of blue holiday lights
- Velcro wall hooks
- glow-in-the-dark moon, stars, and planets
- glass prism and string for hanging

Children need 10 to 12 hours of sleep a night to be healthy and to be able to pay attention in school. You can help your kids get a good night's rest by making their room cozy and peaceful. One motif is "sleeping under the moon and stars." Find just the right sheets, pillows, pillowcases, and snuggly covers to make this "magical" bed. One pillow is placed supporting the left side of the child's body, the other supports the right side, and the third is for the head. (This gives the full "sleeping on clouds" effect!) Next string blue holiday lights around the windows or the top of the room to lend a blue glow at bedtime. Use Velcro hooks to attach the lights to the ceiling or walls—the adhesive is easily removable. Glow-in-the-dark stars and planets are also soothing. Make sure to unplug the blue lights when the kids fall asleep. To make morning time as pleasant as bedtime, purchase a glass prism and place it in a sunny window. When the sun comes streaming in the window, 1,000 rainbows dance on the walls. (Of course, this only works where sunlight is available.) This combo makes children feel well rested and cheerful in the morning . . . and reduces our parental stress as well!

240 ✳ Essential Bath Oil

Materials
- 1 or more small dark glass bottles
- 6 to 10 drops of essential oil (see lists)
- 8 ounces oil (sunflower, safflower, coconut, almond, or vegetable)
- small funnel
- eyedropper
- decorative label and colored markers

You can make your own bath oils by mixing a few drops of essential oils into a base oil. Remember that essential oils should only be handled by adults. Essential oils can be purchased at health-food stores or herb shops.

These oils are considered relaxing evening bath oils. Make up your own combinations:

rose	ylang-ylang
sandalwood	jasmine
chamomile	lemon
geranium	lavender

How about a refreshing bath oil to wake you up in the morning? Try any combination of these:

juniper	cypress
rosemary	fennel
eucalyptus	peppermint
bergamot	lemongrass

These special mixtures need to be placed in dark glass containers to preserve the oil. Sunlight isn't good for the oils. Use a funnel to put the base oil into the bottle and a dropper for the essential oil. Make sure you wipe the extra oil off the outside of the container. Make a decorative label with a special name for your blend and attach it to your container. Beautiful!

241 ✳ Music to Soothe Your Soul

Materials
- portable sound system
- blank cassette tape
- batteries

Did you know that you can change how you feel just by selecting the right kind of music? When we want to exercise we listen to fast music with a strong beat. Frightening movies often have scary music in the background to enhance the effect—and it works! Some say even plants respond to soft, gentle music and tend to grow better when it is played regularly. Have your kids make their own tape of natural sounds by taking a tape recorder into the woods to record the birds or to the ocean to record the sounds of the surf. Some people find rainfall relaxing. The goal is for the kids to associate the peacefulness they experienced when making the tape with quiet times when they later listen to the tape.

242 ✳ My Arms Are Heavy . . . I Have No Worries

Materials
• soft mat or blanket

The most powerful organ in the body is the brain. It controls almost everything we do. You can teach your children to relax when confronted with a stressful situation by coaxing their bodies into a deep relaxation state. Have your child lie in bed or on the soft grass with eyes closed. Tell her that she is going to try a technique of thinking about each body part as being heavy and relaxed. Have her say and then think about these words: "My eyes feel heavy and relaxed. My forehead is free of tension. My cheek muscles are relaxed. My jaw feels no pain or tension. I feel peaceful and calm. My shoulders and neck are heavy and free of muscle aches." Now keep going, taking your time, coaching your child through each body part down to her toes. Remind the child to take deep breaths throughout the session. Check in periodically and ask how she feels.

243 ✴ Yoga for You and Me

Materials
• Soft mat or blanket

Yoga is an exercise form that comes from India. It combines stretching and relaxing. In addition to being very calming, it can be challenging as well. Try these with your children. Remind them to breathe in and out deeply during these movements. Work on making the mind quiet and still.

Try these poses with the deep-breathing technique:

Tree (Vrksasana) Start by standing with weight evenly distributed between both legs. Shift weight onto the left foot and draw the right leg up, placing the right foot on the inner thigh of the left leg. Turn the knee out to the side. Place palms together at midchest. Breathe out and press hands together over your head, arms straight up. Balance and try to hold pose as still as possible. Can you identify the parts of the tree?

Tree

Bird (Bakasana) Crouch down so that you are sitting on your heels. Place hands on the floor in front of you. Rock forward and breathe out so that the weight of your body is supported by your hands. Balance on hands in the crouched position to look like a bird. Keep back and neck as long, straight, and parallel to ground as possible. Ask your child where the wings and legs of the bird are.

Bird

Turtle (Kurmasana) Sit with legs straight out in front of you with knees slightly bent.

Bring your chest to your legs and reach under
your knees, placing hands next to hips with
palms facing upward. Try to rest your head on
the floor between your knees. Can you slowly
straighten your legs? Breathe out to relax and
melt into the floor. Does your turtle have a
rounded shell? Is the head poking out or
hiding? Ask your child for these answers.

Turtle

Mouse (Pindasana) See if your children
can get this little mouse to sleep. Start by
kneeling with a straight back. Sit down on
your heels with knees and feet close together.
Exhale and bring your chest down to the floor,
arms stretched out in front. Hold and relax,
breathing in and out. When fully relaxed into
position, put hands next to hips and rest like a
baby mouse.

Mouse

244 ✻ Candle Campfire

Materials
- 1 or more candles in holders
- tin pie plate or ceramic or metal dish
- matches
- 1 pillow for each participant

Well, maybe this isn't a campfire, but it is a nice way for the
family to "chill out" together. Place your candle in its holder and
place it on a fireproof plate or dish—not paper. Arrange the pillows in a circle around the candle. Adults light the candle, someone dims the lights, and everyone sits on a pillow. The family can
have a peaceful moment together watching the candle burn, or
you can have a family meeting to discuss plans and dreams, or

maybe you can just sing a song together. Make sure the candle is put out before the family circle time ends. Some families like to hold hands in the circle, and at the end of the time they pass a squeeze around.

245 * My Relaxation Book

Materials
- scrapbook, or colored paper, hole puncher, and 18 inches of ¼-inch-wide ribbon
- crayons, markers, and glitter glue
- pair of scissors
- glue
- magazines and other items the child selects

This is a collection of memories that bring back feelings of relaxation and stress-free times. Choose a premade scrapbook or, even better, make your own. Punch holes in the sides of colored paper (be sure the holes line up). Let the kids pick out the order of the colors. Together, thread a ribbon through the holes—voila! Ask your children to think of their senses: sight, smell, touch, sound, and taste. What things make each sense feel relaxed? Have them cut out pictures of things that visually give a mellow feeling (meadows, mountains, oceans, flowers, and so on), and glue them in the book. Next, add items to the book that when touched are relaxing (cotton from flannel pajamas, silk from a milkweed plant, wings from an already deceased butterfly). Certain smells invite pleasant, relaxing memories—spray a little of Auntie's perfume or Grandpa's cologne on a page. Be creative. Maple syrup reminds me of sleeping in on a Sunday morning, and the scent of strawberries reminds me of a wild field. These would be difficult smells to put on paper, but a picture rendition could be cut out instead. Don't forget sounds and tastes. Pictures probably work best here, too. Have your child add crayon, marker, and glitter glue decorations. Make sure to include all of the child's favorite things! When your youngster sits down and goes through the book she will recall that warm and fuzzy glow!

246 ✳ Flute and Zither Harmonies

Materials
- musical instruments
- shoe box or oatmeal or other cereal box
- cardboard tube
- 4 large elastic bands or string
- 2 aluminum pie plates
- 1 cup dried beans (dried peas, lentils, or rice will also do)

- glass beverage bottles and water
- strong tape
- pair of scissors
- colorful scarves

Do you have a recorder at home? A zither, a pan flute, or a guitar? If not, try making musical instruments out of shoe boxes, elastic bands, cardboard tubes, bottles, or whatever! To make a guitar, tape an empty cardboard shoe box or cereal box closed. Make a hole on the small side of the box—it should be the diameter of a cardboard tube. Insert the cardboard tube into the hole until it is sturdy (two to three inches). Tape the tube in place. Cut open the large rubber bands and tape one end around the top of the tube. Stretch the bands taut and tape the other end to the box. These should look and function, more or less, like guitar strings. (String will also work, but not as well.) Place dried beans (or a substitute item) in a pie plate. Place another pie plate on top. Seal very well with tape all around the edges. This makes a "quiet shaker" for rhythm. Fill glass beverage bottles with different levels of water. Instruct the kids to blow gently across the top for a homemade flute sound. (Use caution with the glass bottles so they don't break.) Have the kids invent music that calms the most wild of beasts or lulls a baby to sleep. They can gather a group of friends and create flowing tunes together. Children can dance to the music with colorful scarves. Show them how to make circles and waves with the scarves that match the sounds and rhythms of the music.

247 * Be a Bernstein, Mehta, or Osawa

Materials
- radio, CD player, or audiocassette player
- chopstick, drumstick, or any small, thin stick

Some experts say that orchestra conductors have the least stress and the greatest sense of fulfillment in their work. How lovely it must be to be surrounded by music all day! Watch an orchestra perform on television, on a video, or at a live concert with your child. Point out how the conductor leads the orchestra to play louder and softer. Note how he uses his arms and whole body to stretch out a phrase of music. "Tra la"—he ends all musicians on the final beat. Conducting a symphony is like taking an exercise class—it is a lot of work. Give each kid a chopstick, put on some classical music, and let them conduct a song or two. Maybe they will become the next world-famous conductor!

248 * Dr. Herbert Benson's Special Idea

Materials
- chair with cushion or soft mat for floor

Dr. Benson felt that people are often sick as a result of stress and that they could get better more quickly if they could learn to unwind. Dr. Benson came up with a technique of tightening muscles for several seconds, feeling the tension, and then fully relaxing that body part. He suggested that we do this to each body part, one at a time. Sometimes we don't even know that we are feeling stressed, and this is a good way of noticing the tension and letting it go. Have your child sit in a chair. Rub his shoulders and neck. Do you feel tense muscles? Tell him to tighten the muscles, count for 10 seconds, and then fully relax that area. Did you feel a difference? Did he? Practice tightening and relaxing throughout the day. You will get the hang of it!

249 * Ultimate Mother's Day Gift

Materials
- basket with handles
- live greenery and flowers
- homemade items: potpourri sachet (see Activity 233), bath oil (see Activity 240), audiocassette (see Activity 241), gift certificate (crayons, markers, paper, pair of scissors), and envelope

- ribbon
- tea cup or mug, tea, and hot water

What mom or grandmother wouldn't appreciate a gift basket that contained a homemade potpourri sachet, bath oil, and an audiocassette? Line a basket with fresh flowers and green leaves. Make the potpourri sachet, bath oil, and music tape and place them in the basket. Include a homemade gift certificate good for a deluxe massage or foot rub that the child will give the recipient. The child can cut out a piece of paper four inches by eight inches and use markers and crayons to decorate the edges with flowers or designs. In the middle, she should write (in her best handwriting):

This certificate is good for one massage
(or a foot rub).

Given to:_____ By:_____

Date:_____ Certificate expires:_____

Place the certificate in an envelope and tuck it in between the other gift items. Wrap a ribbon around the handle of the basket and make a pretty bow. Have the kids deliver it with a cup of tea and a hug!

250 ✳ Stress Ball

Materials

- balloons, 3 per ball
- flour, approximately
  ½ to ¾ cup per ball,
  depending on the size
- teaspoon
- small funnel
- pair of scissors
- pencil

These handy little stress relievers are an "instant" project for kids, and they make unusual gifts to give away! The finished product will be a small, squishy ball that sits in the palm of your hand. Squeeze the ball and relieve your tension. Begin by blowing up the balloons to stretch them out and then deflate them. (Young children should not blow up balloons.) Insert a funnel into the neck of a balloon and spoon in flour until a small ball (the size of your palm) is formed. Use the pencil to push the flour down the funnel's neck if it gets clogged. Cut off the "lips," or opening, of the balloon and put another balloon over the opening so it faces the other way. Push the first balloon inside the second. Use a third balloon to do this one more time—make sure you remove the "lips" of the second balloon as well. Knot the end of the third balloon—leaving the lips on! These extra layers of rubber make the stress ball more resilient. Now you can squeeze all your stress out!

X

Sports and
Adventure Travel

A family vacation no longer means packing up
the station wagon and sitting by a motel pool
for a week. These vacations are action-packed
with adventure, education, history lessons, and
athletic pursuits—guaranteed to provide your
family with phenomenal experiences they'll never
forget. This is serious living for active families!

251 ✷ A Volkssporting We Will Go

Materials
- sturdy walking shoes (if new, break them in before
  first hike)
- water bottle (recommended)

- walking stick (optional)
- layered clothing, according to weather conditions
- hat (optional)
- sunglasses (optional)
- sunblock (recommended)

Walking is easy, efficient, and economical! If your family is into organized walking for health and recreation, consider joining the American Volkssport Association (AVA). *Volkssport* is a German word for "the sport of the people." As one might guess, it is a noncompetitive group activity that encourages everyone, regardless of age, to join any one of the 400 clubs established in the United States. Most of the walks range from 3.1 miles (5 kilometers) to 12.4 miles (20 kilometers). It is recommended that your children start with the shortest walks. Once they get a taste of success they will surely want to try another one of the 3,000 scheduled events. These events can all be done at your own pace, and they are scheduled to take place at beautiful scenic or historic sites. The organizing group is responsible for making sure that the trails are safe and clearly marked. Meet up with new and old friends at any of the checkpoints and enjoy refreshments together. Participants receive a "record of achievement" book when they register with Volkssport. When you present your book at the event's sign-in, you will receive a set amount of points that later qualifies you for awards (pins, patches, and certificates). Children of all ages love this! Your kids may link up with other "sole mates"!

Contact Information:
American Volkssport Association
1001 Pat Booker Road, Suite 101
Universal City, TX 78148
(800) 830-WALK

252 ✷ Wind and Water Fun

Materials

- ask what you will need to bring

What happens when a sailor and a surfer put their heads together to create a new sport? They come up with windsurfing! How can a child possibly maneuver a big board with a large sail in the ocean? The windsurfing professionals at *Windsurfing* magazine write in an article called "Everything You Want to Know About Windsurfing" that it is not a strength sport, but rather "a finesse sport where 100-pound girls can windsurf as easily and as well, if not better than, 200-pound football players." Windsurfing is great exercise that tones the entire body, *and* it is great fun! Children can take lessons or attend "Kids Camp."

Contact Information:
American Windsurfing Industries Association (AWIA)
1099 Snowden Road
White Salmon, WA 98672
(509) 493-9463
www.awia.org

253 ✻ Ranchin', Ridin', and Ropin'

Materials
- ask what you will need to bring

Live out a childhood fantasy with your child! You can go back in time and experience the Old West by taking a vacation at a dude ranch. Horseback riding, cattle drives, roping lessons, rafting, fly-fishing, trap and skeet shooting, gold panning, and covered wagon trips can all be found by contacting Old West Dude Ranch Vacations. Different packages offer a variety of activities. Ask for the "family fun" vacations. Your children will learn new skills and stretch and strengthen their muscles from head to toe in the process. What a great journal your child will have to share with his class!

Contact Information:
Old West Dude Ranch Vacations
10055 Westmoor Drive #215
Westmister, CO 80021
(800) 444-DUDE
www.gorptravel.com

254 * Swim with Flipper

Materials
- ask what you will need to bring

Swimming is a great aerobic exercise. Your entire family can enjoy this healthy activity, paddling around with gentle dolphins. "Dolphin Discovery Camp" is located in Roatas, Honduras. The program is designed for kids from 8 to 14 years of age. Many other activities are offered as well: hiking, beachcombing, nature hikes, snorkeling, and glass-bottom-boat tours. There is something offered for all ages!

Contact Information:
American Wilderness Experience
2820-A Wilderness Place
Boulder, CO 80301-5454
(800) 444-0099
www.awetrips.com

255 * Row, Row, Row Your Raft

Materials
- ask what you will need to bring

Have you considered "family adventure travel" on the great rivers winding through some of America's great sites and national parks? Try a "sea kayak" (great to do with children), a "paddle raft" (with a group), or a "dory" (where you let the guide do the tough work). These trips teach teamwork and cooperation as well as physical skills. Because these trips are specifically designed for families with children (even as young as four years old), the guides are understanding and supportive of your special needs and concerns. They even bring a bag of games and toys! The staff guides you through warm waters in scenic settings rich with wildlife (such as the Grand Tetons National Parks or Jackson Lake). The pace is easy for children and first-time paddlers. Healthy, hearty meals are provided at beach campsites. Trips are scheduled on specific dates. You will need to call to find out what each adventure includes. Ask about "family friendly programs" and let the bonding begin!

Contact Information:
O.A.R.S.
P.O. Box 67
Angels Camp, CA 95222
(800) 346-6277
www.oars.com

256 ✽ Treetop Adventures

Materials
- ask what you will need to bring

Can you imagine surfing from treetop to treetop? Would you like to have a camp-out sleepover party *in a tree*? How about just scampering up and down enormous trees in Atlanta, Georgia? Your family can learn how to respectfully climb these giant trees with the utmost safety at Tree Climbers International (TCI)

Climbing School. Your teachers will show you how to use ropes, harnesses, and other safety gear. In addition, each person will learn about trees and nature. All this *and* a great workout!

Contact Information:
Tree Climbers International
209 Arizona Avenue
Atlanta, GA
(404) 377-3150
www.treeclimbing.com

257 ✽ Oregon Trail Hike

Materials
- sturdy walking shoes (if new, break them in before first hike)
- water bottle (recommended)
- walking stick (optional)
- layered clothing, according to weather conditions
- hat (optional)
- sunglasses (optional)
- sunblock (recommended)
- camera and film (optional)

Here's an activity in which parents will find a great U.S. history lesson combined with a fabulous physical education experience! This is perfect for a family vacation or for home schoolers. The Oregon Trail is a 2,170-mile route from Missouri to Oregon. The early pioneers traveled out west in the 1840s to seek their fortune and to create a new life. Let your children's imagination travel with them as they hike the primary trail system. There are 300 miles of "discernible ruts" traveled by the wagons on this primary trail. Wagons were not used for passengers but rather to haul essentials. Both young and old pioneers had to walk the route. Your children can experience the same without all the hardship! Along the way are 125 historic sites to study. Parents can enhance the educational aspect of this trip by ordering study material (video and workbook) in advance. Begin a physical-conditioning program at home in preparation. Start by hiking short trips on flat land. Increase the distance and add mild hills to your day hikes. Add a backpack with some light supplies such as a water bottle or canteen, a notebook and pencil, a camera, and binoculars. Once you arrive at the Interpretive Center in Baker City, Oregon, pick one of the three levels of trails to tackle. All are barrier free with a slope no greater than 5 percent. The loop is 4.2 miles long. You can obtain the study materials and additional information by contacting the Interpretive Center.

Contact Information:
Oregon Trail Interpretive Center
P.O. Box 987
Baker City, OR 97814
(503) 523-1845
www.or.blm.gov/NHOTIC

258 ⋆ Attention Aspiring Trapeze Artists

Materials

• ask what you will need to bring

Do you wish to experience, at least once in your lifetime, flying through the air with the greatest of ease? You and your children can learn how to swing on a trapeze, walk a tightrope, cycle, juggle, and clown around at the circus school at certain Club Med Resorts. Once everyone has perfected the triple midair somersault you can try some other activities. Even children can learn new sports such as waterskiing, sailing, golf, and tennis. Try in-line skating or BMX bike riding on the "half-pipe" (a large cylinder cut in half). Skaters and cyclists ride up and down on the inside of the pipe, gaining momentum, and practicing trickier stunts. There are numerous other activities for those who don't like to lounge around the pool: horseback riding, baseball, basketball, football, archery, kayaking, and "Keepfit" classes. Even the little ones (starting at age two years) can participate in sports.

Contact Information:
Club Med Inc.
75 Valencia Avenue
Coral Gables, FL 33134
(800) CLUB-MED
www.clubmed.com

259 ★ Swim with the Manatees

Materials

- swimsuits
- hat
- sunglasses
- sunblock
- camera and film (optional)

What a treat to be up close and personal swimming with these huge but gentle sea creatures. Manatees are unusual-looking mammals that reside in the Florida rivers. There is a great need to learn about manatees and to help protect them. While they appear rather clumsy on land, once they slink into the warm waters they become as graceful as ballet dancers. Share this unique experience by contacting River Safaris—they will make special arrangements for you.

Contact Information:
River Safaris
10823 Yulee Drive
P.O. Box 800
Homosassa, FL 34487
(800) 758-FISH
E-mail: riversafaris@hitter.net

260 ✳ "Hike," "Gee," "Haw"

Materials

• ask what you will need to bring

Does this sound like a foreign language? It is a language that only Alaskan and Siberian Huskies understand. You can take your family dogsledding without having to travel to Alaska! The Continental Divide Dogsled Adventures company has full- and half-day programs available—even for children under age 10. If you sign up for an overnight trip, you will stay in a *yurt*, a traditional nomadic round dwelling. So learn what *hike, gee,* and *haw* mean as you tread the backcountry of the Wyoming wilderness.

Contact Information:
Continental Divide Dogsled Adventures
P.O. Box 84
Dubois, WY 82513
(800) 531-MUSH
www.dogsled.com

261 ✳ Turtle Trek

Materials

• ask what you will need to bring

Would your kids like to stay up past their bedtime and go for a late-night hike to see 300-pound turtles nesting? You betcha! If you plan your trip at the right time you might also see the turtle hatchlings emerge. Wow! That makes it worthwhile being groggy in the morning! There is only one nationally recognized location for this spectacle: The Bald Head Island Conservancy. The conservancy tags the flippers of the turtles, records information, and protects these awesome creatures in a safe environment. They will share their appreciation and knowledge with you in a special evening program. Plan to arrive at the conservancy site at Bald Head Island at 9:00 P.M. for a 45-minute program followed by an educational nature hike to see the turtles and hatchlings. In order to prepare for the hike, take daily strolls as part of your everyday activities—leave the car in the driveway and walk home together from school or walk to the local grocery store with backpacks. See how much fun walking and talking can be! You should contact Bald Head Island Conservancy in advance.

Contact Information:
Bald Head Island Conservancy
7000 Federal Road
Bald Head Island, NC 28461
(910) 457-0089
www.bhic.org
E-mail: email@bhic.org

262 ∗ Hi-Ho, Hi-Ho, a Hiking We Will Go

Materials
- ask what you will need to bring

Join the Appalachian Mountain Club (AMC) for family hiking trips along paths from Washington, D.C., to Maine! Established back in 1876, the AMC provides educational programs, runs a Junior Naturalist Program (for ages 4 through 12), maintains huts and lodges to stay in, and, of course, clears all the hiking trails your feet can handle. The AMC program is one your family can grow into. Begin with learning basic backpacking, map and compass reading, bird-watching, or wildflower identification, and work your way up to an overnight stay in a hut or a lodge. If you want to try on your own or if you are experienced, purchase one of their guide and map books. See you on the trail!

Contact Information:
American Mountaineering Club
Route 16
P.O. Box 298
Gorham, NH 03851
(603) 466-2727
www.outdoors.org

263 ✳ A Family That Surfs Together . . .

Materials
• ask what you will need to bring

Get wet together *and* have a great time in the process! Adults, can you imagine going back to camp with your child and learning an activity you've always dreamed of being able to do? Ride the waves with your child at Summer Fun Surf Camp. This camp has sessions for children over 10 years and adults (at different campsites). Camp is run all through the summer months; however, not every session is open to adults. The location is San Clemente State Park in California. You will find other fun fitness activities included such as bicycling, skateboarding, and playing beach games. You will also be able to collect professional surfers' photos and autographs. Wetsuits and surfboards are provided . . . just grab your sunblock and swimsuit! Here's the plan: learn to surf and you will have a family beach activity to last a lifetime.

Contact Information:
Surf Fun Summer Camp
P.O. Box 254
San Clemente, CA 92672
(949) 361-9526

264 ✷ Build a Community Playground

Materials
• KaBOOM will send you a complete list

Do you want to build a great play area for the kids and foster terrific community spirit at the same time? KaBOOM is a nonprofit organization dedicated to seeing that every community has a safe and fun playground for the children. So put out a call to your neighbors, area businesses, and community leaders and enlist their brawn and bucks to build the world's greatest play area! Call KaBOOM for all the instructions you will need, including information on funding and grants.

Contact Information:
KaBOOM
2213 M Street NW, Suite 300
Washington, DC 20037
(202) 659-0215 ext. 225, or (312) 876-5885
www.kaboom.org

265 ✶ Dig This

Materials

- ask what you will need to bring

Children love to dig in the dirt with the hopes of finding old relics or buried treasure. Parents love for their children to learn about American history in a fun, hands-on way. Put the two together and throw in a physical activity of day hikes and you have a trip to Raven Site Ruin in Arizona! Six hundred years ago the Anazi and Mogollon Indians made pottery on this site. Today, children nine years and older are allowed to participate in a morning dig with trained archaeologists. In the afternoon, families can take a hike to see the ancient rock drawings called *petroglyphs*.

Your family will love the beauty of the area—mountain rivers, clear lakes, fresh air, and extinct volcanoes.

Contact Information:
Raven Site Ruin
Highway Contract 30, Box 30
St. Johns, AZ 85936
(520) 333-5857
www.ravensite.com

266 ✳ How Fred Flintstone Really Lived

Materials
- ask what you will need to bring

Did you know that many people enjoy a form of recreation and exercise called *spelunking*? Spelunking is a delightful name for cave exploration! The Drift-A-Bit Company has organized tours to teach you all about interesting caves and rock formations. They will provide some cool equipment for you and the kids to borrow including helmets, lights, and knee pads. The gear alone gives you a hint that you will be getting a workout! You can explore a maze of underground caves in West Virginia by calling Drift-A-Bit Company.

Contact Information:
Drift-A-Bit
P.O. Box 885
Fayetteville, WV 25840
(800) 633-7238
www.driftabit.com

267 ✳ Calling All Mermaids and Mermen

Materials

• ask what you will need to bring

Can you imagine staring nose to nose with a parrotfish? Can you imagine extending your hand with fish food and having thousands of our finned friends instantly get chummy with you? Young children can don the shallow water diving helmet and walk on the ocean floor breathing as naturally as on land. The special helmet, invented by Bronson Hartley, a marine biologist, works similarly to a glass turned upside down in the bathtub—air stays in it. In addition, fresh air is continuously pumped into the helmet. Your head stays dry, you can wear glasses and contact lenses, and you don't need to know how to swim. You probably want more information before you'll allow your kids to hang out underwater, so contact Undersea Adventures.

Contact Information:
Hartley's Undersea Adventures Ltd.
P.O. Box SB 194
Sandys, SB-BX
Bermuda
(441) 234-2861
www.hartleybermuda.com

268 ✶ Love a Llama

Materials
- sturdy walking shoes—if new, break them in before first hike
- water bottle (recommended)
- walking stick (optional)
- layered clothing—according to weather conditions
- hat (optional)
- sunglasses (optional)
- sunblock (recommended)
- camera and film (optional)

What is highly intelligent, sweet, gentle, and doesn't complain about carrying the groceries? Not your children, you say? Llamas don't mind helping you out as you hike the backcountry of the Sierras. Half-day trips are recommended for families with children. You'll enjoy the serenity and peacefulness of the beautiful surroundings, and your kids will be tickled by the interactive personalities of the llamas.

Contact Information:
Leelin Llama Treks
P.O. Box 2363
Julian, CA 92036
(800) LAMA-PAK
E-mail: leelin@llamatreks.com

XI

Things to Make and Build

Building projects are great for the weekend or during a vacation. Your final product can be enjoyed for a long time to come. Let everyone chip in and help out!

269 ✴ Easy-Does-It Balance Beam

Materials
- 4″ × 6″ × 8′ lumber, fir or any hardwood (ash, oak, birch, maple)
- 1″ × 6″ × 3′ lumber, same as above
- tape measure and pencil
- saw (hand or circular)
- electric drill/screwdriver

- 8 2½-inch all-weather deck or drywall screws
- indoor/outdoor carpet remnants with low pile
- marker
- carpet cutter and glue
- sandpaper
- plane
- polyurethane and brush (optional)

Here is a building project that can be simple or fancy in design. Make sure the eight-foot piece of wood (your beam) is sturdy and free of splinters and sharp edges. Cut a 1″ × 6″ three-foot plank in half using either a hand or circular saw. Place each piece one foot from the end of the beam as a cross support. (Use the measuring tape and pencil for this. Note that your beam will only be a few inches off the ground.) Use an electric screwdriver to attach four screws through each cross support and into the beam. Trace the shape of each cross support (1″ × 6″ × 18″) on the backside of the carpet using a marker. Cut the carpet to fit the size of each cross support. Glue the carpet to the underside of the support, so that when the beam is turned upright, the carpet will protect your floors and keep the beam from sliding. Once the glue is dry (according to manufacturer's directions) turn the beam upright and plane and sand every corner and edge. Round off the corners and run your hand over the entire beam to check for sharp edges or splinters. You can polyurethane (follow manufacturer's directions) the beam if you like. If you "poly" the top surface, sand it to take the sheen off—you don't want a slippery surface! Balance beam work is tricky under the best of circumstances! You and the kids can now practice walking forward and backward, stepping sideways, hopping, skipping, tiptoeing, and doing "dip" steps on your new beam.

270 * My Own Backyard Skating Rink

Materials
- 6 pieces 4″ × 6″ × 12′ lumber
- 8 metal corner braces
- 4 metal mending plates
- 1 package (50 to 100) 1″ drywall screws
- electric screwdriver
- 10′ × 100′ × 6 mm plastic (poly tarp)—cut down to size or use super duty painter's tarp
- duct tape
- hose and water

Build this outdoor skating rink and hope for frigid weather! These directions are based on a 12′ × 24′ rink. You can scale the plans up or down to suit your yard. Place the rink in the flattest part of your yard. (Purchase the appropriate size tarp according to your dimensions.) Place the 4″ × 6″ × 12′ pieces of lumber in a rectangle. Make sure they are lined up squarely. Use two braces at each junction (one higher than the other) to secure the lumber together for the rink's perimeter. You will use two 90-degree angle brackets for each of the four corners. Use two mending plates at the junction where two 12′ lengths are end to end to make the 24′ side. (Mending plates do not have an angle in them.) Both corner braces and mending plates have holes for screws. Attach the plates and brackets to the planks with an electric screwdriver. You should now have a terrific rink shape! Lay the waterproof plastic or painter's tarp (usually blue) on the ground. Make sure that two feet of tarp hangs over all the edges. Cut and tape together as needed. Tuck the extra material under the wood to keep it from blowing away. (This job requires a few helpers.) Once your rink is ready, use your hose to fill the rink evenly with one inch of water. Let it freeze, and add another inch of water.

Let that layer freeze and do it again. Keep adding layers as needed. Now get those skates on and make the best of freezing temperatures!

271 * Bigfoot's Coming

Materials
- 6 open-back slippers
- 2 pieces 1″ × 6″ × 6′ lumber
- electric screwdriver
- 1 package of 1-inch drywall screws

For this project you can recycle some old slippers that you haven't had the heart to throw away. Take three pairs of slippers (the open-back style works best) and place them on the long boards at even intervals, with the front and back ones six inches from the ends of the board. Now use your electric screwdriver to bolt the slippers in place. Use three or four screws per slipper. Make sure you are drilling the screws from the slipper down into the wood and not the other way around. You don't want to step on the sharp end of the screw—ouch! Now have three kids slip into the six slippers (they don't have to fit their feet). Try walking forward, staggering backward, sauntering sideways, taking big and little steps, moving with quick shuffling steps, and advancing by big giant steps. This activity takes cooperation and timing! The kids can call out "right, left, right, left" together or have one child as the designated "coxswain." Try singing a marching song to keep the beat. Find out what works best to get "Bigfoot" across the field!

272 ✳ Storkie Stilts

Materials

- measuring tape and pencil
- hand or circular saw
- 1 piece 2″ × 4″ × 6′ (or shorter) lumber—
  you will need to cut this down to size
- 2 pieces 2″ × 2″ × 6′ lumber
- electric drill/screwdriver
- 6 3-inch screws
- sandpaper and plane
- polyurethane and brush

Let your kids teeter around on these sturdy stilts! Measure and then cut two 2″ × 4″ × 6″ pieces from the 2″ × 4″ × 6′ piece for the foot blocks. Attach each foot block to a 2″ × 2″ × 6′ piece of lumber, one foot from either end, with an electric screwdriver and three screws per stilt. Younger children may do better with the foot blocks lower to the ground (six to eight inches from the end). Plane and sand all the edges of the stilts, rounding off the corners. Double check for splinters and sharp edges by running your hands over all sides of the wood. Seal the wood by putting on a coat or two of polyurethane (follow the manufacturer's directions). Let it dry thoroughly between coats. Take the storkie stilts and the excited kids out to a grassy yard or field and let them practice walking about. Hold the stilts for them to help them mount one at a time. Support the kids at the waist as they learn to lift both their leg and the wood at the same time. It takes a little getting used to, but once accomplished, they'll never forget!

273 ✻ Walking Sticks

Materials
- straight, strong branch (1-inch cross section)— choose length according to kid's size
- bells, acrylic paint, yarn, felt, glue (your choice)

You can't climb the Alps or tackle Mount Kilimanjaro without a proper walking stick. Walking sticks help set your pace and assist with balance. In many cultures walking sticks are part of an outfit, as important as the hat or pocketbook. Your kids can enjoy decorating their own sticks. First find a sturdy stick without any sharp points or leaves on it. It should be approximately one foot higher than hip level. Next adorn it with bells, paint, colorful yarns, or felt . . . anything goes! Most important, remind the kids to provide their sticks with plenty of exercise! Take it on long walks!

274 ✴ Cheerleading Pom-Poms

Materials
- 4 or 5 clean plastic grocery bags
- pair of scissors
- 1 roll strong cloth tape

Rah! Rah! for recycling a few of those bags you can't bear throwing away! Cut plastic grocery bags into one-inch strips. Wrap tape around the bottom six inches of the pom-poms. Use as many bags as you want—the more strips you use the fluffier the pom-poms will be. Next crinkle the plastic strips in your hands to give a full, not droopy, effect. Make up some cheers! Here are some you can teach your future cheerleaders:

G-O-GO (name of team) GO FOR IT!

Push 'em back, Move 'em back, way back!

Fight, Fight, Fight, (name of team) UNITE!

275 ✳ Silent Jump Rope Partner

Materials
- wood post
- ¼-inch eyebolt
- 3-inch hook fastener
- measuring tape or yardstick and pencil
- electric drill
- 12 to 15 feet of clothesline rope

Jumping rope is a great workout whether in the gym, the playground, the backyard, or a spacious room at home. In some areas of the United States, it is a favorite competitive sport. Children can find skipping rope a fun activity to work on all by themselves or with a group. If you only have two kids, you can rig a silent "third" partner. Make a swivel bolt using the eyebolt and hook fastener. Select a site to attach the bolt, such as a wood post. You could also use the side of a garage or the wooden support of a deck. Mark two to three feet up from the ground with a pencil and measuring tape. This is where you will drill and fasten the eyebolt (with hook fastener attached) tightly in place. Tie the rope through the hole and knot securely. The bolt will rotate with every turn so that the rope will never become twisted and tangled. If this is impractical, settle on teaching the children these verses and lend a hand as one of the rope swingers!

Here is a verse for "straight jumping." (Try this jumping on both feet, hopping on one, or running in place.)

"A" my name is Alice
My husband's name is Alfonso
We live in Albuquerque
And we eat apples

Go through the alphabet, filling in names that begin with the letter you are on.

For more information on jumping rope contact:

Buddy Lee Jump-Aerobics
P.O. Box 3
Woodbridge, VA 22194
(800) 953-JUMP
www.buddyleejumpropes.com

Contact the American Heart Association for information on the Jump Rope for Heart program for your school. (See Activity 50 for contact information.)

276 * Batting Tee Made Easy

Materials
- extra large coffee can (empty) with plastic cover
- pair of scissors
- 3-foot cardboard tube, the kind that holds an architect's blueprints
- small stones or sand, enough to fill can
- Wiffle bat and ball

Make a hole in the coffee can lid with scissors (it should be big enough for the cardboard tube to fit through). Fit the tube through the hole. Place the cover with the tube already in it over the can and push the tube down to the bottom of the can. Before you snap the lid down, fill the can with small rocks or sand to give it some weight. Now you can snap the lid firmly into place. Set it upright and balance your whiffle ball or softball on the top of the tube. Practice your swing! Adjust the height by cutting the tube. You might want to make several "removable" tubes to accommodate the different heights of the children.

277 ∗ Tin Can Stilts

Materials
- 2 empty coffee cans with plastic lids
- screwdriver
- hammer
- 5 yards of rope cut into 2 equal pieces

Take two empty coffee cans and poke two holes per can, one on each side of the unopened end. You can use the screwdriver and hammer to do this. (This should be done by an adult for safety reasons.) Take one piece of rope and thread it through both holes of the can and pull it through so that each side of the can has the same amount of rope. The rope ends should come up to hip height on the child. Cut the rope to meet this requirement. Knot the ends together to make a large loop. Now do the same for the other can. Have your child stand on the cans and pull up on the loop to walk around. Adjust the rope length if needed. Have your child try walking in a straight line, sideways, backward, big steps, and baby steps. Hint: If you glue the plastic lids on the coffee cans, you can use the stilts inside without marking up the floor.

278 ✤ Rhythmic Gymnastics Ribbon

Materials
- 14- to 16-inch wooden dowel (½-inch diameter)
- cloth tape
- 1 ½- or 2-inch-wide satin ribbon between 8 and 18 feet long, depending on the child's height and coordination
- pair of scissors

One of the most graceful sports in the Olympics is rhythmic gymnastics. Dance routines are created using balls, hoops, wooden clubs, and long ribbons on sticks. Children will love experimenting with this apparatus and creating their own style and movements. Make your own ribbon stick by taking a thin wooden dowel and taping a long satin ribbon to one end of it. Begin by wrapping the cloth tape around the end of the ribbon

for one inch. (You can scrunch up the end of
the ribbon or fold it over to make this
step easier.) Then continue taping
the ribbon for one or two inches
around the end of the wooden
dowel. It should be securely
taped by wrapping the tape
around the stick several times.
Try the following fun moves
individually and then put them
together in a combination!

Swirls Hold the wooden stick in one hand and make large arm
circles in front of you. Try making large circles overhead so you
look like a helicopter propeller.

Figure Eights Holding the wooden stick in one hand, make a
figure eight in the air. Try it low down near the floor, at hip
height, and high above your head.

Big Waves Using one hand, hold the end of the wooden dowel
and create big waves. Try making little waves. Can you make
ripples down low near the ground so they look like ripples on the
water?

Slithering Snakes How would a snake look slithering through
the grass? Use your wooden dowel and make this motion.

Name and Letter Game Can you spell out your name or the
letters in the alphabet?

279 ✳ Balance Board

Materials
- wooden rolling pin
- 2½- to 3-foot wood board approximately the same width as the rolling pin

The hardest part of this project is parting with your favorite rolling pin—more than likely it won't be returned in the same condition as it was taken. Look for a flat surface to practice this balancing act. You will also want a wide-open space, free of furniture and other hazards. Start by placing the board tilted up across the rolling pin. Have your child place one foot on the "down" side of the board. Now have her carefully place the other foot on the "up" side and slowly press down to balance the board parallel to the floor. (You can stand behind her and hold her steady at the waist.) Have her try holding still and then rocking back and forth. Did you ever imagine that your child's future might be as a circus star?

280 ✳ Gone Fishin' Rod

Materials
- 8- to 12-foot tree branch
- spool of fishing line
- #10 snell hook
- plastic bobber or bottle cork
- coffee can with lid, filled with dirt

Double your fishing fun by first making a rod and then trying it out! First find out if you need a fishing license in your area.

(Call your town or city hall for this information.) Second, find out where the best fishing spots are and if it is legal (and safe) to fish there. Now you are ready for the "reel" fun! You can make your own fishing rod with an 8- to 12-foot tree branch—one without twigs sticking out of it! Make sure you take it from the ground or an already dead tree, no need to harm a living one. Go to a sporting goods store for the fishing line, hook, and plastic bobber or a bottle cork. Take 10 to 12 feet of fishing line and twist one end around the end of the branch. Knot it securely so the fish won't be able to pull it off. Tie the bobber or thread the cork through the line about three feet higher than where you are planning to attach the hook. (The hook dangles off the end of the line.) An adult should tie the sharp hook to the end. When you are ready to go fishing you will need to dig up some slimy worms from under a rock and place them in the coffee can. (Make sure you put the lid on the can!) Pack a healthful lunch and enjoy the day fishing!

281 ✳ Homemade Barbells

Provided they can follow your instructions and safety precautions, children as young as three can benefit from *light-weight, high-repetition* resistance (strength) training—a strong body is less likely to be injured in sports. Follow proper form and the safety recommendations below and, most important, go slowly!

Safety Tips Make sure the children start with a light barbell.
Emphasize low weight with more repetitions (8 to 10) rather
than heavy weights that they can only lift once or twice. Knees
should be slightly bent with feet shoulder width apart. Weights
should be lifted slowly and rhythmically with a relaxed grip.
There should be no straining, arching of the back, or swinging
of the weights to lift them. Check and make sure there are no
objects or people in the way. Place a mat on the floor or do over
a rug so the child can set down the weight. Encourage the child
to stop when he or she feels tired or has any sudden, sharp pain.
Never allow a child to overdo it. Remember, we have our whole
lifetime to get into shape, and we don't have to be a champion
weight lifter in one day!

Materials
- electric drill
- screwdriver (optional)
- 1-inch-diameter wooden dowel (36 inches in length)
- 2 small screws (1½ inches long)
- 2 weight-lifting clamps
- a variety of small weight-lifting plates (found at a sporting
  goods store)—two of each of your choice of 1, 1¼, 1½, or
  2 pounds
- small exercising mat or rug

You can make barbells at home with a little effort. An adult
should use an electrical drill to make starting holes for the screws
eight inches from each end of the dowel. Use either the drill or a
screwdriver to twist the screws approximately one-half inch into
the dowel. The screws will prevent the weights from shifting to
the center of the bar. (Leave one inch sticking out of the dowel.)
Place the desired weight-lifting plates next to the screws and then
add one clamp to each end. The clamps prevent the weights from
falling off the end of the bar while still allowing you to change the
plates as needed. Start your children off *light* with one- to two-

pound weights. Remember to multiply the weight you select by two, since this is the total weight to be lifted (one weight on each end of the dowel). The amount you select should be determined by the child's size, previous training, and natural strength. Both adults and children can do these exercises. Adults can add on heavier weights or use an adult-sized barbell. Do these exercises every other day to give the muscles a chance to "recover." It is during the "recovery" phase that muscles grow stronger.

Bicep Curl While standing, hold the barbell in both hands down by the hips. Palms should be facing away from the body. Slowly lift barbell to shoulders by bending elbows. Return to original position. This is one "rep" (repetition).

Bicep Curl

Overhead Press

Overhead Press Place barbell at shoulders with elbows bent and palms facing out. Press barbell overhead, hold for one second, and return to starting position.

Upright Rows Pick up the barbell with an overhand grip (your palms will be facing your body). Bring your elbows out to the side as you lift the bar to midchest. Lower the bar slowly to the starting position.

Upright Row

282 ✳ Wrist Curls

Materials
- sandpaper
- 1-inch-diameter wooden dowel
  (12 inches long)
- 5-foot length of rope
- cloth or electrical tape
- 3-, 4-, or 5-pound weight-lifting plate
  (found at sporting goods store)

Many sports require strong, flexible wrists. Often these smaller muscles are neglected. Here is how your young athletes can strengthen their wrists for tennis, hockey, gymnastics, and many other sports.

Use sandpaper to smooth a wooden dowel. Thread the rope through the hole of a small weight-lifting plate and knot it tightly. Take the other end of the rope and tie it to the middle of the dowel. Wrap several layers of tape around the place where the rope is knotted to the dowel. Hold the dowel with both hands, elbows tucked securely by your sides. The weight on the rope should dangle between your feet. Palms should face away from your body, and your forearms should be parallel to the floor. You are now ready to roll the weight up to the dowel by doing alternate twisting of one hand at time. Hold a contest to see who can roll the weight up the fastest: Mom? Dad? Brother? Sister? Grandmother? Does your family have Superman-sized forearms yet?

283 ✴ Wheelies

Materials

- wheelbarrow wheel (approximately 8 to 10 inches in diameter)
- wooden dowel 18 inches long (diameter sized to fit the wheel hole)
- sandpaper
- moleskin fabric and pair of scissors (optional)

- acrylic paint and paintbrushes (optional)

No, you won't need your bicycle for this! You will need a small wheel from the hardware store (the kind used to replace wheelbarrow wheels) and a wooden dowel that will fit through the hole in the wheel. Try out the fit before you buy it—it has to be very snug! Smooth the edges of the wooden dowel with sandpaper (this will prevent blisters or sore hands). You can also use adhesive moleskin and make handgrips if you want to be fancy. Use acrylic paint to decorate the wooden dowel if you want. Let the paint dry overnight. Then push the dowel through the wheel and make sure the wheel rotates freely as you hold the dowel. This is a fun piece of equipment the entire family can use—take turns doing a variety of exercises! Depending on how you use the wheelie, different muscles will be used. Here is one exercise to try:

Arm Rollers Kneel on the floor or a rug, sitting on your heels. Place the wheelie on the floor and hold it with both hands in front of your knees. Roll the wheelie forward lifting your hips off your heels. Your weight should be on the wheelie as you roll it as far in front of you as you can go. Now pull it back into place. Use your arms and upper-body muscles for this exercise.

284 ✱ Pillowcase Punching Bag

Materials

- 2 to 3 old pillowcases
- several buckets of sand
- 1 or more full rolls of cloth or electrical tape
- 8 to 10 feet of rope

Who doesn't feel the need to throw a jab at a punching bag now and again? Here is a quick and easy way to make a punching bag that can be disposed of as easily as a grumpy moment! Take two or three old pillowcases that are free of rips and holes. Place one inside the other to make the punching bag stronger. Fill the double- or triple-layer pillowcase with sand—no rocks please! Four inches from the top you can begin to wrap the cloth or electrical tape. Fold this four-inch pillowcase "tail" in half, making a loop for the rope to thread through. Now tape the loop securely at the bottom to hold it tight. Continue downward, taping around every inch of the punching bag. This will give it extra strength. Thread through the loop a heavy-duty rope. Use the best knots you know to tie the rope to the bag. Then tape around your knots and continue to tape partway up the rope for at least one foot. Tie the rope very securely around a strong tree limb. The bag should hang down to eye level. Of course, this will need to be adjusted if there is more than one user. Practice each punch and then put different punches together in combinations.

Jab Hold both fists in front of face with elbows bent. Punch straight forward and return to bent-elbow position.

Jab

Roundhouse Punch
Punch around from the side in a circular motion.

Roundhouse Punch

Uppercut Punch Scoop punch upward with fist facing inward.

Uppercut Punch

XII

Splish, Splash—
Bucketfuls of
Good Times!

These games and activities for the beach,
pool, tub, or sprinkler will drench you with
good times!

285 ✴ Drip, Drip, Drop

Materials

- bucket or cup
- water

Here is a cooling and invigorating version of "Duck, Duck, Goose." You will need eight or more participants. Have everyone sit in a circle with eyes closed. Choose one player to be the "big cloud." The "big cloud" carries a bucket or large cup of water and walks around the circle. As she passes each player she dribbles a drop of water on his or her head and says the word "drip." The anticipation builds as the players squirm wondering if they will be the victim of the cloudburst. Whenever the cloud chooses she empties the entire bucket or cup over the head of one of the sitting participants. At this time she shouts out "drop" and runs in a full circle to claim the participant's abandoned seat. If the participant catches her before she sits, she is out. If not, he becomes the new "big cloud" and she remains sitting in his place. This game can be played until everyone has had a chance to be thoroughly soaked! Be careful not to run on a wet, slippery surface.

286 ✳ Ping-Pong Lottery

Materials
- 25 Ping-Pong balls, plastic eggs, or corks
- indelible marker
- swimming pool (or lake)
- 1 sieve, strainer, or net for each player
- small prizes for winners

What's the chance that you can win the lottery? Pretty good if it is Ping-Pong lottery. Gather 25 Ping-Pong balls, plastic eggs, or corks and number them 1 through 25 using an indelible pen. Now toss the balls into the pool (or lake). On the count of three, all the players jump into the pool feet first and scoop up as many balls or corks as they can in their sieve, strainer, or net until all are collected. Climb out of the pool and tally the scores. The highest score wins the Ping-Pong lottery. The winner receives a tax-free prize!

287 ✳ Every Drop Counts

Materials
- field or yard
- metal or plastic measuring cups (or buckets), 2 per team
- 1 cone or box per team
- water

Play this game and practice conserving water! You will need two teams of players. You can do this with as few as two players or have many more. (If you have an odd number of players one person can go twice.) The more players you have the harder this game becomes! Place both teams at one end of the field, three yards apart. Twenty yards away place two cones or boxes, one for each team. The cones or boxes should be in line with each team and separated from each other by at least three yards. Give the first person in each line a measuring cup with exactly one cup of water. The first person on each team runs down to the other end, circles around the cone or box, runs back, and pours the remaining water into the cup of the second player in line. The second person—now first in line—runs up and back with the water cup. (The first runner gives his cup to the third person in line and goes to the back of the line.) Go through all the players and then compare the amount of water remaining. Add variations by doing the sideways slide step, walking backward heel-to-toe, or tiptoeing. You can try the race again using buckets and measuring eight cups of water into each one. The chances are greater that you will get soaked! Whichever team has the most water left wins the water conservation award!

288 ✳ Thar She Blows

Materials
• any body of water

Whales are the largest mammal on earth. So how does this gentle giant attract a mate? By breaching! Breaching is the powerful thrusting of his tail, which drives the enormous body out of the water. It is kind of "show-offy"! Your kids can practice "breaching" like a whale. Have your kids begin by sitting under the water in a squat, rear ends resting on heels. They then push off and break through the surface with all their might, trying to get their entire body above the water level. Do 10 breaches in a row and aim to go higher with each attempt. Pushing against the force of the water strengthens your legs and is easy on the joints. This makes breach jumping a great exercise for the whole family!

289 ✳ Statue

Materials
• any body of water

This game is usually played on land, but it is more of a challenge and a riot in the water. Have all the children go into the water up to midchest. Instruct them to swim, paddle, run, or walk through the water. They must stay continually moving. When the person on land shouts, "Freeze!," all bodies must stop in the middle of their movement and hold the position until the "OK!" instruction is given. At that time the participants may continue moving. Once "freeze" is shouted, no one can move even the smallest bit or that player is out. Players who are out must come out of the water as a penalty. The last person in the water wins and rises to the rank of new instructor. What makes this game difficult is that the motion of the water makes balancing and staying still close to impossible. Make sure everyone gets a turn being the instructor!

290 ⚓ Deep-Sea Treasure Hunt

Materials
- swimming pool or lake
- airtight plastic bags (large size), 1 for each child
- trinkets (several for each bag)—pencils, erasers, plastic rulers, small boats or figures, jewelry
- black, bold marker
- flat rocks, 1 for each child
- penlights and batteries (optional)—look for these at bargain stores

This game can be played in deep water by excellent swimmers or shallow water with beginners. Use this at a pool party as a way to pass out goody bags. Fill plastic bags with small trinkets— plastic or wood items are a good bet since they won't be damaged by water. Write each child's name in marker on a flat rock and add it to the bag. Remove any excess air from the bag and place the bag at the bottom of the pool (or a cordoned off, shallow side of a lake). If this is an evening pool party you can add a small, battery-operated, waterproof penlight to the bag as the "special gift." The bottom of the pool will be lit up by the penlights. At the end of the party have the kids go into the water and search for their loot bags. If they find someone else's bag they should just place it back where they found it and not say a word. This way the kids will get more exercise swimming until they locate their bags. This is a grand finale to your successful pool gathering!

291 ✳ Message-in-a-Bottle Relay

Materials

- 3″ × 5″ index cards, 1 for each player
- markers
- airtight plastic bags (small), 1 for each player
- 12″ lengths of string, 1 for each player
- 2 plastic bottles with caps (2-liter size)
- swimming pool
- pair of scissors

What will the message in the bottle be? No one knows until the game is over! Give each child an index card, marker, and plastic bag. Have them write a full sentence of their choice on the card. Place the card in the bag and squish the air out of it. Zip it closed. Roll the card and bag up tightly and then tie a string around it so the card stays in a "tube" shape. Remind the kids that the tube must fit through the narrow neck of the bottle. Divide the kids and messages into two groups. The two teams stay at one end of the pool, the "mainland," and the two separated piles of messages are placed at the far end of the pool, the "island." Give the first person in line a plastic bottle (with cap screwed on). At the command "ready, set, go" the first kids swim or walk to the end of the pool, capped bottle in hand. They remove the cap, select one message from the pile, stuff it into the bottle, replace the cap, and swim or walk back. Once back, the bottle is passed on to the next person in line. She swims or walks with the bottle (now containing one message), adds another one to the bottle, and returns back home. Each person does the same until all the messages are transported safely from the island to the mainland. An adult should carefully cut the plastic container open with scissors. The team that returned first gets to open and read their messages first (in random order). Does the "message" make any sense? Kids will get a good laugh at the nonsensical message.

292 ✷ The "Feet First" Championship

Materials
- swimming pool or lake
- paper and pencils
- 10 pieces of cardboard (8″ × 10″)
- black, bold marker

Here is a competition modeled after a diving meet, however, it is done with safety in mind as the competitors must enter the water feet first. Have all the entrants practice jumping into the water feet first in the most original way they can come up with, using their cleanest form (pointed toes and precise positioning). Try a pencil jump (straight body), a straddle jump (legs wide apart), a jackknife jump (legs come straight out in front, touch toes then straighten body back to the pencil position), a full turn (360-degree rotation while maintaining pencil position), or a scissors jump (legs pass back and forth). The children should use their imagination and creativity. Meanwhile, the scorekeeper makes the scorecards. Write the numbers 1 through 10 on separate pieces of cardboard. The numbers should be large and bold. The scorekeeper's job will be to show the judges' scores and keep track of each jumper's standing. The judges also have their job at this time. They must make a judging sheet for each athlete. The sheet will contain the athlete's name and have columns for originality (how unusual or different), execution (how well done), difficulty (how hard to do), safety (did they enter the water feet first?), and personality (did they smile and look confident?). Under each column the judges will make notes about the athlete's performance in these areas. The judge can then read the notes and come up with an overall score. One is low and 10 is high.

You are now ready for the competition to begin. Each contestant does one jump. After each jump the judges pass in their "judging sheets" with the final score circled. The scorekeeper adds all the scores together and divides the total by the number of judges. The final figure is flashed and recorded. The round is repeated until each athlete has done three different jumps. All three jump scores are totaled up for a final score. The highest score wins. Remember, safety and personality are just as important as originality and execution!

293 ✳ Motorboats Brrr

Materials
- shallow pool or lake
- kickboard

Your toddler will enjoy pretending he's a motorboat, and you'll be pleased that he is learning how to put his face in the water. Let your child stand in the water waist-deep holding the "motorboat" (kickboard) in front of him. Show him how to blow bubbles by dipping his chin and mouth below the water's surface and gently blowing out air. Have him add a low tone to his voice. For the next step have him push off his feet and rest his belly and chest on your outstretched arms. He adds the bubbles, tone, and kickboard as you gently glide him through the water. Let him

steer the motorboat in differents direction and soon he'll be hooked
on putting his face in
the water!

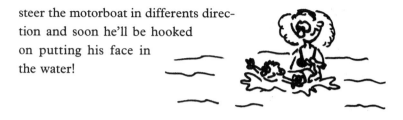

294 ✷ Ring-Around-a-Rosy

Materials
• shallow pool or lake

This simple game can be played with one or more toddlers
and an adult. Stand in a shallow pool or lake (no deeper than one
foot) and have all the participants hold hands. Walk in a circle as
you sing this variation of the song "Ring-Around-a-Rosy":

*Ring-Around-a-Rosy, a pocket full of posies
Ashes, ashes, we all get wet!*

At the word *wet* have all the children sit or squat in the water.
Now stand up and sing the same song but walk in the other direction. Try doing the song squatting and moving like a duck. Pop
out of the water on the last part of the song and change the words
to—"we all stay dry!"

295 ✳ Baby Play

Materials
• swimming pool or lake

Babies naturally love water—after all, they spent 40 weeks bobbing around inside mother. Four to five months old is the ideal age to start babies in the water, according to *Teach Your Child to Swim*. Make sure the water is tepid since babies do not shiver to keep warm, which makes them more vulnerable to the cold. The length of time babies should stay in the water varies with the age of the baby.

Child Less Than 6 Months
Ten minutes for first visit, maximum of 30 minutes after several visits

Child 6 to 18 Months Fifteen
minutes for first visit, maximum of 30 minutes after several visits

Hold the baby close at all times, talking soothingly and maintaining eye contact—this will put baby at ease. To introduce baby to water, sit on the edge of the pool or lake and hold her securely on your lap. Sing the following song to help your baby get used to the water:

> *This is the way we wash our hands, wash our hands, wash*
> *   our hands.*
> *This is the way we wash our hands so early in the*
> *   morning.*

Gently rub water on the baby's hands as you sing. Go on to a different body part and repeat the song, changing the lyrics according to the new body part. This is a good way for the baby to feel the water temperature and relax. After the baby is comfortable you can carry her into the water and play a few games. Gently bob up and down as you hold the baby close. Hop through the water with feet together and sing:

Here comes Peter Cottontail, hopping down the bunny trail.
Hippity-hoppin' all along the way.

Swish the baby from side to side and make soothing whooshing noises. Hold the baby several inches from your face, blow bubbles as you draw her near, and then kiss her nose. Going to the lake or pool regularly, repeating the same routine and games each time, and keeping the baby safe and comfortable will help your baby love swimming.

296 ✳ Crocodile Rock

Materials
• kiddie pool

Get ready to crawl all over and around the kiddie pool for this activity with your toddler! This exercise helps your child prepare for floating. The water needs to be shallow so that he can put his hands on the floor of the pool and keep his head out of the water. Begin by kneeling in the water with your child and have him put both hands on the bottom of the pool. Help your child to extend his legs behind and go into the push-up position. His feet may drag along the bottom behind him. Show him how to use his arms to pull himself through the water like a crocodile. Thrash around like a croc by keeping your feet together and swishing hips side to side. Lower your chin just beneath the surface of the water and then lift your head to open and snap shut your jaw. Soon your child will feel comfortable in the prone position needed for floating and you will be able to support his chest as he glides along the surface. Walking along the pool's floor is a great arm strengthener, too!

297 ∗ Supersynchronized Swimming

Materials
- kiddie pool
- video camera (optional)

Try making up a synchronized swimming routine in your small home pool or at the "kiddie" pool at a swimming club. (The kids can even practice on a rainy day on the living room floor!) Synchronized swimming is an Olympic event that requires a team of swimmers to do movements exactly the same way at the same time. One easy move is to make a star: have everyone sit in a circle, legs and toes facing the center. Arms and rear ends rest on the bottom of the pool—this is why you need a shallow pool. There should be a yard or more between each set of toes. On the count of three everyone opens his legs so that each person's toes touch those of his neighbor's. From above, it will look like a star. Next try leg kicks, first the right leg then the left. Repeat. Can everyone swivel in a circle on their rear ends and then end together at the same time? Everyone should end facing the center of the circle. Let the synchronized swim team make up its own coordinated moves and then perform them. Grab the video camera to show them how great they look!

298 ✳ It's Raining, It's Pouring, and Everything Is Just Ducky

Materials
- rain
- swimsuit, rain slicker, and boots (recommended)

There is nothing more fun than putting on your swimsuit or rain slicker and rubber boots and going puddle jumping with your whole family. A warm spring rain is the best time. See who can make the biggest splash in a puddle. Try leaping from one puddle to the next with your hands on your head. Can you hop from puddle to puddle on one foot without losing your balance? Jumping jacks are fun to do in the center of a pool of muddy water! Play "Duck, Duck, Goose" standing up! Young children will love this, and it is a great way to put them in touch with Mother Nature!

299 ✳ Really Great Pyramids

Materials
- sandy beach
- camera (optional)

This is great fun at the beach. The sand makes a nice, soft landing mat. All ages and skill levels can participate, as well as any number of kids you can recruit! (Use it as an icebreaker during vacation.) Start by building the base of the pyramid with the largest kids kneeling shoulder to shoulder on the ground. Next make the second layer by having midsized kids carefully put their lower legs in the middle of the backs of the first layer and their hands between the shoulder blades. (Everyone is kneeling on all fours.) If these first two groups are holding up well, add a third tier of little ones. Parents need to act as "spotters" and help position the kids. The younger ones will need extra help getting up and down from their places as well. Extra kids can do splits, poses, and one-leg stands in front and at the side of the pyramid. Quick, grab your camera! This is a Kodak moment that doesn't last! Undo the pyramid by helping the top layer off first and the middle layer next. Try different configurations that the kids design together.

As a variation, make this the ultimate family holiday card—use all family members, even grandparents and the pets in simple poses!

300 ✳ Sprinkler Obstacle Course

Materials
- variety of sprinklers
- garden hoses—as many as you need

What a way to beat the summer heat! This will be a blast for the whole neighborhood. It requires teamwork and cooperation. Ask neighborhood friends to pitch in sprinklers, hoses, and water. Try to gather a variety of sprinklers; oscillating ones that arch back and forth, rotating ones that spin the water in a circle, and spitting sprinklers that flick back and forth. I also like the flower and frog ones. Find a central location where you can stretch hoses from your neighbors' yards into one area. Now set up "Sprinkler World"! Oscillating sprinklers can wave back and forth opposite each other. Run under and beat the tidal wave. Crawl around and under the spinning sprinkler and avoid getting spit at by the spitting sprinkler. Create your own arrangement based on the area you have, the number of water sources, and the variety of sprinklers you have collected. Have fun!

301 ✳ Beach Blast

Materials
- ocean or lake with sandy beach
- towels
- low beach chairs
- drinking water to prevent dehydration

You don't need to just sit when you go to the beach. You and the family can get a great fresh-air workout. Try a zigzag run up and down the hills for a great leg workout. (It is a good idea not to disturb the dunes.) Twist up a towel and wrap it behind your neck, holding each end in one hand. This works like the "ab" machines advertised on TV. Lie on your back and do crunches with slightly bent knees. You barely need to leave the ground to feel your stomach muscles tighten—no one will know what you are doing! Do beach chair dips by scooting forward on low beach chairs. Keep your hands on the armrests and your knees bent in front of you. Your weight should be on your arms. Work your triceps by lowering your bottom to the sand and then pressing up to straighten your arms. Try as many as you can plus one! Have the whole family join in—see who can do the most. How's that for a guilt-free day at the beach?

302 ∗ Pool Golf

Materials
- swimming pool with a deck
- balloons, wood blocks, bubble wrap
- several yards of string
- weights (rocks or bricks, for example)
- large plastic bowls
- foam egg containers
- glue
- flat pieces of foam
- plastic golf ball and clubs
- paper and pencil

Guaranteed to provide hours of poolside fun and relief from a heat wave! Place different objects such as balloons, wood blocks, and bubble wrap in the water and anchor them down with string attached to a weight. Other objects such as plastic bowls and foam egg crates will need to be glued to a flat piece of foam so that they float. Puncture the foam in the middle and thread string through the hole. Glue the object to the top and let the string come out the bottom. Attach a weight to the bottom of the string. All weights should rest on the bottom of the pool. Now that you have a course, you will need to assign a number of points to each floating object. (Write these points down on a piece of paper to avoid arguments over the scoring system.) Some of the objects will need to be hit in order to gain points while other objects will receive points if the golf ball lands in them (such as a bowl). Take turns hitting the ball with the plastic club from outside the pool into the golf course. Give the golfer plenty of room to swing the club. Make sure the kids call out the target that they are aiming for *before* they swing. Keep track of the points. Let the kids be inventive as they search for pool targets.

303 ✳ Beach Air Bowling

Materials
- ocean or lake
- plastic or paper cups
- small stones, well-rounded sea glass, or shells

Here's a game that doesn't require lugging extra equipment to the beach. After lunch, when you are done with your drinking cup have the children bury the cup up to the lip in wet sand. The kids should then stand back 10 feet and try throwing shells or small stones into the cup. If that is too easy, take one big giant step back. Try again. Can the kids do it blindfolded? Pull a hat down over their eyes and try. Make it a splashing success by filling the cups up with ocean water! Be sure to clean up the cups when you're done.

304 ✷ Underwater Funfest

Materials
- swimming pool or lake

Here is a noisy game that you won't hear! Gather a group of friends. Have them climb into the pool and hold hands in a circle. Pick one person to be the official "hummer" and all the others will be the "figure-it-outers" for the first round. On the count of three, everyone takes a deep breath, goes underwater, and sits cross-legged on the bottom of the pool or lake. The "hummer" hums out a tune and the listeners try to figure it out. Everyone pops back up and shares his or her guess. The person who guesses correctly becomes the new "hummer."

305 ✸ Funny Fingers

Materials
- swimming pool or clear lake
- goggles, 1 pair for each player

It is hard to see underwater—that is what makes this game a challenge. Two children wearing goggles hold hands and face each other. On the count of three they take in a deep breath and kneel on the bottom of the pool. One child holds out a certain number of fingers and then the other child nods acknowledgment that she has seen it. Both pop to the surface. The child who is guessing reports what she has seen. The other child then asks, "Is that your final answer?" and then confirms or corrects her. Now they switch roles! This game also helps the kids work on breath control!

306 ✸ Noodle Stretches

Materials
- swimming pool or lake
- foam noodle or waddle

These noodles (sometimes called "waddles") aren't good for eating, but they are great fun in the pool! Here are some stretching exercises you can do with foam noodles! They are good props for kids to invent their own exercises. Here are a few to try together.

Side Bend Stand in the pool with the water at chest height. Hold the noodle in both hands, arms over your head. Hands should be two feet apart on the noodle. Stretch while still holding the noodle overhead, stretch to the left, bending at the side. Try it going to the right. This stretches out your waist. Make sure you do not bend forward!

Side Bend

Inside-Out Straddle Stretch Hold the noodle across your chest at midchest with your elbows above it and hands close together. Float on your back with legs in front. Then open your legs wide and "straddle through," going from lying on your back to your front. You are now floating on top of the noodle, which is still across your chest. Straddle through again and put your legs together in front of you so you are floating on your back again. This takes a little practice, but it is a great workout for your inner thighs!

Inside-Out
Straddle Stretch

Swish Stretch Stand in the water up to your chest with feet apart, for balance. Hold the end of the noodle out in front of you with two hands. Swish the noodle from side to side with big sweeping gestures. It takes some work to do this, but it stretches and strengthens your sides in the process!

Swish Stretch

307 ✳ Seal Swim

Materials
- kiddie pool
- 1 balloon or plastic ball for each child

Can you act like a seal? Use a plastic ball or blow up a balloon (adults should do this for small children) and knot the end to make a ball. Make sure each "seal" has a ball and place it in the water. Have all the seals get into the pool by lying on the pool deck's edge and then rolling or flopping into the water with legs together. Then they move around the water using arms and hands as flippers. Kids can try to keep their legs together and have them work in unison so they look like a tail. Now they can push the balloon around in the water just using their nose! Can they go from one end of the pool to the other acting like a seal? If so, "arf" once!

308 ✳ Get-Dressed-Quick Contest

Materials
- swimming pool
- 1 item of lightweight clothing per child

This contest takes place in the shallow end of the pool so all players can safely put their feet on the bottom. Place several clothing items at the opposite side of the pool. Some creative lightweight choices include hats, gloves, tank tops, and shorts. Divide the group into two teams. At the command "Go!" the first kid in each line walks, runs, or swims to the other side of the pool, grabs the first piece of clothing available, and puts it over his or her swimsuit. Each goes back to his or her teammates, takes the item off, and passes it to the next person. The second person puts the item on and walks, runs, or swims down to the pile of clothing, adds a second piece to his existing wardrobe and then goes back to the group. This happens until the last person in line is wearing all the items. The winner is the team that finishes first. After the contest is over, the kids can carefully climb out of the pool and show off the latest in swimwear fashion!

XIII

Stretch to the Max— Flexibility Exercises

Flexibility exercises help prevent injuries, improve athletic performance, and are a great "cooldown" after a good workout. Involve the whole family or group for these low-key exercises.

 Read Activity 309 before you try any of the other activities in this chapter!

309 ✹ Top-Secret Hint

Materials
• rubber putty

Shhh—don't tell anyone, but the secret to becoming more flexible is to stretch your muscles when they are already warmed up. If you stretch *before* you exercise you will not get as far as when you do most of your stretching *after* your muscles are warm. Scientists know this from actually taking the inside temperature of muscles. Put some rubber putty in the freezer overnight. What happens in the morning—does it stretch or snap in half? Let's try a "human" experiment. When you wake up in the morning, put one leg up on your bed and see how far down your leg you can reach without straining too hard. Later on in the day, when you're warmed up, try the stretch again. When was it easier to stretch, in the morning or in the afternoon? Some people only stretch *before* they exercise, and they only achieve 10 percent of their potential flexibility. If they waited until *after* they exercised they would be much more flexible—closer to 90 percent of their maximum flexibility.

310 ✷ Rib Cage Wiggles

Materials

• none

Here is a great stretch to help wake up the body in the morning. Do this with your child when you first climb out of bed or just before a family breakfast. Stand with your feet apart, reach both arms overhead, and lock your fingers together. You now have to do two things at once: you need to make small circles high overhead with your hands and at the same time circle your rib cage in the same direction. Now reverse and go in the other direction. Keep stretching up as high as you can all the time. Can you do this with your hands going in one direction and your rib cage going in the other direction? This requires talent and concentration!

311 ✳ Test Your Family

Materials
- medium-sized strong cardboard box
- wooden measuring stick
- 1- to 2-inch-wide packaging tape
- marker

Kids almost always beat their parents on this one! This is the stretch and reach test done at many fitness centers. It measures how "stretchy" the muscles are in the back and legs.

Place a cardboard box on the floor upside down. Tape a wooden measuring stick to it

Fun Fact: Boys and girls are equally flexible until approximately age 12. At that point, or when puberty starts, girls produce a hormone called "relaxin," which gives them greater flexibility than boys at that stage.

with wide packaging tape (see illustration). The measuring stick should hang over the edge 12 inches. Trace two feet on the side of the box with a marker. This will indicate where to put your feet for the stretch and reach test. If contestants can touch their fingertips to the 12-inch mark, they get three stars. If they can reach past their toes with straight legs, they get four stars. If they can't reach the box and they are close to the six-inch mark, they get two stars. If they can't touch the beginning of the stick they don't get any stars. Practice this hamstring and lower back stretch with or without the box twice a day—morning and night. After everyone works on stretching for two weeks, do the test again. How did everyone do? Did the moms do better than the dads? Did the kids do better than the parents? Did the girls beat the boys?

3l2 ✴ Inside-Out Stretch

Materials
- 4-foot broomstick or 1-inch-diameter wooden dowel

Fun Fact: Our shoulders can do this exercise but our knees cannot. The reason is that our shoulders are *ball-and-socket joints* that can move all around. Our knees are hinge joints and work like doors opening and shutting.

Hold a broomstick over-head with your arms very wide apart. Now bring the broom down the front of you to your hips and then all the way over your head and behind to your lower back. Can you bring it back over again? Do you feel like you just turned inside out? No? Then make it harder! Move your hands closer together and try again. See how close you can bring your arms and still do this. Some gymnasts can do this with their arms straight up. They need very flexible shoulders to do the uneven bars. Watch gymnasts perform on TV or at a competition and see how flexible their shoulders are—even the boys!

313 ✳ String Bean Stretch

Materials
- chin-up bar at home or monkey bar at a playground

Did you know that in the morning you are about a half-inch taller than you are at bedtime? During the day, your spine rests on itself and becomes slightly compressed. At night it stretches out again because the bed is bearing the weight of your spine. You can stretch your back out during the day by hanging on a chin-up or monkey bar and relaxing. Gravity will pull your body downward and lengthen your spine. Now hang with your feet wide apart and let your body twist from front to back and back to front. After a few minutes you will be totally stretched out and your back will feel great. Ahhh, I needed that!

314 ✷ Partner Bridge

Materials

- none

Stand back-to-back with someone who is almost the same height and weight as you. Hook elbows. One person bends forward (knees slightly bent) hoisting the other person off the ground. Do this slowly and gently to stretch out the back. Switch positions and repeat. Be careful not to lift someone who is too heavy for you!

315 ✷ Push Me, Pull You

Materials

- none

This is another partner stretch to do slowly and gradually after you have warmed up. Take your buddy and sit on the floor, face to face, in a wide straddle. Reach out and grab each other's wrists. Rock side to side, forward and back. Try making circles—small ones at first and then larger ones as your muscles loosen up. Can you each touch your nose to the ground? OK, this time without cheating, keep those knees straight!

316 ✳ Lead Your Class

Materials

• none

Have your child ask her gym teacher if she can volunteer to lead the warm-up stretches in class. Help her to be well prepared. Discuss all the parts of the body that need to be stretched out. Work from the middle of the body (torso) out to the limbs. For example, start at the waist, then do the hips, sides, upper leg, shoulders, arms, lower leg, ankles, and wrists. Did you miss anything? Hold each stretch for 20 to 30 seconds. Don't bounce. You and your child get an A+ for the day—good job!

317 ✳ Achilles' Weak Spot

Materials

• none

Stand facing a wall and place your toes so they touch the wall. Place your hands on the wall, push-up position. Now take a baby step backward, keeping your heel on the ground. Do it again with the other foot behind. Is your heel still on the ground? (The leg that is not being stretched may bend slightly at the knee.) Keep going backward one small step at a time until you feel your heel start to leave the floor. How far from the wall did you get? Stretch your heel down slowly and hold for 20 seconds. Now do the other leg. This is a great stretch for the lower calf muscle and the Achilles tendon. Runners do this stretch all the time . . . maybe that's why it is called the runner's stretch!

Fun Fact: Achilles lived in ancient Greece and he had a weak spot on his body: the tendon that runs from the heel bone to the calf muscle. This lucky guy had a whole myth written about this weakness and even had a tendon named after him!

318 ✴ Piano Player Exercises

Materials

- none

Yes, you can warm up almost every one of your 640 muscles . . . even your fingers. It's good to keep *all* your muscles flexible and agile—even the smallest ones—and here's how. Close your fists tight, and then spread your fingers out wide. Do this 10 times. Now keep your hand wide open and touch all your fingers to your thumb, one at a time. Go up and down your fingers like you are playing the scale on a piano. Make your fingers look like a monster hand. Keep your fingers wide apart the whole time that you do the touches. Now let's do the wrist. Join your hands together by interlocking your fingers (basket style) and circle your wrists around in both directions. Now you are ready to play one of the hardest piano pieces: Beethoven's *Moonlight Sonata*!

319 ✳ Houdini Handshake

Materials

• none

Houdini, the magician, was unusually flexible. This helped him to get out of a lot of his "predicaments," such as being handcuffed inside a straight jacket. See if you and your child are as flexible as Houdini. Place one hand behind your head and down the middle of your back. Reach up the other way with your other arm. Can you touch both hands together? Try it the other way, switching the top arm to the other side. Is one side more flexible than the other? If so, can you explain why?

320 ✳ Bridges and Cats

Cat

Materials
• none

This is a group exercise to stretch out everyone's back. Folks with tight backs should do the cat stretch. Those who have backs like rubber bands can do the back bridges. A cat stretch is done on all fours lifting your belly up to the ceiling—you need to hold your stomach in as far as you can and round your back. The bridge starts by lying on your back and placing your hands under your shoulders and your feet near your thighs, like a back bend. (Don't assume the position until you have been instructed.) Choose the smallest person in the group for the "crawler." Now everyone has to line up together, alternating "bridges" and "cats." At the count of "three" the participants will either do a bridge or a cat stretch and hold it until the crawler has had a chance to go through the whole tunnel. When he announces that he's made it through to the end, the tunnel can collapse!

Bridge

321 ✳ Neck Pretzel

Materials
• None

This isn't as painful as it sounds! Reach your left hand behind your back, trying to place it on your right, back hip. Place the other hand lightly on top of your head and tilt your head to the right. Do you feel a gentle stretch down your neck and across your upper shoulder? Hold for 30 seconds. Repeat on the other side. This is a great stretch if you have been sitting at a desk or in front of a computer or reading at the library for a long time. Now make half-circle dips with your head—go left to right and right to left. But never put your head all the way back, it is bad for your neck.

322 ✳ "Ain't No Mountain High Enough, Ain't No Bridge Wide Enough . . . "

Materials

• none

Can you and the kids do a bridge that repeatedly turns inside out until you go all around a full circle? This is hard! Start in a bridge (a back bend with hands and feet on the floor). Next reach over your chest with your arm and bring the same side leg over at that time so that you are in a "mountain" position. (You are on all fours looking at the ground with your rear end high in the air—you should look like a mountain.) From the mountain position flip yourself back into the bridge. Flexible children will have an easier time than stiff adults, so go slow! Keep going with the same arm until you make a full circle, all the way back to where you began. This is a fun and crazy group activity!

323 ✷ The Stork Stretch

Materials

- none

This requires balance and flexibility. It will stretch out the quadriceps in the front of your thigh. Actually, this isn't one muscle but, rather, four (*quad* means "four"). Stand on the left leg, bending the right one behind you. Grab your right foot with your right hand. Pull your foot gently upward, but keep your knees together. While still holding your balance, lower your right leg, then bring the same knee to the front of your chest. Squeeze it tight with your arms. This will stretch out your gluteus muscles. The gluteus muscles are the ones you sit on—your rear end! Now switch sides. You need to be an equal opportunity stretcher. If you can successfully do both sides, you'd make a great stork!

324 ✷ Four-Way Stretch

Materials

- none

This is an awesome stretch for your lower legs, and it will help prevent your twisting your ankle. It's great for skating or soccer practice! Start by sitting down with your legs stretched out in front. Take a deep breath in and while you exhale rest your chest on your thighs (or as close as you can get). After a minute, point your toes down to the floor—hold for one minute. Try a variation with flexed feet, pointing your toes back to your nose. Hold the position for a full minute and try to relax! Now put your heels several inches apart and point your toes in toward the center. Breathe in and then out and hold the stretch for 60 seconds. The last exercise is to keep your heels in the same place but grab your insteps and make your toes point out, Charlie Chaplin style. Keep this position for one minute. Now your lower legs are really stretched out! It is important to stretch in all different angles, because we don't just move in straight lines.

325 ✷ Gumby and Pokey

Materials

- old pantyhose
- pair of scissors

Find a pair of old, unusable nylon pantyhose. Cut the legs off and discard the panty part. Twist the two legs once around each other to form an X. Sit toe to toe with someone who is the same height with the X between you. Both partners keep their legs straight and grasp an "end" in each hand. Take turns pulling each other forward. You should be like a seesaw going back and forth. In the first round you should each hold the stretch for 5 seconds. Hold the stretch for 10 seconds in the second round. Gradually build up to a full 60-second stretch. This will really increase your hamstrings' flexibility!

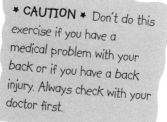

326 ＊ Oh, My Aching Back Stretch

Materials

• none

This is one good way to stretch out the lower back. In fact, it is recommended by the YMCA in their book *YMCA Healthy Back Book.* Lie on your back with your knees up to your chest. Roll your knees to the right, keeping in the tucked position, and look to the left. Hold for 30 seconds. You'll feel your back relax as all the muscles get stretched out. Now switch over to the other side and hold.

＊ CAUTION ＊ Don't do this exercise if you have a medical problem with your back or if you have a back injury. Always check with your doctor first.

327 ✳ Baby in a Basket

Materials

- none

Babies are remarkably bendable! They can easily put their feet near their ears with no problem. As we get older, we stop stretching as much and we lose a lot of our flexibility. Can your kids still do the baby in a basket? Have them lie on their backs, bringing both knees up to the chest, and then straighten legs so feet are by their ears. Superflexible kids can actually rock with their feet behind their heads!

328 ✳ Cobra Snake Stretch

Materials

- none

This is one for (almost) everyone in the family . . . except for someone with a bad back. Lie on your stomach with hands by your hips. Press up and arch your back. If this is too difficult, you can do a modified cobra by keeping your elbows on the ground and arching halfway up. Some kids are so flexible they can bend their knees and touch their head to their feet. It is important to keep your back flexible and strong so that the everyday stresses on the back don't lead to injury. Start kids doing these back-conditioning exercises while they're young.

329 ✳ Rock 'n' Roll Back Stretch

Materials

- none

Lie on your belly and reach back to grab your ankles, one in each hand. Slowly start to roll forward and back, keeping your back arched. Do you feel like an inside-out tire?

330 ✸ Pancake Split

Materials

- none

This exercise is easy for young kids and unimaginable for most adults! Start by sitting in a wide straddle, reach your arms forward, and slowly walk your hands in front of you until your chest is on the floor. Take deep breaths to relax. When you exhale, let your body sink down to the ground. Do this for five minutes. Concentrate on totally relaxing the muscles in your inner thighs—these muscles are called *adductors*. (They bring your feet together.) While you are in this position rock yourself forward so that from a bird's-eye view you look like the letter T. Then push yourself forward and slowly bring your legs behind you. Practice this every day and you will be able to do a pancake split (also known as a straddle split).

331 ✳ *Don't* Do These Exercises

Materials

• none

Below are a few exercises children and grown-ups should *not* do. Adults may remember doing these in their childhood gym classes—sports medicine experts have since learned that they can cause injuries. They can put stress on the ligaments that support your knees or they can put pressure on the nerves in your neck.

Hurdler's Stretch This is done by sitting with one leg out in front of you and the other bent underneath you so that your heel is next to your hip. This exercise puts stress on the knee ligaments.

Hurdler's Stretch

Inside-Out Cobbler Many children like to sit like this when they watch TV. This is a kneeling position with the feet next to the hips. This also stretches out the ligaments supporting the knee.

Inside-Out Cobbler

Overhead Plow This is done by lying on your back and bringing your feet overhead until your weight is resting on the neck and shoulders. Very flexible people can put their feet on the ground past the top of their head. This is not good for the neck.

Overhead Plow

332 ✳ Chicken Wings

Materials

- none

Can you touch your chicken wings together? These are really your shoulder blades (*scapulae* in Latin lingo!). They do look like chicken wings, don't they? Who can touch their elbows together behind their back? Mom? Dad? Sister? Brother?

333 ✳ Hug-a-Tree Day

Materials

- none

Find a tree that isn't too big and wrap your arms around it so that your hands can meet. Move your toes so they touch the bottom of the tree and lean back in an arch so that you are looking up toward the sky. As you go farther back in your arch, you can let your hands walk down the tree—hold on tightly and don't let go! What do you see: branches, leaves, clouds? Hold this position and sway back and forth. Enjoy the view as you enjoy the feeling of your back stretching out!

334 ✳ Dead Man's Hang

Materials

- none

Have you ever stretched so quickly you felt a tight pull in a muscle? That pain is your body protecting you from pulling or tearing a muscle. In our muscles, ligaments, and tendons we have tiny sensors that tell our brain if that area is being stretched too quickly. The brain then sends down a message for the muscle to tighten up fast, and that is what you feel. This is why you should never bounce in a stretching position. To do the dead man's hang, stand up straight, then flop forward very slowly (keep your legs straight) and take deep breaths in and out to fully relax. Hold your position for at least one minute. Did you notice how you were able to stretch farther once you relaxed?

335 ✳ Hockey Player's Warm-Up

Materials

- hockey stick or broomstick

Place your hockey stick or broomstick behind your head and hold onto it with your arms far apart. Put your feet two to three feet apart. Slowly twist your body so that the right end of the stick is on the far side of your left foot; plant the stick firmly on the ground. Keep your body twisted, bend forward at the waist, and

look up. You will feel a great
stretch through your hips,
waist, ribs, shoulders,
and neck! Undo yourself
slowly and then stretch on
the other side.

XIV

School's Out—Yahoo!

Open to this chapter when there's a snow day,
early dismissal announcement, or a planned
school holiday or vacation. It is filled with
quick and easy activities for hours of
healthy entertainment.

General instructions for this chapter Keep in the closet a
cardboard or plastic storage box filled with inexpensive and
simple items for that unexpected "no school" day. Stockpile the
box in advance with all the items listed in the master materials
list. Bring the box out when the kids are showing signs of severe
boredom and cabin fever. (Make sure they are not allowed to
preview the box at any other time.) Use a room with lots of open
space (playroom or large basement) and remove any clutter or
furniture in the way. (Noncompetitive versions are included to
minimize quarreling!) Relax and have a cup of tea—your kids
are all set!

Master Materials List

- cardboard or plastic storage box for all items
- 1 section of newspaper
- 1 package of 25 lunch-sized paper bags
- 20 disposable rubber gloves (available at pharmacies)
- chalk, string, or yarn (for finish line)
- 6 to 8 inexpensive shower caps
- 1 roll cloth or masking tape
- 1 roll green paper streamer
- markers, a variety of colors including black
- 1 package of 100 round coffee filters
- 1 air pillow packing material
- 100 bathroom-sized paper drinking cups
- 1 package of 25 paper plates
- old sheet
- 3 Ping-Pong balls
- 1 box plastic freezer bags (1-quart size)
- 2 small plastic eggs, beanbags, or small toys
- rope
- 100 index cards (5″ × 7″)
- 6 to 8 used dryer sheets
- at least 2 balls of yarn
- 9-inch round balloons (recommended size)

336 ✳ Newspaper Frenzy

Materials

- 1 section of newspaper
- 1 paper lunch bag for each player

What causes more excitement than a stock market crash, the first man landing on the moon, or the blizzard of '78? This easy game of "paper ball"! This modified version of basketball allows your kids to throw newspaper balls to their heart's content, and they won't destroy the house. The first task is to make 25 paper balls per player. Cut or rip each large sheet of newspaper into four equal pieces and have the kids scrunch the paper into compact balls. The tighter the balls are the easier they will sail through the air. (The kids should wash their hands after "scrunching" to remove any newspaper ink.) Write each player's name on one paper bag. Place the first player's bag at the base of the far wall. Have the first player back up 8 to 10 feet, depending on the size of the room and the age and skill level of the entire group. Give the first player 25 paper balls. The goal is to "free-throw" all the paper balls into the paper bag. Close up each bag without counting the paper balls until all the players have had their turn with their own bags. The final score isn't tallied until the round is over. This adds suspense and drama to "Newspaper Frenzy"! After everyone has completed round one, place the paper bag farther away (or if your room is small, place the paper bags several feet higher for a greater challenge). A quarrel-free version would be to have all the kids pool their balls together by emptying the bags onto the floor and tallying after each round and to see if they can better their collective score. Now that's front-page news!

337 ✳ Doctors in the ER

Materials

- 20 disposable rubber gloves
- chalk, string, or yarn
- 1 shower cap per player
- cloth or masking tape

This is one of the silliest games your kids will ever play. To start the fun, each child must wear a shower cap (or an operating-room cap if you can get them). Inflate 20 rubber gloves. Tie the ends into a knot. Have the kids designate a center line with a piece of chalk (for vinyl, cement, or wood floors) or a long piece of string or yarn (for a carpeted floor). To play "Doctors in the ER" start with two players—one player on each side of the line. The players gently tap the glove back and forth into the air using an open hand. The players need to be alert to keep the "sterile" glove from landing on the floor. If the glove lands on the floor it has to be taped to the hat or any piece of clothing belonging to the "doctor" who dropped it, and a new glove has to be used. After 20 gloves are used up, see who looks silliest. The winner is the "doctor" with the fewest gloves. The quarrel-free version would be to have the kids put the gloves on each other and then together decide who looks the silliest. Warning: This game is not recommended for hospital use!

338 ✳ Snake-in-the-House

Materials

- 1 roll green paper streamer
- 3 black markers for each child

Now you can say "yes" to having snakes in your home! Cut the paper streamers into two-yard lengths. Give each child three or four "snakes" to decorate. Use the marker to make eyes at one end and create interesting patterns down the backs. (A variety of color markers might make for even more creative snakes.) You can refer to a reptile book for ideas and to facilitate more of a learning experience on this "no school" day. Next stretch and twist the paper. Now roll up all the snakes. Each child should have his or her own snake creations in hand. All the children stand on the edge of the imaginary 10- to 12-foot-diameter snake pit. The first child throws one snake into the pit. It should unravel as it becomes airborne. All the children then go *one at a time* running and jumping over the streamer, being careful to respect the sleeping snake. One snake is easy—but what about two? Three? Four? Repeat the pattern, adding snakes one at a time and then crossing through the pit, until all the handmade snakes are in the pit. If a child disturbs a snake, that child is out. The child who remains at the end is the winner. A quarrel-free version would be to not keep track of who steps on a snake, just hop over and enjoy the fun of the challenge!

339 ✶ Rock Bridge

Materials

- 100 round coffee filters

Fun Fact: According to the *Guinness Book of World Records,* the longest pedestrian and bicycle bridge is located in Madison, Illinois. The Old Chain of Rocks Bridge is 5,350 feet long.

If you can part with 100 round coffee filters, your kids can make their own "rock bridge." Have the kids flatten all the filters—stomping on them works just fine—and place them, one by one, in a long chain. Make sure they can go from one to another with no problem. This chain can travel through rooms and even between floors. How about a trip up and down a hallway? Into a closet and out again? Try going over the bed and around a rug. After the bridge is constructed, the kids line up at one end and make their way along the coffee filters using any body parts they want. The trick is not to fall off the bridge. After all the kids have successfully made it from one end to the other, they can reconfigure the bridge and do it again. You get a lot of "mileage" from this box of filters! Quarrel-free version: Downplay falling off the bridge and focus on the bridge construction part.

340 ✴ Soft Soccer

Materials

- 1 air pillow packing material

A parent's dream comes true: gentle and soft indoor soccer. You will need six players—although you can get by with more or less. Each child has a part as either a dribbler or an obstacle (stationary object). Each participant takes turns being a different obstacle such as a tree, rock, bridge, tunnel, or goalpost. The "tree" stands with feet together and hands stretched out at shoulder height. A "rock" curls up tightly on the floor. The "tunnel" stands with feet wide apart and hands on hips. The "bridge" assumes a gymnastic back bend on the floor (lie on back, knees bent, and hands under shoulders, then push up into an arch and hold the position). Two people are needed for the goalposts. They stand four feet apart and lean into each other placing hands on the other person's shoulders. The obstacles can be placed in any order or pattern to suit the room size. Establish the route to be followed—in, around, and through the obstacles—before you begin. The dribbler places the pillow pack at his feet and gives soft, controlled kicks, steering the pillow along the course. At the end of the course he shoots the pack through the goalposts. The person who goes through the course with the fastest time wins. Add on to the final time a three-second penalty if the pack touches an obstacle and a five-second penalty if the dribbler touches an obstacle. Skill is as important as speed in this game! Quarrel-free fun: Work as a group and total the number of goals scored. Try again and again to better the group's score.

341 ✳ Paper Cup Split-Splat

Materials
- 100 bathroom-sized paper cups

Take out a column of 100 paper cups from your storage box. Let the kids arrange 25 of them all over the kitchen floor in a "modern art" (i.e., random style) pattern. On the count of three the kids hop from one cup to the next trying not to crush them. Of course, most, if not all, will be flattened. Challenge the kids by having them do the split-splat different ways. Set out several more replacement cups and try a variation: put the cups farther apart, use only the right foot, hop from one to the other. Try it in a squatting position or with both legs held stiff. The game is over when the cups runneth out. This is a quarrel-free game—everyone who plays automatically wins just by participating!

342 ✳ Who Can Hold the Wall Up the Longest?

Materials
- none

This is a great leg strengthener that usually ends in giggles. Place back and shoulders against a wall, scooting feet out a foot or two (depending on the child's height—taller children need to move their heels farther away from the wall). You're going for the "I'm-sitting-in-a-chair" look so knees should be bent at 90-degree angles. How long can this position be held? This strengthens the quadriceps (thigh muscles), which need to be strong for many sports, such as skiing and soccer. It also makes a fun contest at a party or gathering, and you can include the grown-ups. For a quarrel-free version, have each person go individually and keep track of their time. Add up everyone's time, take a half-hour rest and try again. Was the group stronger or weaker the second time around?

343 ❉ Winter Blues

Materials

- 2 paper plates or quart-sized plastic bags per skater

Chase away the winter chill (or summer boredom) with some invigorating exercise! This skating activity can be done during any season. Try skating on the kitchen floor with feet in plastic bags or on two paper plates for "plate skates." Suggest the kids try making circles, spinning in place, and skating forward and backward. Make sure they are far away from furniture and sharp edges . . . no big leaps either, please!

344 ✳ A Through Z Exercises

Materials

• none

Create every letter in the alphabet using just human bodies! The letter L is easy, but how does one make the letter Z or Q? Here's a hint: When all else fails try forming the letter lying down. While the kids squirm, wriggle, and problem-solve, they are getting a good body and brain workout—improving strength, flexibility, agility, and body awareness, as well as a review of the alphabet and formation of letters!

345 ✳ Parachutes and Popcorn

Materials

• 1 old sheet
• 2 or 3 Ping-Pong balls

What do parachutes and popcorn have in common? Not much, except for this game. This is a popular gym class game. Here is how you can do it at home. You will need at least four people, a sheet (without rips or holes), and Ping-Pong balls. Each person holds a side and a corner of the sheet and stretches it taut. The Ping-Pong balls are placed in the center. All the kids shake little waves into the sheet causing the balls to pop up in the air like popcorn. The object of the game is to keep the balls "popping" and avoid having them jump off the sheet onto the floor.

346 ✳ Summer Snowballs

Materials

- snow
- plastic freezer bags (1-quart size)
- mittens or gloves (optional, but recommended)

Are your kids home because of a snow day? Do you have extra freezer space? Try this! Make one or two dozen snowballs, wrap them securely in a plastic bag, and pack them into the *back* of the freezer (they are less likely to melt if they are in the back). On the hottest day of the summer, bring them out! This will be the hit of the neighborhood! Put on your mittens or gloves and make miniature snowpeople or snow animals, or play a gentle game of toss into a trash can. It is important not to throw them at each other since they may have become icy and hard while they were in the freezer.

347 ✳ Penguin Predicament

Materials

- 2 small plastic eggs, beanbags, or small toys per penguin player
- piece of string or rope, 6 to 8 feet long

Fun Facts: Penguins waddle because their knees are inside their bodies! The daddy penguins guard the eggs, and when they want to move around they place them on top of their feet.

Here is a fun and educational way to learn about our friends from the Arctic. Try this contest: Place the "penguins" in a line at one end of a room or in the yard. Give each child two small objects such as plastic eggs to put on the tops of his or her feet. Set up a string or rope finish line several feet away. The person who crosses the line first with the "eggs" in place wins. Congratulate the proud (and coordinated) penguins! Quarrel-free version: Work as a team to transport as many eggs to "safety," without falling off the feet, as possible.

348 ✳ Fitness Flash Cards

Materials
- 50 index cards (5″ × 7″)
- marker, crayon, or pencil

You've seen spelling, phonics, and math flash cards, but have you seen flash cards that teach fitness education? Here they are! Take 25 5″ × 7″ index cards and divide them between all the participants. Give each person a marker, crayon, or pencil. Have the participants write the name of an exercise, such as jumping jacks or push-ups, and draw a simple illustration of that exercise. Pass out a second set of 25 cards. Have everyone write down specific instructions: "Use a two-pound weight and do five arm lifts,"

"Don't use hands while doing this exercise 10 times," "Do this while running," "Do this in place," "Do this to the tree and back twice." Now shuffle each set of cards separately and place the cards in a stack, side by side. Go around the circle and have each person select one card from the exercise description group and one card from the instruction group. Now put them together and see if that person (or everyone) can do the exercise! To make it really difficult take two instruction cards for every one exercise card. You may have to do cartwheels up hill with one foot! Pretty hard!

349 ✳ Take Your Child to Class

Materials

• none

Have your child accompany you and participate in a fitness class you take. Ask the instructor permission *in advance* so that your child is not disappointed. Your child might really enjoy water aerobics, tai chi, yoga, softball, cardio kickboxing, ballet, or square dancing! Exercising together is great for quality time.

350 ✻ Climb a Tree Today

Materials
• good climbing tree

When was the last time you climbed a tree? Go to a park or find a tree on your property that is just waiting to be climbed. Help your children climb up safely first, get them situated, and then join them. Spend time in the tree together, enjoying the view, getting caught up on the day's events, and relaxing. When it is time to go, climb down first and help your child down if needed. Climbing trees builds strength, coordination, and confidence!

351 ✻ Climb the Doorways

Materials
• doorway

Kids love to scoot up doorways, posts, and even firehouse poles! Let them try climbing up the doorway like a spider—under your watchful eye. Find a doorway that is not too wide. Have the child place both hands and one foot as high as possible on the doorway. Then boost the other leg as the child pushes out against the door frame. Remind her to keep pushing out as the arms and legs climb higher. Believe it or not, it takes a lot of upper-body strength—and a good amount of bravery—to do this. Parents can step in to catch or to assist the scampering spider!

352 ✳ Machine Madness

Materials

- 12 index cards
- marker

This game is good for a rainy day when everyone claims horrible boredom! It offers physical exercise without tearing the house apart. Grab index cards and write down the names of electrical appliances and household machinery: blender, dishwasher, washing machine, dryer, electric can opener, juicer, vacuum cleaner, lawn mower, hedge trimmer, or Weedwacker. (Shhh—don't tell what's on the cards!) Have everyone sit in a circle. Put the cards facedown in the center of the group and let one child select the top card. Using both body movement and vocal sounds the child must act out the movements of the machine. The other kids must guess what machine she is. The person who guesses correctly gets to choose the next card. It takes skill, coordination, a good imagination, and sometimes a lot of endurance to act out the machine until it is figured out!

353 ✳ Unlimited Partners

Materials

- none

There are so many tricks you can do with a friend—the possibilities are unlimited! Pair two children together who are close in height and weight. Let them try these stunts to build cooperation as well as coordination. Have the two children face each other (toe to toe) holding each other's wrists. While maintaining this stance they both squat down to their heels and back up without losing balance or control. This must be done at the exact same time and very slowly for best results! Once this is mastered, have the kids stand back-to-back with shoulder blades touching and heels two feet away from the other person. The children should look like an upside-down letter V. At the count of three, they slowly sit down back-to-back. Knees should be bent at 90-degree angles and their backs should be entirely in contact. Do the kids look like matching bookends? Holding this position for as long as they can will strengthen their legs and torso.

354 ✻ Dryer Sheet Mambo

Materials
- 6 to 8 used dryer sheets

Save those dryer sheets to build foot and toe dexterity! Have two children lie flat on their backs, head-to-head with legs extended straight out. Put a pile of three or four "previously used" dryer sheets at the feet of each child. The first child (the giver) picks up a sheet using only his toes. The giver then lifts his feet overhead and passes the dryer sheet to the "receiver," who has also lifted her feet overhead. After the dryer sheet has successfully "changed feet," both parties lower their legs. Now the "giver" becomes the "receiver" and they try again. Make this more challenging by passing different objects. After a half hour of this, the stomach muscles will be tight and toned. The kids won't even know that this was a bonus to "dryer sheet mambo."

355 ✳ Wild 'n' Wooly

Materials

- 2 balls of yarn per 2 players

You will need an even number of players. Grab two yarn balls out of your "emergency kit" ("school's closed" box) and let the kids rewind them so that they are loosely balled up. The looser, the more challenging this game becomes. (Since the children will exchange balls there is no advantage to "trickery" when rolling up the balls.) Two children stand one yard from each other and each one has a ball of yarn. They count "one, two, three" and then throw their yarn balls simultaneously to each other. They take one giant step back and then exchange balls again. After a predetermined number of exchanges, compare the "tail" on the yarn ball. Whichever tail is longer is the losing ball. The kids never lose, only the balls—so no quarreling!

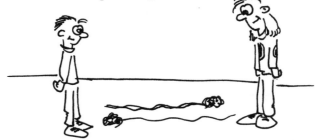

356 ✳ Spider Wall Crawl

Materials

- pillow (optional)

Make sure the kids have clean bare feet or are wearing clean socks for this one! Choose a room or hallway with clear wall space. Remove any furniture that is nearby. Have your children squat or kneel with their backs one foot from the wall. (Little ones might need a helping hand with the next part. Place a pillow on the floor between their hands in case they come down too quickly.) Lean forward putting all weight on both arms. Lift one leg up behind and place it on the wall. Bring up the second foot and place it on the wall. Make sure that the arms are held straight and push out of the shoulders. Slowly walk up the wall like a spider, one leg following the other. Once this skill is mastered, the spider can walk sideways against the wall—moving both arms and legs. Come back down the wall one leg at a time and return to the squatting position.

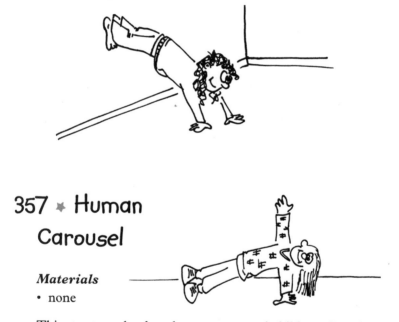

357 ✳ Human Carousel

Materials
• none

This stunt can be done by one or several children. Start in a push-up position with arms straight. Separate feet slightly to aid with balance. Shift weight onto one arm, freeing up the other arm to be held straight up toward the sky. As you do this, twist the body so that you are completely sideways. Now move in a circle, switching hands as needed. Now go in the other direction. Little ones can join in by just lying on their side and squirming in a circle. Any variation is acceptable and encouraged!

358 ✱ C'mon Join the Train

Materials

• none

The push-up train that is! Here is a stunt that was done in circus "strongman" shows and by acrobatic stunt teams and is now seen in aerobics competitions. This is a "shoes off" activity. Have a group of 7 to 10 kids make a circle lying on their stomachs head to toe. Select one child to be the conductor. When the conductor yells "T" the kids go into the push-up position with arms held straight. At the command of "R" all participants place one leg up on the shoulder of the person behind them. (Be careful to land the foot gently on the shoulder.) When "A" is called out the second foot is placed on the other shoulder. At the sound of "I" all participants bend their elbows and lay their chest on the ground. The conductor should quickly call out "N" signaling the pushing up and straightening of the arms. Make sure each child is the proper distance from the person in front of and behind her and that the torso is held stiffly. Often the train ends in a wreck with the kids roaring with laughter!

359 ✳ Skin-the-Cat

Materials

• none

This is a trick almost all parents have been asked to do by their child at one time or another. Here is how to do it! Stand facing your child and hold hands. Bend your knees and lean back slightly. Your child should place one foot on your thigh and bend her climbing knee. Holding on to each other tightly, have the child climb up your body using her free leg. At your midchest area she tucks into a ball and rotates through your arms, landing on her feet. (Make sure you are squatting low enough so that her shoulders are not strained in the process.) As she lands on the ground, release her hands so she can stand up. You are now both in your original starting positions. If you are able to do this easily you can add a reverse skin-the-cat. You must first do the regular skin-the-cat, and then before you release hands, your child gives a little push off her feet, tucks into a ball with her rear end coming toward you, climbs back down your body and legs, and lands safely on her feet! Ta-dah!

360 ✳ Soccer Circle

Materials

• 9-inch round balloon (recommended size)

Beginners can practice their passing skills by making a soccer circle! This can be played indoors in a wide-open room. Blow up a round balloon and knot the end. Have the children stand in a circle and hold hands. They should be close together (shoulder to shoulder). The children gently kick the balloon around the circle, passing to each player down the line. After the balloon has been successfully circulated the children all take a giant step back and kick the balloon around once again. (They may need to drop hands.) Keep playing until the passing gets sloppy or you run out of space. The key is to keep control of the balloon. Try kicking with the other leg in the opposite direction. Why not pass the balloon by bouncing it off the knee? Keeping control of the balloon is the challenge! This is good preparation for community soccer or the after-school sports program.

361 ❉ Snow Porkypines

Materials
- waterproof snow mitts (recommended)
- snow
- pine needles

This is great fun on a snow day! Don your most waterproof mitts and make "porcupines" out of snow. Find an area in your yard where this challenge can be done safely. Pat several handfuls of snow into football shapes. Place the clumps on an elevated object—trash can, cardboard box, or log. Gather long pine needles and press them into and all over the backs of the snow porcupines. Make several snowballs and stand back 10 feet from the targets you just made. Take turns throwing the snowballs at the "porkypines" at this close distance and then move back as the accuracy improves. Work as a team to knock the porkypines off their sites. Make sure those who are waiting their turn keep out of the line of fire. Practice until you run out of targets or your waterproof mitts give out!

362 ✶ Citius, Altus, Fortius

Materials

- computer
- website: www.olympics.org

Spend a quiet moment in front of the computer learning about the Olympics and all the hoopla! You can find out about the history of the Olympics; the countries that participate; and the Olympic flag, motto, and oath. You can also read all about the athletes. Register to receive the E-mail newsletter. Explore the kids section, play the "sport-zone" trivia game, or look up the "kid's guide to sports." You can even find out about volunteering. Bookmark this address and you'll learn that the three Latin words *Citius, Altus, Fortius* mean "swifter, higher, stronger"!

363 ✴ Travel Smarts

Materials

• none

Plan ahead for your next airline dining experience, and cut out the extra calories and fat by ordering special in-flight meals. Most airlines have a variety of alternative meals to suit the needs of their passengers. Some airlines have more than 20 options to choose from, including low-sodium, low-fat, wheat-free, vegetarian, kosher, and children's meals. The kids' meals are geared toward the taste buds of typical American children—they are loaded with fat, sugar, and salt. Think low fat or low calorie when you are high in the sky and you will get a fresher, more nutritious meal. Another bonus, especially when traveling with kids, is that special meals are served before the regular fare (so your kids won't squirm as they wait for the cart to come down the aisle). Special orders must be placed with the airline at least 24 hours in advance. It is helpful to notify the flight attendant where you are sitting and that you have ordered a special meal. Drink extra water or fruit juice to keep from getting dehydrated, and "Ladies and gentlemen, enjoy your flight!"

364 ∗ Hurray for Volunteering

Materials

- none

When school is out for the summer, your kids will have plenty of time to spare. What's a better use of free time than volunteering to help out an organization? Volunteer in the Special Olympics as an official "hugger," and hug the athletes as they complete their events! Play a game of one-on-one basketball with a wheelchair athlete or go tandem bicycling with a seeing-impaired person. How about pitching in at the Paralympics? Or schussing down the slopes in Winter Park, Colorado? Whether you are coaching a sport or helping to clean up after a tournament, you will find volunteering fun, helpful, and a great way to enlarge your circle of friends. There are hundreds of ways to get the whole family involved!

Here are some organizations to contact:

Disabled Sports USA
451 Hungerford Drive
Rockville, MD 20850
(301) 217-0960
www.dsusa.org

International Paralympic Committee
Adenauerallee 212-214
53113 Bonn
Germany
+49 (228) 2097-200
www.paralympic.org

National Sports Center for the Disabled
P.O. Box 1290
Winter Park, CO 80482
(970) 726-1540
www.nscd.org

Special Olympics International
1325 G Street NW, Suite 500
Washington, DC 20005
(202) 628-3630
www.specialolympics.org

United States Association for Blind Athletes
33 North Institute Street
Colorado Springs, CO 80903
(719) 630-0422
www.usaba.org

United States Cerebral Palsy Athletic Association
25 West Independence Way
Kingston, RI 02881
(401) 874-7465
www.uscpaa.org

Wheelchair Sports, USA
3595 East Fountain Boulevard, Suite L-1
Colorado Springs, CO 80910
(719) 574-1150
www.wsusa.org

365 ∗ Travel Fit

Materials
- jump ropes (one for each member of the family)
- cassette tape
- sneakers

Traveling families can keep fit on the road by packing jump ropes into the behind-the-seat compartment in the car. When you pull into a rest area, double tie those sneaker laces, grab the jump ropes, and find a safe, grassy location to hold a "family jump-a-thon." If you can park near the spot, turn on your radio or pop in a tape to jump to. Be considerate if there are others around and keep the volume down. See who in the family can jump the longest without stopping or tripping. Try reversing the swing (backward) or crossing the rope as it passes in front of you. Can you and the kids do a double bounce for every single swing over your head? That's tricky! The kids will enjoy jumping as a family, and the exercise break will do everyone a world of good.

You can order a jump rope music tape (with instructions and rope) to bring along:

"Red Hot Peppers Book, Music, and Jump Rope"
Sportime
One Sportime Way
Atlanta, GA 30340
(800) 283-5700
www.sportime.com

Recommended References

Many of these books, magazines, and resources inspired the ideas
or provided information for this book.

Books

Anderson, Bob. *Stretching*. Bolinas, CA: Shelter Publications,
2000.

Andes, Karen. *The Complete Book of Fitness*. New York: Three
Rivers Press, 1999.

Baechle, Thomas R., and Barney R. Groves. *Weight Training: Steps
to Success*. Champaign, IL: Human Kinetics, 1992.

Bellerson, Karen J. *The Complete and Up-to-Date Fat Book*. New
York: Avery Publishing Group, 1997.

Clapp, James F. III, M.D. *Exercising Through Your Pregnancy*.
Champaign, IL: Human Kinetics, 1998.

Cole, Joanna. *Anna Banana*. New York: Beech Tree Paperback
Books, 1989.

Cook, Brian, and Gordon Stewart. *Get Strong*. Victoria, BC,
Canada: 3 S Fitness Group, 1981.

Cooper, Kenneth H., M.D. *Kid Fitness*. New York: Bantam
Books, 1991.

Cumbaa, Stephen. *The Bones and Skeleton Book*. New York: Workman Publishing, 1991.

Davison, Bev. *Creative Physical Activities and Equipment*. Champaign, IL: Human Kinetics, 1998.

Dorland. *Dorland's Pocket Medical Dictionary*. Phildelphia: W. B. Saunders Company, 1968.

Drake, Jane, and Ann Love. *The Kid's Summer Games Book*. Buffalo, NY: Kids Can Press, 1998.

Duff, John F. *Youth Sports Injuries*. New York: Macmillan Publishing, 1992.

Einon, Dorothy. *Dorothy Einon's Learning Early*. New York: Checkmark Books, 1998.

Esche, Maria Bonfanti, and Clare Braham Bonfanti. *Kids Celebrate*. Chicago: Chicago River Press, 1998.

Evans, Mark B. *Natural Home Remedies*. New York: Hermes House, 1996.

Faigenbaum, Avery D., and Wayne L. Westcott. *Strength and Power for Young Athletes*. Champaign, IL: Human Kinetics, 2000.

Falk, John H., and Kristi S. Rosenberg. *Bite Size Science*. Chicago: Chicago Review Press, 1999.

Guyton, Arthur C. *Textbook of Medical Physiology*. Philadelphia: W. B. Saunders, 1976.

Hacker, Patty, et. al. *Gymnastics Fun and Games*. Champaign, IL: Human Kinetics, 1996.

Hamilton, Leslie. *Child's Play*. New York: Crown Trade Paperbacks, 1989.

Hetzer, Linda. *Rainy Days and Saturdays*. New York: Workman Publishing, 1995.

Hilton, Joni. *Family Fun Book*. Philadelphia: Running Press, 1998.

Hinson, Curt. *Fitness for Children*. Champaign, IL: Human Kinetics, 1995.

Jacobson, Michael F. *What Are We Feeding Our Kids?* New York: Workman Publishing, 1994.

Jennings, Debbie Sowell, and Suzanne Nelson Steen. *Play Hard, Eat Right: A Parent's Guide to Sports Nutrition for Children*. New York: John Wiley & Sons, 1995.

Johnson, Rebecca, and Bill Tulin. *Travel Fitness*. Champaign, IL: Human Kinetics, 1995.

Jordon, Dorothy. *Great Adventure Vacations with Your Kids*. Hampstead, NH: World Leisure Corporation, 1997.

Kite, Patricia L. *Gardening Wizardry for Kids*. New York: Barron's Educational Series, 1995.

Kohl, Mary Ann, and Jean Potter. *Cooking Art*. Beltsville, MD: Gryphon House, 1997.

Kraemer, William, and Steven J. Fleck *Strength Training for Young Athletes*. Champaign, IL: Human Kinetics, 1993.

Lehne, Judith Logan. *Never-Be-Bored Book*. New York: Sterling Publishing, 1994.

Lyght, Charles, M.D., ed. *The Merck Manual of Diagnosis and Therapy*. New York: Merck & Co., 1966.

Moore, Carolyn E., Mimi Kerr, and Robert Shulman. *Young Chef's Nutrition Guide and Cookbook*. New York: Barron's Educational Series, 1990.

Moquette-Magee, Elaine. *200 Kid-Tested Ways to Lower the Fat in Your Child's Favorite Foods*. Minneapolis: Chronimed, 1993.

Morris, Neil. *Where Does My Spaghetti Go When I Eat?* New York: Reader's Digest Kids, 1995.

Orlick, Terry. *Cooperative Sports and Games Book*. New York: Pantheon Books, 982.

Prudden, Bonnie. *How to Keep Your Child Fit from Birth to Six*. New York, NY: Ballantine, 1986.

Prudden, Suzy. *Exercise Program for Young Children*. New York: Workman Publishing, 1983.

Rice, Wayne, and Miki Yaconelli. *Play It: Great Games for Groups*. Grand Rapids, MI: Zondervan Publishing, 1986.

Rojany, Lisa. *Exploring the Human Body*. New York: Barron's Educational Series, 1992.

Sachs, Patty. *Pick a Party*. New York: Meadowbrook Press, 1997.

Samman, Patricia. *YMCA Healthy Back Book*. Champaign, IL: Human Kinetics, 1994.

Schultz, Danielle. *Terrific Topics—Food and Nutrition*. Greensboro, NC: Carson-Dellosa, 1996.

Sears, William, and Martha Sears. *The Family Nutrition Book*. Boston: Little, Brown & Co., 1999.

Schwarzenegger, Arnold, and Charles Gaines. *Arnold's Fitness for Kids*. New York: Doubleday, 1993.

Smith, Richard, and Ron Van Der Meer. *The Good Health Kit*. New York: Henry Holt & Co., 1987.

Spalding, Anne, et al. *Kids on the Ball*. Champaign, IL: Human Kinetics, 1999.

Stewart, Mary, and Kathy Phillips. *Yoga for Children*. New York: Fireside, 1992.

Stillwell, Jim L. *Making and Using Creative Play Equipment*. Champaign, IL: Human Kinetics, 1987.

Treat, Rose. *The Seaweed Book*. New York: Star Bright Books, 1995.

Usberg, Emily. *Peak Performance*. New York: Simon and Schuster, 1989.

Warner, Penny. *Birthday Parties for Kids*. Rocklin, CA: Prima Publication, 1996.

Watson, Franzesca. *Aromatherapy Blends and Remedies*. London: Hammersmith, 1995.

Webb, Tamilee. *Step Up Fitness Workout*. New York: Workman, 1994.

West, David. *Brain Surgery for Beginners*. Brookfield, CT: Milbrook Press, 1993.

Winston, Mary, ed. *American Heart Association Kids' Cookbook*. New York: Random House, 1993.

Magazines

American Baby
Primedia, Inc.
249 West 17th Street
New York, New York 10011
(212) 462-3500
www.americanbaby.com

Child Magazine
375 Lexington Avenue
New York, New York 10017
(800) 777-0222
www.childmagazine.com

Family Fun Magazine
244 Main Street
Northampton, MA 01060
(413) 585-0444
www.familyfun.com

Family Life
1633 Broadway 41st Floor
New York, New York 10019
(212) 767-6000
familylife@aol.com

Healthy Kids
Primedia, Inc.
249 West 17th Street
New York, New York 10011
(212) 462-3300
www.healthykids.com

KidCity Magazine
One Lincoln Plaza
New York, New York 10023
(888) 362-KIDS
www.kidcity.net

Parenting
1325 Avenue of the Americas, 27th Floor
New York, New York 10019
(212) 522-8989
www.parenttime.com

Parents Magazine
375 Lexington Avenue
New York, New York 10017
(212) 499-2000
www.parents.com

Sesame Street Parents
Children's Television Workshop
One Lincoln Plaza
New York, New York 10023
(212) 595-3456
www.sesamestreetparents.com

Sports Illustrated for Kids
1271 Avenue of the Americas
New York, New York 10020
(212) 522-1212
www.sikids.com

Walking Magazine
45 Bromfield Street, 8th Floor
Boston, MA 02108
(617) 574-0076
www.walkingmag.com

Organizations

Aerobics and Fitness Association of America (AFAA)
15250 Ventura Blvd., Suite 200
Sherman Oaks, CA 91403-3297
(800) 446-2322
www.afaa.com
(a website for fitness professionals but also contains
useful and interesting articles)

American Academy of Pediatrics
Department of Federal Affairs
601 13th Street NW, Suite 400 North
Washington, DC 20005
(202) 347-8600
www.aap.org
(contains excellent and timely information and
resources for parents)

American Alliance for Health, Physical Education,
Recreation and Dance (AAHPERD)
1900 Association Drive
Reston, VA 22091-1599
(800) 213-7193
www.aahperd.org

American Council on Exercise
5820 Oberlin Drive, #102
San Diego, CA 92121
www.acefitness.org

IDEA—The Fitness Source
6190 Cornerstone Court East, Suite 204
San Diego, CA 92121-3773
(800) 999-IDEA
www.ideafit.com
(a website for fitness professionals but also contains
useful information for anyone)

National Youth Sports Safety Foundation, Inc.
333 Longwood Avenue, Suite 202
Boston, MA 02115
(617) 277-1171
www.nyssf.org
(learn how to make sports participation safe;
excellent links to useful information such as youth
fitness guidelines)

Nutrition Action Newsletter
Center for Science in the Public Interest (CSPI)
1875 Connecticut Avenue NW, Suite 300
Washington, DC 20009
(202) 332-9110
www.cspinet.org
(website containing important nutrition news and
letters all ready for E-mailing to your legislators—
including information on children; contact CSPI for
their newsletter or to obtain nutritional
information)

Youth Fitness Resource Center
(AAHPERD, Cooper Institute, Human Kinetics)
P.O. Box 5076
Champaign, IL 61825-5076
www.americanfitness.net